From Bär to Bear

Hans B. P. Thielemann

Hügelwilhelm Publishing Co.
813 Country Oak Drive
Redding, CA 96003-2747 USA

Published by
Hügelwilhelm Publishing Co.
813 Country Oak Drive
Redding, California 96003-2747
USA

Layout by Janice C. Thielemann

Cover design by Hans B. Thielemann

Printed in the United States of America

DEDICATION

This book is dedicated to the millions of people who, unlike myself, did not survive World War II in Europe.

I dedicate it also to my wife, Janice, who encouraged me to continue with my autobiography and helped me with her patience and extensive knowledge of computer software. She always had good ideas for text, formatting, and graphics.

Life can only be understood in retrospect, even though we have to live it forward and don't know what is coming towards us.

Preface

My life has had so many unanticipated events that it reads like a fictitious novel; it was above all affected by the actions of political demagogues and my determination to survive. I survived Hitler, I survived Stalin and I will survive many presidents in the White House.

As a teenager in Nazi Germany I learned to speak "politically correct" to keep my ass out of a concentration camp. Living through six years of World War II, I had to get accustomed to the fact that whole cities could "disappear" in a few hours of Allied bombings and yet, people survived. During my four years of service in the German Luftwaffe at the Russian front I had many close calls, but survived.

After the end of the war I survived a Russian jail and a POW camp; and when I came back, I had lost my family, my home and property and my country. I was homeless, but had to survive. All these trials and tribulations left many physical and psychological wounds and yet I am still around.

Eight years after World War II ended I came to Canada and the United States, because I wanted more freedom and I knew the US Constitution's first amendment would allow me to express my opinions. Unfortunately during the last 10 years "political correctness", in numerous forms and fashions, has become the "In Thing" in the USA. It distresses me, because it again makes the truth elastic.

Now living in the world's only Superpower that is envied by the rest of the world, we are facing many forces which try to damage our status and inflict damage in our society. Only being prepared for such events and not fall apart when they happen, will enable us to survive. People in the United States have to realize that life has unanticipated and often deadly consequences.

During the 81 years of my life the world population has tripled from two to six billion people, and aided by world spanning "information" systems, it is now much easier to manipulate and influence the masses. The World Trade Center disaster and the anthrax problem were examples of how the media was able to brainwash millions of people into near panic.

The constant repetition of slanted political, religious and economical information can effect every one of us. Our biggest problem is therefore finding the facts and question pundit opinions. Eternal vigilance is the only way to preserve freedom, be it on the personal, national, or international level !

The reason for the Bear symbols on my book is that my life seemed to be influenced by the Bear of Berlin, Germany where I was born. Next by the Russian Bear because I was a soldier in Russia during WWII and a POW after the war. Finally by the California Bear because I immigrated to California.

Contents

1. My childhood in Berlin 1
2. Politically Correct? 25
3. Dig, Dig, Hurrah 49
4. To Hermann Göring-Meier 61
5. To Russia Without Love 67
6. No Relief for Leningrad 77
7. Russian Army Turns the Tide 85
8. Another Furlough 93
9. The Beginning of the End 101
10. Courland, Latvia 109
11. The End is Here 117
12. Hike West, Young Man 121
13. I Am a Hobo 133
14. NKVD Commissar Krapnikov 139
15. Even the Sun Dimmed................................. 145
16. Food, the Lack of It...................................... 151
17. Back in the Same Cattle Car 159
18. The Colors Never Change 169
19. To be Human Again 181
20. To Start Life Over 185
21. Last Stage Before Exit 209
22. Go West, "Old Man" 225
23. This is the Promised Land? 237
24. Back to Civilization 267
25. Poor Old German Immigrant (P.O.G.I.) 283

The trouble with the world is that the stupid are cocksure and the intelligent full of doubt.
Bertrand Russell

1

MY CHILDHOOD IN BERLIN

On the 16th of December 1923 rain was coming down on Berlin, Germany, when Hans Bernhard Paul Thielemann was born. Hans was baptized with Spree River water, supposedly to confirm that he was born in Berlin. One month before his birth Germany's worst inflation had ended, but the economical and political situation was anything but solid. Hans didn't care about that yet.

His parents and paternal Grandparents occupied a large apartment at Georgen Strasse No. 43 in Berlin NW 7 . The apartment building was only 2 blocks from the Kupfergraben, a branch of the Spree River, that surrounded the Museums Island with the Bode-and the Egyptian Museum. Hans grew up with his mother and grandparents. He didn't see his father often because he was a sales rep for a big machine manufacturing company (Deutsche Werke) and was traveling, often in foreign countries. During father's absence his paternal grandfather Johann Maria Joseph Bernhard Thielemann was often substituting father and took care of Hans. According to my parents, I was growing up fast and started walking when I was "only" 9 months old. Grandfather Thielemann and his wife Elise, Anna, Klara Scholz had three kids, two girls and one boy. Klara, Bernhard and Hanna, all were married and six months after my birth Klara and Hanna had kids too.

I remember actual happenings of my early childhood when I was about 12 months old. I was a rather rambunctious kid and after my first successful attempts in "vertical locomotion" I was determined to expand my exploration areas. My exploration was blocked however by the guardrail surrounding my playpen. It didn't take me very long to find a way to overcome that obstruction.

I leaned up high against the guard and that tipped the whole playpen on its side and if I crawled very fast I was out. Since the playpen righted itself after I got off the guardrail, my escape was not noticed right away. A whole new world opened up for me now if I walked around quietly. Pretty soon my adventures into adjacent rooms were causing me some pain, because I bumped into some furniture or tripped over obstructions. This always caught the attention of my mother or the grandparents and they curtailed my freedom again. But as I advanced in age, I was allowed more exploratory space.

I have to explain the layout of the big apartment (approximately 2,500 square feet) we lived in. The rooms were arranged in L-shape, with the larger rooms up front facing the street for the owners, and the rest of the rooms in the "L" for their servants. The servant quarters also had a small kitchen and bathroom. This wing was occupied by my parents, while the grandparents lived up front. Now being "very experienced" in upright locomotion I had an enormously large area for my exploratory roamings. My prime target were the grandparents, whom a called Oma and Opa.

As a small kid I had already acquired very specific tastes for food, and in general Oma cooked food that I liked better than my mother. This was primarily due to the fact that mother had less household money than the grandparents.

Opa had been the chief butler of the Empress of Germany for more than thirty years and after their abdication and move to the Netherlands he joint the Reichsbank (the federal bank) of Germany in Berlin. Due to his long association with the Royal household he knew a lot of VIPs in Berlin including Hjalmer Schacht who was the president of the Reichsbank. From where he lived, he could walk to work, and every day he came home during the noon brake (1:00 to 3:00 pm) to eat. Oma had to have dinner ready at exactly 1:15 for him.

When I became aware of that daily schedule I turned into an opportunist. If the smells from my mothers kitchen indicated that she was cooking stew again which I disliked, I wandered up front to Oma and asked what she had for dinner. When that was more to my liking, I asked if I could eat with them. This was never denied. When my mother could not find me, she walked up to the grandparents dining room to look. After she opened the door I would yell "I eat already", which of course didn't sit too well with her. But Oma smoothed the embarrassment out immediately and no quarrels started.

In 1924 Wolfgang and Ellen were born, which gave me two cousins. Wolfgang's mother was Klara, the older sister of my father and Ellen's mother Hanna was father's younger sister. Since the three of us were born within 6 months they called us the "three musketeers". Ellen's parents moved from Berlin to Ahlfeld, so we three cousins were rarely seen together.

Wolfgang lived near by and as we grew up, we had all sorts of fun together. At times our mothers would take us out for a walk. Wolfgang 6 months younger than I was in a stroller, while I had to walk. They would take us counter clock wise "around the carré" as they said. Their carré was in the center of Berlin and about 3 km long. We walked east along Georgenstrasse to Friedrichstrasse, turned left and went up to Unter den Linden Boulevard and past the Zeughaus we turned left again into Am Kupfergraben following it to Georgenstrasse and back to home. This was one of the busiest street carrés in Berlin, and acquainted us with the traffic at a very early age.

When my father was home he would take me along on his bicycle if he had some errants to do. On one of those trips he pointed a Negro out to me, who was walking along the street. It was the first one I had ever seen. He was probably a musician at one of the famous night clubs, such as the "Wintergarden" or the "Kabaret der Komiker" or "Haus Vaterland". Opa also acted as a "tour guide" and showed me Berlin by riding on streetcars with me. In summertime some streetcars ran double decker cars and the upper decks had no roof. This was like riding in a convertible and a splendid way to see all the buildings and monuments in Berlin.

Wolfgang and I often played on the floor of the grandparents living room, but at times there were strict prohibitions to our crawlings. That was at a time when the news came over the radio. My father had hooked up a detector and connected several earphones to it, which made it possible for the whole family to hear Radio Berlin. If we hit the table, the detector lost the station and my father called us to order and fiddled with the detector to get the broadcast back again. Opa usually fell asleep during these sessions and woke up when the news was finished. He then asked everybody what the radio had said and, getting different answers from everyone who had listened, he decided that he simply had to read the Morgenpost (newspaper) to see what was really going on.

During one of my "explorations" at home I went out the front door and was trying to leave the building. There were several granite steps down to the sidewalk and I fell down the stairs, head first and banged my head on the ice scraper (for cleaning the shoes in winter time). I didn't remember anything of that crash, but woke up with terrible pains at a doctors office who was stitching the skin of my forehead. I had of course a concussion and was severely restricted in my explorations after that.

Much later in my life my father often sarcastically said: "I think your crash as a kid did some damage to your brain" after I had done something stupid.

When I was about four years old mother took me downtown for shopping. We took the streetcar to Leipziger Strasse and did window shopping along that busy area. We visited the biggest department stores like Wertheim, Tietz, and the many specialty stores. Then we had lunch at some of the first fast food stores, like Aschinger and one store that really intrigued me, a store where sandwiches were sold by vending machines. Even the beer came out of a tap when you put your glass under it and a coin into the slot. None of the tables had chairs they were stand up eating platforms. My favorite store was a big Italian ice cream parlor which had dozens of different flavors. To buy shoes for me and Wolfgang we went into a big store called Leiser and they had an X-ray machine that would show, how our feet fit in the shoes. Wolfgang and I didn't believe that we could see our own toes in the shoes, and wiggled our toes, to ascertain these were our feet. Much later these machines were outlawed because of the radiation.

Moving from Berlin

My father who had been out of a job for a short period, was hired by the "International Harvester Company", probably because he was fluent in English. His job change however meant we had to move into the "province" as he put it. We would be living in Breslau, Silesia.

Father had rented a big downtown apartment on the fourth floor, and mother was bragging that the master bedroom was 12 m (almost 40 feet) long. The apartment had been completely repainted and looked very nice, but soon turned into a disaster. We had the worst house pest, bedbugs! The damn painters had even painted over the bedbugs and when they moved we had an interesting wall pattern. My mother cursed the painters when she woke up in the middle of the night, grabbed a ladder and smashed the bugs at the top of the wall. That did not accomplish anything because there was an unending supply of the bloodsucking beasts. Next morning she called the manager and raised hell about the infestation and demanded that an exterminator come immediately. He came and we had to move to a hotel for two days. We could come back after it was safe to re-enter the apartment. In those days the poison that was used was also very toxic to human beings. All mirrors and pictures in the apartment had to be taped so they wouldn't get damaged by the gas.

After we got back it took only 48 hours and the bedbugs attacked us again. They had only been disturbed by the exterminator and started a counterattack. Now my father had to get into the act. My mother complain bitterly about this damn apartment he had rented, but he said, he didn't get stung and added that he wasn't as sweet as she was and consequently the bedbugs only bit her. His remark infuriated mother even more and he quickly had to take some action. Breslau was ill-famed for its bedbug contamination and he got another exterminator who was recommended by his colleagues. This man looked at the place and started to remove all baseboards and the jute tapestry in one room before he gassed the place again. This time the bugs were exterminated and he vacuumed the dead ones up, because some of them are not quite dead and recover, he said. His more vigorous approach worked and we were able to sleep peacefully after that battle was over.

I celebrated my 5th birthday and had to go to Kindergarten now. It was the first time in my life that I had to play with kids I wasn't related to. I discovered that I could get along better with girls, than with boys and I liked two girls right away. Ursula was a red head and also an only child and she lived near our apartment. Our mothers talked to each other and thought it would be good if we would play alternately at our or her place. We really got along very well and the mothers were pleased.

As kids of that age we were both in the "discovery phase" of our lives and we discovered that there were some differences between boys and girls bodies. We explored these differences unperturbed for a while until Ursula's mother noticed what we were up to. After she had talked to my mother about it, we were more closely supervised. However our mothers must have spun out our play in their conversation and decided to start an experiment to find out. They never told us anything about their plot but in my later years it dawned on me what their plot was. They wanted to find out wether I would get aroused looking at a naked girl. During the summer we went to a nearby lake with a beach and they took all our clothes off. This was quite common in those days. Ursula and I played naked on the sandy beach and we built sand castles and didn't even notice that we were naked. At one point however Ursula was facing me and while making improvements at our sand castle she spread her legs and I saw more of her private parts. Suddenly I had a strange feeling, my penis started to get bigger and I had an erection. Our mothers curiosity apparently being satisfied, they prepared us to go home. Our plays were very supervised after that incident.

Since we did not know what their intent had been, we soon forgot about the whole thing, but that I still remember the details after 75 years is remarkable and shows what all is stored in a persons memory. My mother never even mentioned this event to me. Of course I experienced many similar reactions later in my life.

While we lived in Breslau my mother and I went to visit some distant relatives in Silesia. Uncle Max was a chef, cooking for some very rich uppercrust people, who owned a small castle there. They used it for hunting and vacations. He introduced me to some new meals that I had never eaten before. He prepared breast of pheasant with fancy sauces and vegetables that he cooked differently than my mother. I was very fond of that and many other dinners we eat at their house. I got into trouble with their dog however that I was supposed to take for a walk. Hasso, an Irish Setter, tore himself loose from me and chased other peoples chickens. I was not able to catch him and soon these chicken owners called the local cop. He knew already who the owner of that dog was and called them to retrieve their beast. I, who was not familiar with dog handling, got blamed by my mother for it and she had to pay for the killed chickens.

From Breslau we went into the Riesengebirge, a mountain rage that was at the border between Germany and Tschechoslowakia, where we met with Opa and Oma Thielemann. We hiked up to the Schneekoppe, the highest mountain of the range. I was doing well at the high altitude, but had constantly problems with my knees whenever I fell down on these rocky hiking trails. My mother just washed the blood off and put some large band aids over them. The band aids got stuck and when she ripped them off, it tore the wound open again. That was very painful, but when I cried I never got any sympathy from her . She didn't want me to be a wimpy kid.

Moving again

After about 18 months in Breslau my father was transferred by International Harvester Company to their factory in Neuss at the Rhine River. So we had to move one more time. Father was promoted to a much higher level and decided we would live in Düsseldorf, the biggest and richest city in the area.

He had rented a very large apartment and when mother and I arrived we noticed that he had furnished one room as his office with a new, heavy oak desk and matching furniture. We were surprised and delighted that we could afford such high class furniture now.

The apartment was located at a boulevard that had a creek running at its centre. I don't remember the names anymore, but it was a very elegant area. The entrance hall of the apartment building was clad in white marble and my mother instantly had a negative attitude about it, because she said it would be difficult to keep the marble clean. She never saw anything from a positive point of view, an inheritance from her mother, who was constantly bitching about anything. It took a while before our furniture arrived and we got settled with the help of Agathe a maid, whom my mother was now able to hire. The apartment also had a covered back patio.

My first school year

I was six years old and we had to find a school that I was going to attend. That was complicated since the Rheinland is primarily catholic and my mother did not want me to go to a catholic school. She finally located a non religious school that wasn't too far a way, so I could walk to school. School busses didn't exist in those days. I don't remember much about my first days at that school, but was surprised that we had to do our letter writing on slates. That was different and outdated from what I had seen at Berlin schools. I really liked school and had no problems with homework which was always checked and supervised by my mother.

Outside of the school I found a few kids in my neighborhood whom I played with. I had the most unusual toys which came from the International Harvester Company (IHC). They had pickup trucks, tractors and plows in toy size and my father brought home those toys from IHC. Father was in a sales manager position, and had to interface with some of the American managers on a social level. We also got to know their families and kids. At one of their kids birthday parties I got acquainted with American (US) toys. These older US kids had mini automobiles that were pedal powered and steerable like real cars. I thought they were impractical for people who lived in apartments because of their size. I could not imagine me riding on the sidewalk with these toy cars.

When a bunch of kids get together to play, there is always some mischief just waiting to come out. During the summer vacation time the creek that was flowing past our building was cleaned and we created all sorts of problems for the workers who did that job. At another time we went out to the garbage dump area and found all sorts of interesting things there. My mother of course didn't know where I had gone to and was exceedingly worried. Several kid had been abducted during our time in Düsseldorf and that made headlines in the papers.

An incident that drastically changed the family's life.

I started into the second half of my first school year and physical education was added to the curriculum. Long jump, high jump and several running events were now practiced. A mishaps at one of these events would change my life and my family's life. At high jump I made it over the bar, but my landing was askew and I hit the surrounding 4x4 with my right leg. The impact wasn't that hard and there was little skin damage. It felt soar but I could walk away from the incident. After I came home, my mother applied some hot towels to the leg. After getting up the next morning however I was in real pain and could not walk because my right lower leg was inflamed and felt real hard above the calf. My mother ordered me to go to bed and called a doctor. She got an appointment two days later.

When the MD examined my leg he found that there was a considerable amount of pus at my ankle and he made an incision to drain it and send me to get an x-ray to find out if there was some bone damage. When the X-ray picture was evaluated it was obvious that there was a problem with the bone marrow of my fibula, and he would not be able to do anything more for me. He advised us to see the best bone surgeon we could find.

His diagnosis and the way he expressed it was of course a severe shock to me and my mother. My father called Opa Thielemann in Berlin to see whom he could get us in touch with. He knew all the top MDs in Germany from his work at the royal household. Within 48 hours he called back and said we had an appointment with Professor Dr. Bier at the Charité Clinic in Berlin. Professor Bier was the top bone surgeon in Germany and was teaching at the Charité. So my mother and I had to get on the train to Berlin, which was a ride of more than 5 hours in those days. The next day Professor Bier examined my leg and some more X-rays were taken. His diagnosis was that I had osteomyelitis an infection of the bone marrow in the fibula. He said he would try surgery, but told my mother that I might never be able to walk in a normal way again. When my mother started to cry, he assured her that he would try his best to solve my problem.

In retrospect, Antibiotics can cure osteomyelitis today, but in 1930 there was no medication for that disease.

I was scheduled for surgery just two weeks before Christmas in 1930 and would unfortunately have to celebrate my seventh birthday in a hospital bed. There were numerous preparatory steps before the surgery. Medical students performed most of the work and finally an hour ahead of going into the operating room, I was given anesthesia in form of an enema. Finally med student rolled me onto a forum like stage with doctors sitting above my level in circular ranks to watch my surgery. It was like the Forum in Rome where people watched the lions tear the prisoners apart. Professor Bier explain my predicament to the audience and during his lecture my narcosis put me to sleep.

I came out of it 72 hours later when an MD and a nurse desperately tried to talk to me. They seemed to be very concerned about my consciousness, because I had apparently been overdosed which they told me later. It took another 24 hours until I was really alert. I noticed then that my right leg was completely bandaged up to above the knee and was wondering about the reason. Then Dr. Bumm (his real name) who was the assistant surgeon to Professor Bier came, and sitting next to my bed explained what had been done in the surgery. He said there was some good news and some bad news. The good news was that Prof. Bier had been able to open my fibula and remove all the bone marrow and we have to hope, that my body would be able to replace the marrow. The bad news was, that during the surgery a motoric nerve, the peroneus, "jumped over the scalpel" as he expressed it. Consequently I wood not be able to lift the tip of my right foot again. With other words I would have a drop foot, but he was sure I would be able to overcome that impediment.

Several days later he brought me a very big chocolate bar for my seventh birthday, together with a new X-ray that he showed to me and my mother indicating that my body already started a new bone marrow at the top of the fibula.

A few days later he came again and together with the chief nurse cut off the enormous bandages on my leg. I saw for the first time now how much "damage" the medical profession had inflicted on my leg. I had a 44 cm (17") long scar along my leg. I would certainly always been identifiable by that scar. He told me that I was going to be released just a day before Christmas and I was happy about that.

It took me a few months to recover from that surgery. I had to visit the Charité every week so they could check on my healing process. They ran numerous tests around my leg and that cut peroneus nerve, but that was only whitewash my parents thought. I got all sorts of massages at some sports clinic, which didn't accomplish anything. I simply had to accept the fact that my right leg had a permanent impairment and I had to find ways to live with it. I tried different kinds of elastic bandages that I wound around my ankle to give the foot more support. What was most depressing to me was that I would not be able to ski or skate, because I could not control my foot properly and in those days custom boots that would partially compensate for my impairment were simply not made or too expensive.

Another move

My health problem also impaired my father's life. He had to ask for a transfer to IHC's office in Berlin which was a demotion for him. I think we could have stayed in Düsseldorf without any problem, but my mother didn't like the catholic people in Düsseldorf. So my father had to give in. He never mentioned or blamed my accident for that, but he was not happy in the Berlin office.

An additional problem came up now, I had to resume my schooling. I had missed a whole year of school. So my mother went to the local school in Berlin-Mariendorf with me and they tested me to see if I could fit into the second grade without causing gaps in my education. The teachers of my second grade class doubted that, but my mother railroaded them and said that she would take care of the necessary tutoring and assured the headmaster that I would finish in the top 20% by the school years end. That was a tall order and throughout that year my mother gave me no time to play with other kids. I had to study and study to catch up with grade two curriculum. At the end of that school year I was in the top 10% of grade two. That surprised my teachers because they had already noticed during the school year that I was way above the average students in that grade. Wow, I was really proud of that. The negative side was that I was constantly ridiculed by the kids. I was excluded from physical education because of my leg injury and I was obviously smarter than the rest of them. That doesn't get you any friends and I concluded that for the rest of my life I would always be an outsider. In retrospect that was an amazingly correct assumption.

Now that I was caught up with my schooling I had some time to do things that kids do. Two events stand out in my memory, both negative from an adults point of view. The apartment building where we lived was owned by a gentleman, Mr. Hirsch, who lived there too. He was a hobby gardener and practised it right behind his five story building. He also had a big German shepherd dog that made sure that nobody stole any fruit from his master's gardening ventures. Every day Mr. Hirsch took the big dog for an hour long walk around the neighborhood, but at times his sciatica bothered him so much that he could not take the dog out. He then asked other tenants to do that for him, which I thought was quite an imposition. One time my father had the Schnaps-idea to suggest that I take the dog for a walk, even though he knew about my previous experience with a dog down in Silesia. So I had to take the damn beast for a walk and my previous experience was repeated. The dog tried to get away and I tried to hold on to the leash and fell and got some very nasty scrape marks on the leg I had surgery on. I was really pissed off at my father and told him so. I was turned off at dogs for the rest of my life.

The other incident was based on my stupidity. All along our street we had plane trees which have golf ball size seeds in the fall season. We kids used the seeds as projectiles for our sling shots or pitched them by hand. We had a competition in throwing them over the double decker busses that frequented a nearby street. The timing and aim was difficult because the busses approached at about 35 MPH and the seeds were not supposed to hit the bus but to sail right over the top of them. Naturally at times our trajectories were off somewhat and hit the side of the bus. An impact damage was not noticeable, but it landed with a fairly loud bang. The bus driver probably didn't even notice the impact bang over the engine noise, but one day when my trajectory was off the bus driver stepped on the brake jumped out of his cab and went after me. For a moment I was perplexed but then burned the rubber of my shoe soles to get away. The driver was a really fast runner, but knowing all the nooks and crannies of my neighborhood, I escaped. Wow, that scared the hell out of me and prohibited any further participation in that "game".

Grandpa retires

Since Opa's retirement they lived in Bergfelde at the very periphery of Greater Berlin. I had to take the S-Bahn to get there and the trip usually took one hour, if I got the right connections. I had to switch S-Bahn lines twice and sometimes three times to get to Hohen Neuendorf. From that station it was a 40 minute walk through the forest to Bergfelde. If I arrived at the right time I could catch a bus to my destination but most of the time I had to walk. This was a bit scary in winter days when it was dark and I walked very fast to get to the grandparents house. Wolfgang had been "parked" at their home, because his parents had divorced and his mother had to work. We had one hell of a good time when I could visit. Opa had a large garden with all kinds of vegies and fruits. Wolfgang and I picked whatever we liked and that was great, but we also annoyed him because we made "earth movements" as he said. We had dug a big hole near the fence and build a "cave" to play in.

My father was interested in flying, so one day in 1932 we went to the Tempelhof Airport where a school buddy of his was a manager. Dad had made arrangements with Mister von Germershausen who showed us the various airport departments and also went through different commercial aircraft parked in the hangars with us. This was quite a show since one doesn't get into an aircraft unless one flies to another destination. He surprised me by channeling me into a Lufthansa excursion flight above the city of Berlin. I was a bit uneasy about it, because I was the only boy in a class of girls who were seated in the single engine Junkers (probably a G 31). This flight opened an entirely different point of view for me. Seeing buildings and streets from the air was new to me and I enjoyed recognizing distinct areas of Berlin. A teacher who was on board pointed out various outstanding features of our home city.

Several months later there was another opportunity to walk through an airplane. We went out to the large Müggelsee to visit the worlds largest airplane at that time, the Dornier Do-X, a 12 engine flying boat with a wingspan of 157 feet and a power of 7,680 HP. It had been designed for the transatlantic passenger service (100 passengers and 15 crew). The big aircraft had just come back from a 30,000 km round trip to South America, and a continuation north to New York and then back to Berlin.

From Republic to Dictatorship

In January of 1933, when the army's "eminence grise" manipulated and coerced Reichspräsident von Hindenburg to name Hitler as the next Reichskanzler, the trouble began. My grandpa, who was vehemently against Hitler, made his usual sarcastic remarks. He had been the personal attendant of the last German Empress, Auguste Victoria, for over 30 years and couldn't understand how the President of the Weimar Republic, Paul von Hindenburg, was taken in by a man like Hitler. How could he appoint a former deadbeat like Hitler, with hardly any education and an Austrian on top of that, to be Chancellor of Germany? There were endless discussions in the family about the Nazi party, Hitler and his cronies and even though I had no political schooling, the situation disturbed me a lot.

Another job, another move.

Father was looking for a job at a different company and was hired by the Swedish company of Alfa-Laval. They manufactured farm equipment too and brought the first automatic milking machines on the market. We also moved to a different location in Berlin. A large apartment in a new building in Berlin-Baumschulenweg. When we moved into our first floor apartment, the upper two levels were not even finished. The location at the Neue Krug Allee was ideal because across the street was the Plänterwald, a large park area that was bordered by the Spree River and I now had a large green area to roam in.

My Best Friend Dies

Grandpa Thielemann died just a few days after my 12th birthday in 1935. Grandpa had not been well for a few months and the events on the political scene did not help to cheer him up. As I learned from Grandma later on, he had some very upsetting disputes with neighbors who were members of the Nazi party. I think he was so depressed over the political scene that he just lost his will to live.

At his funeral members of the German Royal Family, wearing the military uniforms of the Imperial Army, came to pay their respect. The loss of my favorite person and the pomp and circumstances surrounding the funeral, with the old Imperial German flag being draped over grandpa's coffin, overwhelmed me. Grandpa had been a stand-in father whenever my father was away on business. I was heartbroken.

A new school

My new school was quite a distance from our home and it took a 30-40 minute walk to get there, depending on the weather, . We had no school buses and public transportation was not convenient since I would have to use 2 different streetcar lines to get close enough to the school. It took me a while to get established at that school, but the teachers were good and I liked the curriculum which also included chemistry in a school laboratory. Then new and political problems started at school. After Hitler's power was established all sorts of new requirement were imposed on us. Whoever was not a member of the Hitler Youth (HJ) had school on Saturdays, doing physical education. My parents did not object to me being required to partake, probably for political reasons.

Nazi ideology filters into our life

The family scenes gradually changed too, because the "new order" had penetrated down to the family level. The discriminatory rules that had been decreed by the Nazi government made open discussions dangerous and difficult. Acquaintances disappeared from our family circle, but the family members were afraid to talk about it. Certain books by Jewish authors were no longer allowed in school. The teacher's rhetoric began to be anti-Semitic. My teachers let me know that my Jewish friend should be avoided, but I didn't followed their advice.

At the beginning of the next school year each student in our class had to produce a family tree. We had to come up with documents that proved our "Aryan" ancestry at least back to our grandparents. This meant that birth, marriage and death certificates had to be obtained from registrar's offices wherever these relatives had lived.

All ancestors on my father's side came from an area near the Luxemburg and Belgium borders, about 500 miles away, while the family on my mother's side came from Saxonia. It took a lot of writing and money to obtain these documents. Some branches of my family tree were traceable back to the year 1625. It was clear however that some branches of the family tree on mother's side had been Jewish, but they were beyond the grandparent's level and so I omitted them.

I was upset when the Jewish kid and his parents who lived upstairs, decided to leave Germany. I overheard my parents talk with friends about other Jewish friends, but they talked quietly because they never knew who was listening in. The newest political jokes about Hitler were also quietly shared.

My father said that I would be better off joining a sports club than the HJ. He had been in a rowing crew when he was attending college and thought that would be a good sport for me considering my leg injury. He checked where the next club was located and took me to the Berlin Youth Rowing Club to enroll me. Their boat house was in Oberschöneweide on the Spree River. When he found out that the club's president was a Mr. Buchholz Jr., he was quite surprised. A Mr. Buchholz, Sr. had been father's trainer at the college and he turned out to be the club president's father. When Buchholz Sr. appeared there was a great big reunion and a mini party started right away. Buchholz Sr. had retired from college and was the trainer for this club and he would take me under his wing and introduce me to the rowing sport. I felt right at home there. The club had an indoor "boat" in which I and other members were trained.

Berlin is the ideal city for any kind of water sport. In and around the city are several rivers, numerous canals and a lot of lakes. After basic training we would be rowing to many places and see beautiful areas. The club had a great variety of boats from skiffs to 4 and 8 oar rowing boats with and without coxswain. I took many weekend tours with that club and we went to many distant lakes and camped there. At a bird sanctuary we were attacked by a swan when we came too close to their nest. We were defended by a farmer's dog who chased that huge bird. Their wing span can be up to 6 feet.

More and more political and personal problems

A problem affected my father's new job. The Government decreed that farmers were not allowed to centrifuge their milk anymore to make butter to sell it on the open (farmers) market. They had to deliver the milk to a government agency. Hitler wanted to cut down on all agricultural imports to save money. Germany bought a lot of butter and cheese from Denmark and Switzerland and that had to be paid in foreign currency, which the government was short of. It was one of those typical Nazi government bullshit claims. As a consequence Alfa-Laval had to leave Germany, they could not sell their products anymore. Father was out of a job again and we had to move to a cheaper apartment. My mother found a place just a block away on Neue Krug Allee and so I could stay in the same school. We were terribly cramped there, because we had to move the furniture of a three bedroom apartment into a 1 1/2 bedroom apartment and that wasn't easy. The 1/2 bedroom was my room but I had to share it with the piano, a couch and some other furniture.

The new political situation stirred up everybody except the members of the Nazi party. Our family was split politically, the Thielemann side was against Hitler while my maternal grandma and some other family members were for him. Whenever we had a get together on a birthday or an anniversary, the political opinions exploded and often ended in shouting matches. My mother was often upset for weeks because her mother put Hitler on the pedestal. Another pro Hitler man in the family was my great-uncle Paul Thielemann, the older brother of my grandfather. He was employed in the Reichskanzelei and worked for the State-Secretary Otto Meissner who was in charge of protocol in the German government. Uncle Paul urged my father many times to join the Nazi party but my father didn't want to have anything to do with the Nazis. At these parties however a lot of political jokes were told, but one had to be more and more careful telling them, because the "Party" had their ears open everywhere.

Here are a few of these jokes that I still remember:

Why docs Hitler like to sit on the toilet? Because then he has the whole brown mass behind him.

A Berliner walks into a store and says "Good morning" instead of "Heil Hitler" and the owner comes running and asks, "what do you mean? Is he dead?

Goering and Goebbels die and go to hell. The punishment: for Goering 1,000 new uniforms and no mirror; for Goebbels 1,000 radios and no microphone.

All roads lead to Rome, but all of Hitler's streets lead to Irrland (the German spelling of Ireland).

Karl Valentin (a Munich comedian) goes on stage, raises his arm in the Nazi salute and shouts: Heil...then scratches his head and says dammit, now I forgot his name!

Grandfather Rausch, the black sheep in the family

My maternal Grandfather Paul Rausch a very elegant man, played excellent tennis and was always dressed according to the latest fashion. He was a textile chemist by profession, who had specialized in fur dyeing, a very difficult field. He was working all over Europe. He had well paying jobs in countries that were in the fur business. Furs were the style during the 1920 to 1940 years and especially the upper class people wallowed in them. Wherever he worked he had girlfriends, since his wife didn't want to move to different countries. Grandpa had affairs all over Europe and many times when we traveled in Germany, my mother would say, "There's supposed to be a half brother or sister of mine in that town." Grandpa's last job was in Poland and he supposedly had a stroke there. He was brought back to Berlin to get better medical care. Grandma Rausch was not enthusiastic about having him home after the doctors found that he had syphilis in an advanced stage.

Grandpa Rausch slowly went into the delirium stage and had to be transferred to Herzfelde, one of the "funny farms" of Berlin, where he died the same year. In contrast to Grandpa Thielemann's funeral, his was very small and family oriented. I thought Grandma Rausch was glad to get rid of him, even though it meant that she had to give up her fancy apartment in Lichtenberg. She found an apartment in the same block where we lived. Grandma Thielemann also could not stay by herself in Bergfelde, so my mother arranged for her to move to a nearby flat too.

Now I had both grandmothers practically living next to each other. I called both grandmas "Oma" and to distinguish between them, one was the White Oma and the other was the Brown Oma. Referring to the color of their hair.

Nearly Fatal Pre-Olympics

In early 1936, there was much ado about the coming Olympic games in Berlin, and feverish construction was underway to build the facilities and stadiums for the games. The papers and magazines were full of articles about the various sporting activities, and we kids staged our own Olympic games in the Plänterwald. Since we didn't have any money, we had to devise our own equipment. We used an appropriately sized stone for the shot-put, and came up with a discus and a javelin for the field and track competitions. It was all great fun. However, one of the kids in the javelin competition got angry when I beat him. Just as I turned my back, he threw the metal javelin at me. I felt a piercing pain in my right leg, looked down and saw the javelin stuck through my pant leg. I reached down and yanked it out. Blood was running down my leg and I thought I would bleed to death, so I ran home as fast as I could. Mother immediately put a tourniquet around my thigh. My stockings, shoes and the kitchen floor were full of blood. Mother washed the blood off and had a closer look at the damage. I had been extremely lucky, because the metal entered underneath the main tendon running down the inside of the knee, without damaging the tendon itself. It was just a flesh wound, and mother patched it released the tourniquet, and ordered me to bed. She had worked in a hospital at the end of World War I, and although not a nurse, had sufficient experience to cope with all my childhood mishaps.

And another move

My father had a new job, he was hired by the Shell Oil Company, that was allowed to remain in Germany even though they were a foreign company. The president of that Dutch/British company was an admirer of Hitler, and Hitler needed oil for his armed forces. Father worked in their big, modernistic Shell office building in Berlin, built by Emil Fahrenkamp (Bauhaus) in 1930. He was being trained in the oil and gasoline business. After several months he came home and said that we would have to move again, and this time really into

the "province", as the typical Berliner saying was for anyplace outside
of the German Capitol. Shell had given him his own sales district,
the eastern half of the Province of Brandenburg. We were to be relo-
cated in 1936 to Landsberg/Warthe (45,000 population). Well, that
was quite a change. We had never lived in a city that small before.

Hans and his Father 1924

Grandparents Thielemann, about 1933

Grandparents Rausch, about 1925

Hans in baby carriage, 1924

The three musketeers, left to right, Wolfgang, Ellen, Hans, 1925

Kindergarten, establishing a trend?? 1928

Father and I, after my school accident, 1929

Dad selling International Harvester Company Tractors, 1928

International Harvester Toys, 1929

Hiking with the grandparents in the mountains 1929

Ellen and I. Notice scars on right leg, 1932

When all the trouble started, Hitler came to power January 1933

At the Baltic Sea 1935

In politics nothing is contemptible.
Disraeli

2
Politically Correct?

After Father found housing in Landsberg, mother and I followed at the beginning of the 1936 summer school recess. That gave us plenty of time to get settled before school opened.

We moved into a brand new up and down duplex, another first for us, since we had always lived in large apartment complexes. The owner of the duplex, a dentist by the name of Fichtmann, occupied the ground floor, while we had the spacious apartment upstairs. From the large balcony there was a 180° view of the surrounding suburban area, and a large sandy hill, where until about 1850 condemned criminals had been hanged.

Up to now we had lived in large metropolitan areas, so I had to adapt to the different life style and the people who lived in this small town. Landsberg had only a small streetcar system in the downtown area, about two miles from our duplex. I had to have a bike. Father finally gave in and bought me an old clunker of a bike "to learn on". It was a "museum's piece," as we kids called outdated things in those days and it embarrassed me to ride it in public. After I proved to my father that I could ride properly he said he would buy me a new bike, and I could even select it myself.

My new bike, delivered by one of father's customers, was not the latest in bike technology but it solved my transportation problem. Now I could roam and explore the picturesque town and surrounding areas. The Warthe, a large river, ran through town in an east west direction. It was spanned by a massive stone bridge connecting the two parts of the city divided by the river. The river was navigable for ships up to 200 tons. Barges towed by tug boats, or self-propelled, hauled bulk freight up and down the river. South of the river was a huge, fertile and rather flat valley, shaped during the last ice age by melting glacier water. This valley was subject to flooding every spring, so it was prime agricultural land.

North of the river the land rose several hundred feet into smooth, sandy, pine forested hills, with numerous picturesque lakes. The town of Landsberg (which had a namesake in southern Germany), was old for this part of Germany. The massive, Gothic style Marien Kirche (church) in the center of town had been built in the 16th century, and had been altered and expanded in subsequent centuries.

My father already had numerous business contacts and mother and I met many of them. One of the most interesting people was Peter Bergner and his large family. Mr. Bergner had the largest dry cleaning and dyeing business in town. He employed about 50 people, including a maid by the name of Emma, and a chauffeur.

Peter's second wife, Martha, had been his secretary when his first wife died of cancer. He had a much older son from his first marriage, and four daughters and a son from his second one. The daughters were Anneliese, Ruth, Edith, Inge and son Dietrich (Dieter, Dee). When I first met them, Anneliese, the oldest daughter, was about 20 years old. Dee was seven years old. Peter Bergner, had connections everywhere and was well liked. His only extravagance was a dark blue 1934 Packard sedan of truly impressive size, driven by his chauffeur. The chauffeur compartment was separated from the passenger section of the car by a sliding glass window. The car easily accommodated six passengers. Its massive engine had the most horsepower of any car registered in the county of Landsberg.

The Bergners often invited us to their home, and I got interested in Inge, who was about my age. Dee was a bit too young for me, but later on we became best friends.

The Only Student Not in the Hitler Youth

Starting in a new school always was a grizzly experience for introverted me, even though I had changed schools often, and should have been used to it. There were no coed schools in Germany. To fit into a new school class was difficult, because each class had an established pecking order that was upset by the addition of a new pupil. The "new one" had to be scrutinized and classified to find out if and how he fit in. I had to first deal with the aggressive class bullies. The outcome depended on how they sized me up, and that depended on how I dealt with them. It was an intimidating experience because I had these clowns behind my back, until either I or they, had established a new pecking order. I tried to play it cool until I had sorted out their intellectual capacities. That didn't take long. Scholastically I was more than one year ahead of these boys, because Berlin had far better schools than this small town. I ignored the smart alecks, but once in a while they ganged up on me. They finally classified me as a kid of rich parents, because I wore better clothes, and my father had a car. I didn't have to pay much attention in class, and yet was consistently among the top three students in school and most of the time, at the very top. My biggest handicap was that I was the only student in this school who was not a member of the Hitler Youth (HJ). One student out of 450. Talk about pressure, from the kids and the teachers. I tried to ignore them as much as I could.

The teachers were a special subcategory of homo erectus. In retrospect, they fit Murphy's law which says, "Those who can, do, those who cannot, teach, and those who cannot teach, administrate."

The principal of the school was Mr. Hildebrand, a veteran who had lost an arm in World War I, and was an SA Obersturmführer. He often wore his Nazi uniform in school. He liked me, but I wasn't sure if that was because of my top notch scholastic record. I never felt quite comfortable with him.

Much later in 1945 when the Russian Army occupied Landsberg he committed suicide.

My class teacher was Mr. Zuelke, another Nazi, who constantly reprimanded and embarrassed me because I wasn't a member of the HJ. A funny guy was Mr. Zippel the PE teacher. He was tall and extremely gawky but not a member of the brown shirted Nazi variety. After he came back from the Olympic Games in Berlin in 1936 he was the only one who gave us an honest account of the winners of the Olympic competitions. The most impossible character was Mr. Dietert, whom we called "the Owl," because he looked like one. This could have been because he was teaching natural history and biology. He did some interesting experiments with the class however. When teaching about human perception, he had the class get paper and pencil ready and then he opened the windows for 5 minutes. We were not allowed to speak or make noise, but had to write down all the outside noises we could hear. He then closed the windows, and each student had to write an assay about the noises they had heard, and how the student thought the noise had been generated. Then all the assays were compared, and it was stunning what some students heard and what they thought the source of the various noises were. A very interesting study about differences in human perception.

I finished school and didn't join the Hitler Youth until a law was firmly enforced that decreed that every youth between the ages of ten and 18 was "automatically" a member of the HJ. When I reported to the "brown kindergarten" as I called it, the first question was, "How come you are joining late?" My prompt answer was that it hadn't been compulsory before. That really angered the HJ Führer, who put me in with the ten year old kids, which was the most demeaning insult to me. I towered over everybody. I retaliated by not showing my face very often at their meetings, and the police inquired several times about my whereabouts. I always found some excuses.

My father insisted that I have a private tutor in English so I would be fluent in the language. The Nazi attitude was that German would soon be the most important language in Europe so there wasn't emphasis on foreign languages in the schools any more. Mrs. Peters, my tutor, was an older, frightfully English lady, who drilled me in British grammar and syntax, irregular verbs, plusquamperfects and similar unpleasant grammar subjects. On occasion she told me the latest political jokes about Hitler, which she picked up from friends and relatives in London and from the BBC. She was a good teacher who always checked my homework, and tried to give me a good base in the language. Unfortunately I didn't gain fluency in conversational English because there was no chance to practice it.

To get together with different kids and to continue my favorite sport, I joined one of the local rowing clubs in Landsberg. Here, as in Berlin, I liked working out, meeting new people, and seeing new scenery. All the rowing took place on the Warthe River, which was large and swiftly running. Every spring the river flooded wide agricultural areas despite the fact that they were diked. This was a fun time for rowing out and crossing some of these large flooded areas. There was competition between the clubs as to who would be the first one up the river in spring. The up-river restaurants offered schnapps and the traditional one dozen eggs for the first crew arriving. Yes, even as 14 year old kids we downed the one shot glass of schnapps. This first outing was commonly referred to as the "egg trip", an old rowing tradition, often risky, because large chunks of ice were still floating down the river. If we ran aground while using shortcuts across the flooded areas, the coxswain was obliged to step into the shallow, icy waters and push the boat off the obstruction.

The Olympics and the American Relatives

When the 1936 Olympics were held, I was sorry not to live in Berlin any more. Even though I was excluded from physical education in school because of my earlier leg accident, I was privately active in soccer, field and track, swimming and rowing, so I wanted to watch some of these events. My Aunt Hanna and her daughter Ellen had come over from New York again, and I wanted to see them too. My mother, however, invented all sorts of strange excuses why I should not. Finally I gave up. I found out decades later from Wolfgang that my mother was afraid I would get romantically involved with my cousin, it was one of her Schnaps-idea as my father said. Maybe it was because Ellen's father, uncle Hans was Jewish and mother was afraid of Nazi reprisals. She never told me about her reasoning, she was probably embarrassed.

Aunt Hanne got into hot water with the ever present Nazi party members in Berlin. She refused to raise her right arm to greet Nazi flags that were carried in rallies, etc. They questioned her and she told the Nazis that she and her daughter were Americans and couldn't be bothered to greet a political party's flag. My aunt didn't beat around the bush, and couldn't be intimidated. With so many foreign guests in Berlin for the Olympic Games, the Storm Troopers (SA) didn't dare raise a ruckus about it. My other aunt, Kläre, who was working for the government, was embarrassed about her "little" sister, and kept a distance from her when in public.

A lot of things happened in 1936. The Olympic Games started with an enormous propaganda effort. Hitler reoccupied the Rheinland, and nullified the Locarno pact. Compulsory military service of 24 months duration was decreed by the government. Hitler and Mussolini signed the ill fated "Axis" pact, which would become a troublesome burden to Germany later on. An Anticomintern pact with Japan was also signed, which likewise proved not worth the paper it was written on.

Even though a lot of people in Germany were still enthusiastic about Hitler, there was an increasing fear that his political games would lead Germany straight into another war. The older people were especially opposed to war, they had bad memories of World War One.

I enjoyed going on long bike trips In Landsberg, and often went for 60 mile trips all by myself. I never had a serious accident, even though no helmets were worn. One day however I had the glorious idea of going down a steep and narrow downtown street called Schlachthofgasse. It's lower end forming a "T" with Landsberg's main street. I couldn't stop as I approached the main street, so I schussed across both traffic lanes at right angles and onto Mr. Schumm's Shell filling station, which was across the street. I heard the screeching brakes of an Opel convertible, and saw the driver literally stand on his brake pedal. When I saw what I had done I didn't waste any time and pedaled off at top speed, disappearing into the next side street to avoid the irate driver. Mr. Schumm, who had been filling up a car at the moment when it happened, was panic stricken by what he saw and of course knew who I was. When I arrived home, the "reception com-mittee" was waiting for me, and they hadn't rolled out the red carpet. My father furiously read me the riot act, strictly forbade me to ever ride that street again, and locked up my bike for two weeks. I had learned my lesson, plus I now had to walk for the next two weeks, which gave me time to contemplate my stupidity.

Confirmation

Early in March of 1938 I was almost 15, and was to be confirmed at the large Lutheran Marien Kirche in Landsberg. My parents had dis-agreements about my confirmation. My father had left the Church many years ago and considered confirmation unnecessary. My mother thought that I should be confirmed, and that I could then decide whether I wanted to remain with the church. I went through the nec-essary instructions, and was looking forward to the festivities. Many family members whom I hadn't seen for quite some time arrived in Landsberg for the occasion.

It was customary that all teenagers who would become members of the church were introduced to the congregation by name. When we stood up, the minister asked religious questions. When one of my rowing buddies was introduced, the question was, what is the differ-ence between the "Heavenly kingdom" and the "Third Reich"? He answered, "There isn't any difference, both will last forever." This caused an audible gasp in the congregation and raised numerous eye-brows, but the Nazis in church were pleased. I could see my father's head shaking and his facial expressions giving an indication of an-noyance. I later talked to my rowing buddy and he told me that his answer had been ordered by the minister, who was apparently more often seen in a Nazi uniform than in his ministerial robe.

The family party was a bash, with some embarrassing moments for my mother. Father, probably because of the "Nazi statement" at church, didn't even talk to the pastor when he dropped in. That upset my mother, because father could at least have said hello. The relatives ignored my father's anger and all continued to have a good time. I received a lot of gifts, and also many flowers from my father's custom-ers. I counted a total of 13 beautiful azaleas, which I adored, but I secretly wondered about the ominous number 13.

Starting Professional Education

I finished school in 1938, one year ahead of schedule, and was the top ranking student in my school. My father insisted that I learn a technical profession. I would have liked to be a car mechanic, but my mother categorically declared that she was not going to wash the dirty overalls of a car mechanic, and that was that.

I went to the employment office to see what other apprenticeships were available. I easily passed several technical aptitude tests and settled down to study ophthalmic optics. During my apprenticeship I attended a local technical school and several times a year I had to take special optics courses away from home. The apprenticeship was to last four years.

I hated the political crap that was going on in the Hitler Youth (HJ). I considered the marches and meetings childish, but I had to make at least a token appearance now and then at their meetings. I discovered that I could transfer into the Motor-HJ and I would gain technical automobile knowledge, learn traffic rules and how to ride a motorcycle. This was better than being taught how to serve "Our Führer". Despite the technically interesting subjects, I staid away as often as possible but had to invent all sorts of excuses such as my rowing training, and the heavy schedule of my apprenticeship etc. The police questioned my mother several times about my whereabouts.

Girls, not the Hitler Youth

On top of all these demands on my time and skills, I was going through puberty. I had a number of good-looking girlfriends and mother encouraged me to bring the girls home, so that she could see with whom I was hanging out and whether or not she could live with them, in case there was a need to take her in as a daughter-in-law.

In school and in the family I had learned about venereal diseases and the dire consequences of making a girl pregnant. An enormous amount of fear and apprehension had been instilled in us kids. We were told never to have sex without a condom, but nobody told us how sexual intercourse was done. Most of what I learned was fantasy, in hush-hush talks, with the kids who did it. A few girls got pregnant and that was scandalous. Most kids grew up with negative impressions, even fear, about sex, and avoided it.

In 1938 Germany annexed Austria under the pretense of bringing it home into the big Fatherland. That was followed by the Sudeten "crisis", the Munich conference, and the occupation of the Sudetenland. It was obvious that Hitler would not keep any of his promises and pacts, and that he was determined to go as far as he could get.

Reichskristallnacht

One day I was biking downtown and saw SA men and other people standing in front of businesses whose show windows had been smashed. I talked to the people milling around the stores, who told me about the Reichskristallnacht, the plundering of Jewish businesses and confiscation of their property. I didn't even know that these businesses were owned by Jewish people. I called my mother right away, so she could turn on the radio, to find out what was going on.

At work on Monday morning, my boss, Mr. Buchner, his daughter, and I discussed the situation. They were incensed about this illegal and frightening action. Again the discussion turned towards whether or not there would be another war. We agreed that it looked that way. The cleaning lady, Mrs. Mielke, was beside herself about the possibility of another war. Her son had been drafted into the army, and she worried about him a lot, as did millions of mothers in Germany.

My personal life was far more important to me than the political scene. I had a new girlfriend Steffi, from Austria. I suspected that she had been sent to relatives in Landsberg until things calmed down after the Anschluss in Austria. She was pert and short, blond, quite muscular and totally different from the Landsberg girls. She wore lederhosen and coarse mountain hiking shoes with steel-nailed soles. She didn't take crap from anybody. When the guys got fresh with her she would let go with a hard punch to their stomach. I ogled her from a safe distance, and didn't make any attempts to meet her. This went on for quite a while until she noticed my inattention. Then she started hanging around where I worked, particularly around quitting time.

One night I came out of the store to go home and Steffi was showing off in a most peculiar way. She would run and then go into a skid on the smooth, granite covered sidewalk, sending showers of sparks from the steel nails under her shoe soles. Guys did that occasionally, but girls? I thought it was a bit theatrical, but the fact that she was different made her interesting.

I asked her for a movie date. We became good friends. She turned out to be feminine, even romantic but just a bit too gushy. She apparently put that rough behavior up for self-defense, to keep the guys she didn't like at a distance. Being Catholic, she didn't believe in premarital sex or even petting, but wanted to get married as soon as possible and have children. I dated her for a while but lost interest because I didn't want to get married that young.

My father didn't like the political situation and could not refrain from making sarcastic remarks about the Nazi nonsense. One day he asked at a neighborhood store for a "Hitler herring". When the owner's wife, Mrs. Ihlenfeld, looked puzzled, she asked her husband, working in the back of the store, if they carried Hitler herring. He came up front to see who the joker was that asked for it and when he saw my father, he said to his wife, "Give him a Bismarck herring without a head." His answer had them all in stitches.

In early 1939 my father told us we had better prepare for a war, because Hitler was doing the same. My parents had lived through World War I, and so they knew what type supplies would be in short supply and could be stored. My father also decreed that we would go on a family vacation.

During July 1939, we set out for the Baltic Sea in father's company car. As we drove north from Landsberg, we met all types of military convoys. Father said he was worried that if the war started while we were on the road, we might not get any gasoline. However, the front wheel drive DKW was extremely frugal in gas consumption (about 30 M.P.G.), and father always carried a spare can of gas in the trunk.

We had selected a tiny Baltic Sea village named Pustchow near Hoff for our vacation spot. Mother and I had been there before, and we stayed with the same family, who farmed and did commercial fishing. We had a simple room with our own kitchen and did our own cooking, since there weren't any restaurants in the village. My father took a liking to the host family and we helped them get the hay in when thunderstorms threatened, or helped to haul in fishing nets.

Mysterious Flying Objects

Below the coastal cliffs was a beautiful white beach. This remote village wasn't frequented by many tourists, so the visitors really stuck out and they sure looked different this year. While on a hike along the sea cliff we noticed new wooden structures that looked like observation platforms, but we could not figure out what there was to observe. Careful questioning of the locals revealed that strange looking small and very fast airplanes were flying parallel to the coast. Some measurements were apparently being taken from these platforms. It took my father's considerable patience to find out that much. It also seemed that some civilians, who looked like summer guests, were really watching everyone. We decided that the airplanes were part of a secret project so we refrained from prying any further. The atmosphere along the coast was not the usual summer vacation party atmosphere.

Years later I learned that Werner von Braun was leading the research and development work of the first pulse jet powered military weapon, later called V-1. This work took place in Peenemünde, about 40 miles southwest from us on the island of Usedom. The test vehicles were flown along the Pomeranian Baltic coast, and observed from the platforms we had seen.

Despite the charged and uneasy atmosphere at the village, we had a good time soaking up the sunshine, and swimming in the beautiful blue green sea. At the end of July 1939, we returned to Landsberg, again encountering military convoys. The masses of military vehicles with heavy artillery pieces driven through Landsberg had caused cracks in houses along the route. People realized that war was imminent. Landsberg was only about 25 miles from the Polish border, and if a war broke out, artillery shells from the Polish side could reach us. There were idiots who claimed that the war would be over in two weeks, if not sooner.

On August 23, 1939, the radio announced that Germany and the Soviet Union had reached a nonaggression pact. Not many details were given about the agreement. First the Nazis made a continuous propaganda effort against Stalin and the USSR, and now they had signed an agreement with them? Who could figure that one out? The guesses were that the war against Poland was now as good as won.

Not even the worst pessimists (or optimists) guessed that this pact would seal Hitler's fate. Stalin was now in the driver's seat, because an economical agreement had also been reached. Germany would receive oil and other important strategic materials from the USSR, so Stalin could influence Hitler's actions.

Three days later it was announced that ration cards would be issued for food, soap, shoes, textiles and coal. "Now you have the shit," declared my mother. The allowances were 1.5 lb of meat, 6/10 lb of sugar, 1/4 lb of jam, 1/8 lb of coffee or ersatz (fake coffee) and 4.5 ounces of soap per week, per person. Everybody said Hitler must be preparing for a long war.

September 1, 1939

On September 1 Hitler ordered the army to invade Poland and the sun started to set for Germany on this infamous day. An immediate blackout was ordered. All street lights were turned off and vehicles had to put black discs with only a narrow horizontal slit over the headlight lenses. Residents were ordered to blacken all windows so that no interior light could be seen from the outside.

Air raid wardens made the rounds in their neighborhood, checking for visible light. This caused a lot of irritation at first, until efficient ways were found to darken houses and apartments. Stores and restaurants had to put black curtains inside of each entrance door so that no light could be seen when the doors were opened. Since most people had vertically hinged, double windows which opened inward, they covered the inside windows with black paper or fabric, and left the outer windows clear. The blacked out windows were left open during the day. In many houses only one room and the kitchen were blacked out, because people didn't have enough money to buy black material for all their windows.

In the streets, curbs around intersections were painted white to make them visible to pedestrians. Everyone had flashlights, but even these had to be dimmed by blue filters. People wore stick-on fluorescent buttons on their clothing so they wouldn't bump into each other in the dark. It was especially spooky during the moonless nights. It was quite an inconvenience, and only we teenagers were having fun, since young eyes are better in dark adaption.

The news on the radio and in the papers now dominated everything. France and England had now also declared war on Germany. The information, or rather the propaganda of the Nazi government, was running at full speed. It fed people all the bullshit they could take, and then some more. Fortunately my parents had a radio with shortwave bands, so we listened to what the propaganda machines of the outside world were cranking out. By believing 50 percent of what the Nazis said and 50 percent of what the outside world said, we were able to get pretty close to the truth.

The first obituaries of soldiers killed in Poland appeared in the papers, and even we kids became aware of the terrible price individuals had to pay to satisfy the ambitions of a few idiotic politicians. Although the war in Poland ended after one month, nobody felt better, we knew that war would continue at the western front. Nothing was heard about fighting there, and everyone hoped a peace agreement could still be reached. That was wishful thinking, Hitler's violent action in Poland had removed any doubt about his true intentions.

Apprenticeship in Optics

I liked working as an apprentice for Mr. Buchner. I learned to cut and edge corrective lenses, repair lens frames, and fit the frames to customer's faces. I also trained in subjective refraction and theoretical physiological optics, and took courses in physical optics.

The son-in-law and daughter of Mr. Buchner, Willy Bauer and his wife who worked there as opticians, and I were enthusiastic photographers. My favorite work was doing photo enlargements, but this was done only for the Buchner family. The printing for customers was done by a professional photographer across the street. At times I was down in the lab by myself, and experimented with various enlargement techniques. That was fun, but it was frowned upon by the boss, because new printing paper was no longer available. One time I had to move the enlarger, and discovered a whole stack of nudist magazines under its base plate. I was sure that they had been left there by Willy Bauer, who had peculiar habits. I suspected that he and his wife had sex in the refraction room at times, because they made strange noises in there. Willy also went on vacation with his stepdaughter Margot, who was my age. They always went to the Baltic during the summer, while Mrs. Bauer went on vacation by herself to Bavaria or Austria. There was much talk about that in town.

The war eliminated my father's position with Shell Oil Company in Landsberg, because the government took over administration and distribution of all gasoline and oil. Gasoline was available only to a few institutions and individuals with a red chevron on their license plates. Only government officials, physicians, essential trucks, and farmers with motorized equipment had these license plates. Many owners of automobiles had to report to the military with the vehicles they owned. Father stayed for a while in Landsberg to convert the local Shell distribution center for the war requirements, then he transferred to the Shell Company's main office in Berlin, which functioned as a government distribution agency now.

Another move

My father was still allowed to drive his company car, but he didn't get commissions any more, so we had to lower our living standards considerably. That meant another move into a smaller, less expensive place. My mother fortunately found an apartment in an older up-and-down duplex in the same street. The best feature of it was the large garden, important during war times. Mother was an enthusiastic gardener, and was looking forward to this with pleasure.

The disadvantage of the place was that it was the only house in the neighborhood not connected to the city sewer. The house had a large concrete cesspool that collected all the sewage, which had to be emptied several times a year. The owner had installed a large hand pump and had bought a number of galvanized sheet metal gutters (like rain gutters) to distribute the contents of the cesspool throughout the garden. Talk about smell! I did not enjoy that type of fertilization, necessary to make our mini-farm productive. The neighbors ran around with clothes pins on their noses when it was pump day.

The downstairs apartment of the duplex had three rooms, plus one bathroom and a kitchen. There wasn't enough space for me to have my own room, so I had to sleep in the living room. The large basement had an old-fashioned laundry room. A huge copper cauldron built into a firebrick base, heated by wood and coal, it was used to boil the laundry. There was also a wood and coal stove in the kitchen, with an additional gas range. It was a move back in time by about 50 years, as well as a move down in size. We also had to chop our own firewood. I couldn't help but make a sarcastic remark to my mother, "Ma'am, permit me to say, we thank our Führer." She gave me a dirty look but had tears in her eyes.

We slowly got acquainted with our new neighbors. To the left were Dutch people by the name of Timmermann. He was a tall, authoritarian looking character, who worked at Landsberg's gas processing plant. Mrs. Timmermann, who always wore black or dark colored old fashioned dresses, seem to be from a different era. She too was tall, and looked like she had come out of a medieval castle. According to my mother she seemed to be pregnant all the time. Mrs. Timmermann could hardly speak German, so everybody had problems communicating with her. They already had three girls by the name of Anni, Hilde and Lotti, and later another girl, Carla.

Above us lived Hildegard Piechatzeck all by herself. Her husband had been drafted right away when the war started, and he was in the air force at the western front. Hildegard was an attractive young woman, blond and slim and always well dressed. She liked to dance, and lived it up while the old guy was away at war, which annoyed my mother. Mother thought that Hildegard had affairs all over town. At one time Hildegard tried to seduce me, but my mother stepped in and broke up the attempt. Mother's opinion was, that at 16, I was too young for sex. Later I often fantasized what would have happened if Hildegard had been successful. I wished she had taught me all she knew about sex. She was lonely, so her amorous advances towards me were understandable. Mother and Hildegard were otherwise on good terms and became good friends.

In 1940 we heard of a big new development being planned around Landsberg. Nobody knew what was going on, but the I. G. Farben

Company, one of the largest chemical concerns in the world, had purchased a huge tract of land northeast of the city along the Friedeberger Chaussee. In a short period of time large buildings were erected for an industrial complex. Under the direction of Dr. Klare it became Germany's largest manufacturing plant of man-made fibers. Dr. Klare was the co-inventor of the Perlon fiber. Perlon was every bit as good as, and in some characteristics better than, Nylon. When fully on stream the Landsberg plant cranked out six tons of Perlon per month, primarily used in parachutes for the Luftwaffe and airplane tire cords. It brought a large influx of workers into Landsberg.

The First Bombs

It was early 1940. The year had started with more bad news. Finland had to capitulate to Russia. Germany marched into Denmark and Norway. Then suddenly on May 10th the much awaited German offensive against France, Belgium, Holland and the British Expeditionary Army began, and to everybody's surprise was won by the end of June. The German Wehrmacht seemed to be invincible, and everybody was certain a landing in Britain would be next. The Luftwaffe continuously bombarded cities in England, and on July 26 the inevitable happened. The British returned the "courtesy", and bombed Berlin, which according to Goering, could not happen. Goering's name after that event was "Meier," because he had bragged in a speech that if the British could get through to bomb German cities, his name was going to be Meier. It again showed what dumbskulls our leaders were.

One night the air raid alarm went off, but was ignored as usual. Whenever Berlin was under attack, 80 miles west of us, Landsberg also had air alarms. Shortly after the alarm, I heard a single airplane overhead and seconds later two explosions. That certainly got everybody's attention. Since I had been outside when the explosions occurred, I had a general idea of the direction were the bombs had come down. Early next morning I hopped on my bike to find the location. About a mile from our house I saw two large bomb craters in an open field. Army officers from the nearby garrison were already looking at the craters and had found parts of a bomb's tail section. This bombing was surely part of a British attempt to remind everyone that Germany was vulnerable, and would soon feel the destruction of war too.

With the Hitler Youth to Poland

The Hitler Youth group that I was a member of planned a trip into occupied Poland. We would use our own bikes to get there. I didn't want to go, but to my surprise was urged by my father to participate. A group of about 20 of us guys set out from Landsberg early in the morning, and crossed the old border post around noon. We continued east to a little town by the name of Pinne. We went to a large country estate with a mansion type home, several guest houses overlooking a pond, and many horses and other animals. Our "Führer" apparently knew the present occupant, or had made arrangements with him. He showed us all to our quarters, and ordered us to clean up and report at the dining room in the mansion at 5:30 pm sharp. I got sidetracked by my bike problem, so I missed the time by a few minutes.

When I did arrive, everybody was already seated at a U-shaped group of tables in the huge dining room. I was embarrassed about my tardiness, quickly assessed the situation, and sat on the nearest available chair. I noticed that my late arrival triggered consternation at the head table. A fat party boss in the usual brown uniform, and various other potentates sat with our Hitler Youth Führer. They frowned at me with displeasure and the Hitler Youth Führer whispered something to the party boss, who was probably a District Party boss, or "Kreisleiter." I pretended not to notice the disturbance at the head table, and casually talked to the kid next to me. He whispered to me that I was supposed to go up to the Kreisleiter, salute, introduce myself, and shake hands. I thought, why didn't they tell me that ahead of time? I wasn't going to get up again, walk up to the head of the table in front of everyone and make a fool of myself, besides that, dinner was starting already.

In came eight uniformed footmen, carrying huge food platters as would have been customary at the four star Hotel Kempinsky in Berlin. I thought, this cannot be true, and my usually camouflaged Berliner arrogance broke through. I thought if they want to play that game, I can handle it. When the servers presented the patters I haughtily took the best pieces of pheasant, venison, and roast beef. I was determined to show them that this pompous exhibition couldn't intimidate me. In other words, I was showing off my social background and impressing the surrounding audience by displaying impeccable table manners. Even the Kreisleiter, who was constantly watching me, seem to notice that I didn't quite fit in with the rest of the group. I practiced a "stiff upper lip" and pretended that this type service was what I was accustomed to at home.

Unfortunately, the after dinner speech of the Kreisleiter did not match the quality of the food and deserts.

The Nazi "Führer" gave a speech detailing the Party's "Ostraum-politik" for Poland. He hashed over all the garbage that I had already heard from the likes of Alfred Rosenberg and other party nincom-poops on that subject. I didn't pay much attention to what he said, because that kind of rhetoric bored the hell out of me. After the speech we were urged to go into town, and see for ourselves how the new Nazi order had changed things. I really wanted to see that, because I had not seen much of a difference on either side of the old border.

We all walked to the little town's center square. Here we were, a bunch of young guys in the uniform of the Hitler Youth, walking along the sidewalk and the Polish people stepped off the sidewalk to make room for us. Some of the older men even lifted their caps and bowed their heads towards us young whippersnappers. I was stunned and ashamed because the Nazis had turned my upbringing upside down. I had been raised to respect the elders, and had never experienced this subservience. I could not believe that people older than I would step off the sidewalk for me. I was disgusted and angry at the local Nazis, who had obviously beaten these people into such obsequious demeanor.

The whole experience deeply disturbed me. I lost a lot of my faith in humanity that day, even though I knew that all through history these things had happened. It was sure different to experience it in person, than to read about it in history books. I felt that even though we were the "victors", we had no right to expect, or extract, such behavior from the losers.

We biked home the next day, and all through the trip there was talk about our experience and now I knew whom I could, and could not trust. As a nonconformist I often opened my mouth too wide and that was getting increasingly dangerous. The secret saying was, "Silence is Gold, talking is Dachau." I understood now why my father wanted me to go and see the situation in Poland.

Military Physical, 1941

I was 17 years old in early 1941 and was called up by the local military draft board for a physical. My parents were anxiously giving me instructions to tell and show the military doctors my leg injury. I did, but they classified me "K.V." meaning, "Able to serve in the war" anyway. These military boards never bothered to determine if a man was physically in good condition, all they wanted was new cannon fodder for the front lines. Their edict was predictable, I was "usable" for the intended purpose (war). At the end of the examination, recruiters from the various branches of the armed forces were waiting to enlist some of the draftees.

If I had to serve, I wanted to serve in an interesting technical field. I talked to the Luftwaffe (Air Force) recruiter and took home enlistment papers. When I told my mother what my classification was, she just wouldn't believe me, and chided me for not properly bringing my leg injury to the doctor's attention. I told her angrily, that if she had gone to that examination, they would have given her the same classification. I didn't see anybody at that physical who did not get the "K.V." status. Maybe if I had come with my head under my arm I would have had a chance.

In the following week I spent a lot of time thinking about what I could do in the military without having to exchange bullets with the other side. I talked to my friends, and most of them said they would just wait and see what branch called them. Others were all gung-ho on volunteering for service in the submarines, the tank force or the SS. I finally decided to sign up for a technical branch of the Luftwaffe, but that meant that I had to sign up for four years. Since I was still a minor, my father had to give his consent. Father had volunteered at the beginning of WWI and he didn't want me to make the same mistake. He said that he would try to get me a job in the defense industry to keep me out of the armed forces. I was apprehensive about that, because the defense industry was increasingly subject to bombing attacks, and the chances of getting killed there were almost as good as in the trenches. Father finally succumbed to my logic, and signed my papers. I was going to live it up in the time remaining.

Other 1941 Events, Hess Flies to England

In 1941 it was obvious that Britain was preparing for an offensive in the Mediterranean area, including Greece.

The radio announced that Rudolf Hess, Hitler's deputy, had "secretly" flown to England. He was immediately pronounced insane by the Nazi propaganda machine, but the German people didn't buy that. The big question on everybody's mind was, "What was the purpose of the flight?" Germany was fighting on too many fronts. Despite severe punishment for listening to enemy radio stations, many German people were listening to the BBC every night and trying to sort out the facts.

Jitterbug

We young guys knew how precious little time of freedom we had left before being in the Armed Forces and the war. We took advantage of everything we could get away with. Some of the American Dixieland hits were very popular with the teenagers. Our favorite was the "Tiger Rag," but when some of my friends started to jitterbug, they were kicked out of the bar. Jitterbugging was considered to be a "decadent" American dance by the Nazi government and was strictly prohibited. This was hilarious because some of the guys kicked out were Hitler Youth Führers.

My home away from home was the boat house of the rowing club, particularly since it was getting into summer. We thought up a lot of pranks while boating and got a lot of laughs out of them. One Sunday a four oar crew with me as coxswain decided to row upstream to Zantoch, a small town at the confluence of the rivers Netze and Warthe. About a mile up the river was a nice secluded stretch of beach, so we pulled our boat up on the west bank of the Warthe river. From there we could see the town of Zantoch. Along the opposite bank was a road on top of the dike, occasionally used by bikers. It was a nice warm day so we decided to skinny dip in the river. There was a practical reason for swimming in the nude. One of the basic rules in rowing is to never wear anything wet that would touch the rowing equipment for any length of time. It would cause painful blisters at the contact points.

After we were cooled off, we sunbathed in the nude, and since we didn't want to sunburn our penis, we covered them with large leaves of wild rhubarb that was growing nearby. It looked cute, five guys sunbathing, with leaves covering the "strategic" body area with the hefty rhubarb stems sticking up in just the right place. We thought it was an ingenious temporary sunshade. Nobody that passed on the other side of the river even noticed, until a group of six uniformed women came along on their bicycles. We recognized by their uniforms that they were from a National Labor Service (RAD) camp in Zantoch. When the women were abeam on the other side, the rowing crew stood up and hollered hello, and when the women looked, we simultaneously lifted the sunshades and waved with them. The result on the other side was instant chaos, they almost ran into each other as they stopped to have a better look. We couldn't hear what they were saying, but it almost looked as if the women were going to jump in the river, and swim over to join us. Unfortunately they decided against it, and continued biking while waving at us and blowing us kisses. We had a good laugh, unpacked our sandwiches and washed them down with some beer.

A few weeks later an acquaintance of mine who had a kayak invited two girls from Berlin to came along on a weekend outing up the river. Gerhard could only accommodate one additional person in his kayak, so he asked me if I would care to come along in a double skull boat and bring the other girl. She could be my coxswain. I said I would consider it, if my friend Max would have time to come along too. The two of us had sculled together many a times. Surprise trips are usually a lot of fun, but in this case I was a bit apprehensive. These two girls probably didn't know anything about boating. I liked to share my time with friends who knew the ropes, and came equipped and prepared.

We were going to take as much food along as rationing would allow, a camp stove, blankets, warm-up suit, swim trunks and even a portable gramophone with some of my records. The girls turned out to be pleasant, one brunette and sexy, the other tall, blond and more of the cool type.

We took off upstream when the sun started to set, illuminating everything with a warm golden light. The farmland along the river receded into a light grayish mist and features faded and became indistinguishable. The world turned down its volume control, and the rhythmic splash of the oars and the soft murmuring of the water were the only sounds surrounding us. Once in a while a cow sounded off out in the fields. It was a scene of peace and quiet, but my thoughts were wandering off into the world of terrible destruction and death on the battlefields. Why oh why God, could the world not be like our surroundings here at this moment? Tears rolled down my cheeks until I reminded myself that I had better enjoy life while it lasted. As we came around a bend in the river we were surprised by a woman standing naked on a stretch of sandy beach, probably cooling off after a hard day of work on the field. We waved and she smiled, and we continued upstream.

It was time for us to find a place for the night and to beach the boats. Since we didn't have a tent along, we looked for a barn where we could sleep. At this part of the river the farm houses were on the left side, while the fields and barns were at the right side of the river. It was almost dark and we were tired. We found an empty looking barn, and pulled our boats up on a sandy stretch of river bank. We ate, and talked quietly, while savoring some beer that we had brought along. We learned that the girls from Berlin had not brought anything along to sleep in, they must have been under the impression that we would stay at an inn. Ursula, the cool blond who was going to be a teacher, was better prepared, because she brought warm clothing. Inge, the brunette who worked in an office, and claimed to be engaged, was a bit flighty and wasn't prepared for anything. After supper, ideas on where and how to sleep were tossed around. Gerhard, who owned the kayak, said we ought to turn both boats over and prop them up so we could sleep under the hull. Since the double skull boat was long enough, Ursula and Gerhard decided to sleep there. Max and I decided to sleep in the barn. Unfortunately there wasn't any hay or straw in it. Inge couldn't make up her mind how and where she was going to sleep. We finally got fed up with her, and just went into the barn and looked for relatively smooth ground, and laid down under our blankets. I was sleeping along one side the barn, Max on the other side. Well, it wasn't long before Inge came into the barn. I told her to stop fussing around, and come and crawl under the blanket with me just to keep warm. She did, and settled down. Max was starting to snore, and I was about to fall asleep too.

After about half an hour Inge propped herself up, and looked down onto my face, apparently waiting for an inviting reaction from me. I just opened one eye and looked back at her, then closed it again. I didn't know how to make love, and was ashamed to admit it. I was sure she was disappointed about this klutz, who asked her to crawl under the blanket with her, and then didn't even give her a kiss. After a moment of hesitation she got up and left the barn. I finally went to sleep and didn't see her until the next morning. She must have slept outside, because she looked rather disheveled. Everyone was teasing her. It was really my fault, because she had apparently expected me to follow her outside, and make love to her there, away from where Max was sleeping. I hadn't gotten the message and lost out.

We had breakfast and then went for a walk through the fields, enjoying the rising sun and the warmth that it brought. Then Gerhard had an idea. If we all agreed to stay another night, he would go to the other side of the river, and talk to the farmer to see if he could buy a bail of straw. Gerhard must have been a smooth talking salesman (his real profession), because he got straw, and also brought one large jar of milk and another one with water, and some eggs. Probably paying with cigarettes or tobacco. We hadn't seen real, rich milk like that since rationing. We were accustomed to "blaumilch" only, as it was commonly called, because there was so little fat in it that it looked blue. Since Inge had been so "awkward," the guys wanted to generously give her another chance, and named her cook for the next meal. She was to create a cream of wheat pudding from the stuff that Gerhard had brought from home and the good milk and eggs he got from the farmer. When Inge started out I watched her closely, because she didn't seem to know how to cook. When she made a move to dump the whole bag of cream of wheat into the boiling milk , I jumped in and took over. I couldn't prevent some of it getting into the milk, but I stirred like crazy, and then added the rest very slowly to prevent big clumps to form. The pudding came out reasonably well and the precious stuff didn't go to waste.

We felt sorry for Inge's fiancee, and hoped that he would find out about her cooking before he married her. We spent that evening around a romantic camp fire and made some hot punch from a bottle of red wine that I had brought. We had a good talk session and Ursula took a real interest in me and asked me to visit her in Berlin. At night we all bedded down on straw in the barn. The girls stayed together under one blanket and we had a good and peaceful sleep.

The next morning on our way back Inge steered the boat, while trying to learn the lyrics from a song playing on the gramophone in front of her. The title was dumb, and the lyrics were even worse. "Why is the banana yellow, and the orange red?" and it continued with "Why does Fritz not sleep at home, but gladly with Christina?" This was easier to figure out than why the banana was yellow.

I told Max, who was in the number one rowing position, to keep an eye peeled on the river ahead of us. Inge wasn't paying any attention, and once we had to work our sculls desperately to keep the boat from hitting the jetty.

Back at the boat house the boatmaster, who was in his mid sixties, had a cow when he saw us pulling in. Mixed crews were forbidden by the club, and the girls were not even club members and the gramophone was of course an absolute no-no in a gentlemen's rowing crew. I knew right there that I would never hear the end of it. When we got the boat out of the water and had lifted it onto a dolly, the boatmaster scrutinized every square inch of its planking, but couldn't detect any "damage". I told him not to worry. I would be called up soon and might not come back alive, so he wouldn't have to put up with me anymore. The boatmaster gave me a dirty look and strode away, probably to write a report about my outrageous behavior.

In September 1941 I worked hard to pass my final written and oral exams to complete my apprenticeship. By the end of the month, I had to go to Frankfurt/Oder to perform additional practical tests at the headmaster's optics shop. After I finished all the assigned work and had passed all required tests, the headmaster handed me my certificate, and invited me to dinner. I was very proud that I had finished my apprenticeship in only three and one half years.

When I got home I found a registered letter from the draft board telling me to report on October 15 to the National Labor Service (RAD) Company K 10/84 in Bomst, about 100 miles from Landsberg. Shit, that was really the pits. I had hoped to have at least a couple of months before being called up.

Landsberg, 1936

Hans at Buchner, 1940

Starting for an eight oar race

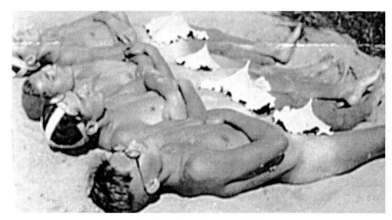

Resting after the race, 1941

Confirmation 1938

Always moving fast 1940

Last family vacation, driving to the Baltic Sea 1939

You will never have a quiet world till you knock the patriotism
out of the human race.
George Bernhard Shaw

3
Dig, Dig, Hurrah

My boss Max Buchner was pissed off, because my apprenticeship contract was to have ended on October 15. He said he had hoped to finally make some profit off my work. That was preposterous since I had made profits for him during the previous two years. He paid me peanuts, less than 5 Reichsmark a week, and claimed he didn't make a profit. The mark up on ophthalmic merchandise was 300 percent.

I didn't give a damn about profits, Buchner was well off anyway. The old fart wouldn't even let me enjoy my last hours of freedom. However since I had my final diploma, I could leave. I wasn't going to work until the day before going off to war, so I packed my tools and walked out.

Most of my friends had also received their induction orders. I called some of them up and suggested we should have a party before going off to our different units.

Since the start of the war against Russia, all public dancing and parties were prohibited. We had to either party at home, or ask permission to use the clubhouse of the rowing club. Permission was granted, and we had some damn good parties there. I had the right connections, and still could get liquor for these bashes.

The official reports were still full of victorious news, saying that the German troops had repelled all Russian counterattacks, and that the Russian Bear was as good as dead, but I couldn't believe that. The radio announcements we heard sounded like an overly optimistic view of the real situation. Hitler had announced demobilization of 70 army divisions. This was either a hoax, or it meant that Germany had lost that many divisions already. I could only talk this over with my parents. Since I had learned to speak politically correctly, to keep my ass out of a jail or a concentration camp. My father had fought against Russia in World War I, and knew the Russians better than anybody else, but he was working in Berlin.

Just 17 years old, and I felt that nothing but black clouds were coming my way. Since I couldn't trust anybody, I started to withdraw into my shell. Father came home for a weekend and he told me about the war. At the start of World War I, he had volunteered to join the Army, and had been wounded five times. He advised me to NEVER, absolutely NEVER, volunteer for anything in the service. He said that volunteers were usually destined to be send on suicide missions.

Off to the RAD

My girlfriend Gisela often came to the house in the evening, and we danced, drank, and talked a lot. I didn't know that her father was an SS officer. Fortunately I never told her about my political views.

On October 15, 1941 my mother and Gisela accompanied me to the station where I boarded the train to go to the camp of the R.A.D. Unit K 10/84, in Bomst just west of the old Polish border.

When I arrived at the railroad station in Bomst, a whole bunch of young man left the train. About 100 draftees walked towards the camp with me, and make sarcastic remarks about the Reichs-Arbeits-Dienst (RAD) to which we all had to report. The peacetime function of that Nazi organization was to teach young people discipline and hard work, mostly on worthwhile public projects such as draining of swamps, road building, reforestation etc. In a way the RAD could be compared to the American CCC camps, however the RAD was much more militarized. In war time RAD units were engaged in paramilitary training, and in building fortifications, roads and runways, sometimes right behind the front lines. Some units worked in the defense industry to fill manpower bottlenecks. In other words, the government used the RAD as defense contractors. At a pay rate of 25 Pfennig, about ten cents per day per draftee, it wasn't surprising they wanted us.

The fenced-in camp we were ushered into consisted of wooden army type barracks and utility buildings. A large open field was to the west, bordered by a big barn by the road into town. Just as in every military camp, there was basic boot camp training. We received our uniforms, fatigues, underwear, socks and boots, gas masks, canteens, and all the other junk that was considered essential for making a trained dog out of a human being. The worst problem was the supply chief who issued all that stuff. He not only looked like an early Neanderthal humanoid, he was only capable of barking one word, "Passt", meaning it fits. He had obviously missed several steps of the human evolution.

We were issued a spade, as well as a Dutch infantry carbine of impressive length. All this equipment was designed to keep us busy and "out of mischief" for months to come. We would be washing, shining, cleaning, polishing, shooting and exercising the equipment. The

"Arbeitsmann" (official title of the "trainees") had to be kept on the run with the aforementioned paraphernalia. May be that's what Hitler meant when he said his party had generated jobs.

I learned a few useful things during boot camp. How to properly handle basic hand tools, how to lift heavy loads without busting my back, how to split wood properly, how to drive a nail without hitting the thumb (hold hammer with both hands), and how to load and push a wheelbarrow. I also learned the names of 59 different soil transportation implements, so the time there wasn't totally wasted.

The Trained Dog Routine

The worst part in any military or semi-military organization, was that the drills turn into a brutal suppression of personalities. Our training was to instill "cadaver obedience", obedience at any cost. So much has been written about this beastly subject that I don't want to dwell on it philosophically here.

Boot camp wasn't too traumatic for me, because there had been so many changes in my life already. For some of the young men, it was the worst thing that had ever happened to them, because they had never been away from home. I tried to make the best of things and kept a low profile, because it was only for six months. I had already been accepted by the Luftwaffe for training in a technical field, so I wasn't worried about what would come after this misery.

To Die for Führer and Fatherland?

It took a while before this heap of civilians settled into a coherent RAD group, and even longer before it could be called a paramilitary unit. After two weeks of sorting the recruits out, and the recruits trying to make sense of all the orders, we were deemed worthy of being sworn in. The RAD oath was identical to the military one. We were supposed to be obedient to Führer and Fatherland, even if it would cost our lives. I mumbled the words as inaudibly as possible. Up to that ceremony we had legally been civilians, even though we had been in the camp for two weeks. After the oath we were under military law, with all the dire consequences should we disobey orders, or leave the unit without authorization.

A Nightly Escape

I had an immediate problem with the latter. Gisela had arrived in Bomst to say good-bye. Her father had been transferred to Prague and she and her mother were very apprehensive about the move. I could not officially leave the camp to meet her. After a bit of information gathering, I decided to leave the camp during the night, and meet with Gisela in the large barn at the end of our exercise field. The camp had a guard posted at the gate, and I had to find out what the routine was, and whether guards were walking through the camp at set hours. This wasn't too difficult, because the guards were also new recruits who didn't know what they were doing. Furthermore, they were constantly harassed to test their alertness by various superiors . The barrack that I was in was at the opposite end from the entrance, farthest away from the guards. Right behind my barrack was a barbed wire fence and beyond it the open field with bushes along one side.

With the gear I had received was a set of sports clothing, boxer shorts, a T-shirt and a warm-up suit, as well as some running shoes. Since the warm-up suit was navy colored and the running shoes were black, I considered that the best camouflage for my night excursion. We had to be in bed by 22:00 hours. I waited till 23:00 hours and got out of bed very quietly. I put on my sports clothes, opened the window, climbed out, closed the window, and listened for a guard walking around. I went through the fence and cautiously walked along the row of bushes toward the big barn. Fortunately it was a moonless night. When I reached the road, I quickly moved over to the barn. Gisela was already at the barn, we hugged and kissed and whispered to each other. The barn was empty, except for some bales of hay in a corner. There was also a partition, and behind it, loose hay on the floor. It was just what we needed, and we laid down and had a long talk.

To my horror she told me that her father was a high SS officer and had been transferred. She didn't want to go to Prague, but had to stay with her parents. We kissed and did some heavy petting, but hearing about her father turned off my love making thoughts. I could imagine what would happen if I made her pregnant. Her father would certainly come after me, and I would most likely have to join the SS as well. Maybe Gisela had hoped I would make her pregnant so that she could stay with my mother, and wouldn't have to move. We should have talked about that before she visited me. Our last get-together lasted until the wee hours of the morning.

I hurried back, just as dawn was approaching. At the fence, I heard a guard walking across a concrete apron, and ducked back into the bushes outside the fence. I hoped he would not check the window of my room and find it unlocked. The guard was not very attentive so I finally made it back through the window and into my bed. I was so pooped that I immediately fell asleep, without even taking my clothes off. The next morning the few men who knew about my escapade wanted to know how it went, but I kept my mouth shut.

A Pissing Contest

With 16 men of various backgrounds thrown together in close quarters, it was just a matter of time before problems surfaced. We had a man named Jurchen, he was a kid from the farm. He was grossly overweight, which during war time with tight food rations was unusual, and he obviously wasn't quite with it mentally. In those days, one had to be very cautious and observant to separate the men who were mentally retarded from the ones who played that role, in order to get out of military service. Jurchen's name was easily converted into Julchen, which in German is an old-fashioned girl's name.

During exercise it became obvious that Julchen didn't know where right and left were, and he became the center of endless teasing. He had been placed in an upper bunk bed, and in the middle of the night he peed right in his bed. His urine rained down on the man in the lower bunk, who jumped up with a loud curse when he realized what was happening. The man in the lower bunk was quite muscular, and in his rage about the involuntary shower, he took his belt with the heavy buckle and thrashed Jurchen. Jurchen's screams woke up everybody, and when they switched the lights on to see what was going on, they either laughed out loud, or cursed Jurchen, depending on temperament. It became such a ruckus that a superior appeared on the scene and analyzed the situation correctly, which was "amazing". He ordered Jurchen to clean up the mess, which was impossible since we slept on straw filled mattresses. When they were soaked, there was no way to dry them out in a hurry. Jurchen had to mop up the floor and take his and the lower bunk's mattress outside to get them dried out. The lower man had to sleep in an empty bed in another room and Jurchen was ordered to report to the dispensary. Of course our sleep was gone and we all cursed Jurchen.

He came back a couple of days later, but was now assigned a lower bunk. He peed in his sleep several nights in a row, until the men finally called on the camp commandant to remove this pissy character from our room. He was taken to an outside hospital for psychological observation, and never came back to the unit. We wondered if he really was a bed-wetter, or had faked it so well that he got out.

The Worst Winter in Decades, 1941/1942

As we continued our training, fall ended and we slid into one of the most severe winters Europe had experienced in decades. We had to exercise outside when it was 10 and 20 degrees below zero. I froze my heels right in the leather boots, because the back of the heels pressed firmly against the frozen leather. All this to "toughen us up" for the war ahead, we were told. Finally we had so many cases of frozen noses and ears, that the camp doctor limited us to no more that 20 minutes outside, and we had to closely watch each other. The moment the ears or the tip of the nose turned white, we had to stop what we were doing, and vigorously rub the frozen body parts with snow to restart the circulation. This was a exceedingly painful procedure. My frozen heels gave me severe pains for years, because we didn't have the proper footwear for these low temperatures. When anybody complained, we were told to imagine how the soldiers at the Eastern Front felt, having to fight in snow and cold down to 40 below zero. I thought, "And where are the SOB's who sent them there?" As far as I was concerned, they should have sent the politicians and generals naked to Russia to fight their goddamn war.

The German losses from the winter weather must have been appalling, but the numbers were not in the official bulletins.

Joseph Goebbels was finally forced to beg the German population to donate every piece of winter clothing they could spare to help save the soldiers at the Eastern Front. Another case of the typical arrogance in the upper echelons of political and military leadership, who thought the war would be over by November 1941. As far as the Russians were concerned, the war was just beginning. They had experienced huge losses in the initial battles, but they were now holding the lines everywhere.

A Dreadful Christmas, 1941

It was now the middle of December, 1941, and my 18th birthday fell flat because we didn't have anything to celebrate with. I was miserable. Then we started to prepare for our first Christmas away from home. We had only the skimpiest amount of coal or wood to heat our barracks, but we got at least a decent Christmas meal, and the parcels from home helped over the worst depressions. We shared what we had with each other and so it turned out as well as could be expected under the circumstances.

Despite the cold we were not allowed to sleep with our clothes on. When we woke up in the morning the single pane windows were obscured by thick layers of ice on the inside! Every night some asshole of a group leader would come around and lift our blankets to see if we had any clothes on. I got so angry that I stayed awake until midnight, and then put all my underwear and the warm-up suit on.

The latrines were in an adjacent building, and if I had to go out at night I had to dress completely before venturing into the subzero temperature. If it was necessary to sit on the 10 holer, I had to check the toilet seat first to make sure there wasn't any ice on it, otherwise the skin would freeze to it, and peel off.

After Christmas we were told that we would be released early, since the allotment of heating material had been completely exhausted, and there was no chance that we would get more. Shortly after that however we were told that we would be shipped out for action. Finally, near the end of January 1942, we were ordered to get ready with all our gear. We traveled by train at night in a northerly and northwesterly direction, but was delayed because of an air raid on Berlin. The next morning the train rolled into Angermünde, which is about 60 miles northeast of Berlin, where we disembarked.

The town of Angermünde, in the Province of Brandenburg, was known for excellent bakery goods and famous jams, so some of the guys remarked we might be needed to stir the cake dough in these factories, and we all laughed. Our leaders herded us on board a narrow gauge train to Pinnow. None of us knew what the hell was going on in Pinnow that could require our presence. I had only heard the name used by a stand-up comedian, who joked that it was the ultimate ass of the world. I thought this "Pinnow an der Knatter", as the comedian called it, was a product of his imagination, and that it didn't really exist. But here we were, right in Pinnow at an Army ammunition factory. Why we were needed there became clear the next morning. We were briefed by an army ammunition expert, who gave lectures on the strict safety rules, and the confidentiality of the work.

The plant was situated in a densely wooded area that offered very good camouflage. There were numerous small, one story buildings, in which various kinds of artillery shells and other ammunition was manufactured. The buildings were widely scattered and were of a special construction. Walls were of cement blocks with the roof trusses sitting on the walls without being tied to them. The buildings had numerous windows which were left open most of the time.

The reason for all these measures was the ever present possibility of an explosion on the assembly lines. The gases of an explosion would lift the roof, and/or blow through the open windows without doing much damage, so the theory went.

My unit was assigned to an assembly line for 75 mm (3 inch) artillery shells. A fireworker, the official name for the army ammunition expert, was in charge of the line, and was going to train and supervise us. He asked everybody what kind of training or profession we had, and assigned certain tasks accordingly. Students were, as always in the armed forces, categorized as unskilled workers. Since I had worked with sophisticated measuring devices, I was assigned the final inspection station where the position of the shell's primer, (which triggered the main explosive) was measured and its location altered when it fell outside an established tolerance. I had to make the necessary corrections so the primer was located within acceptable dimensional tolerances to the fuse.

The corrective action was to remove the highly explosive primer and put washers underneath to raise it, reinsert the primer, and re-measure the corrected dimension. Sometimes several corrections were necessary. We were warned not to drop these primers, because they could explode and blow somebody's leg off. The cement floor of the building was covered with soft, rubber like foot mats to cushion a drop. I was issued a rounded wooden stick, with which to GENTLY, PLEASE, tap the primer into a bore of the shell's explosive core. Wooden sticks were used because any spark in surroundings like that could mean instant death. Well, how would you like to do a job like that for ten cents a day?

Death Manufactured Everywhere

The job bothered me a lot because what I made with my hands could literally kill somebody or cause terrible injuries. However, the other side was doing the same idiotic deeds. I recalled a story by Mark Twain called "The War Prayer". It fit this situation exactly. The stupidity of men and especially politicians was beyond comprehension!

Like everything in life, one gets used to even the most dangerous jobs and becomes callous and even careless at times. Unexpected inspections were the rule. Once a superintendent almost fainted when he saw me tapping the primer rather hard with the wooden stick. He stopped the line instantly with his shout, and proceeded to give all of us another safety lecture. At the end he asked everybody to look out the window, and he grabbed one of the nitro-penta primers and threw it out the window. It landed on a concrete pad about 50 feet away, exploding with a loud bang. For the rest of the day the line slowed down considerably. The fireworker had told us that our line's output was about 30% greater than that of civilian workers, so he gave us permission to take it easy.

The whole ammunition complex was subdivided by barbed wire fences, and in adjacent working areas different ordinances were manufactured. The work crews were different too. Some were German civilian workers, men and women. Other compounds were manned by women of Russian and other nationalities. Our RAD men were forbidden to have contact with these groups. In one group the women all had red hair. The fireworker told us that it was caused by the type of chemicals that went into some of the explosives.

Outside of our work there wasn't much to do. The barracks we lived in were some distance from the factory and reasonably comfortable compared to the boot camp. At least we had enough coal to heat them properly. On Sundays we could catch a ride on the narrow gauge train into Angermünde. The town was very old and quaint, and had been made famous by the jam and marzipan that was manufactured there. My mother sometimes mailed me ration tickets, and I would go into town, sit in a nice café and have coffee ersatz and some pastry.

Sex through the Fence Prohibited

Adjacent to our living quarters were other camps, all separated by high wire fences. One adjacent camp had "Arbeitsmaidens", the female members of the Arbeitsdienst, the same organization we were part of. Even though we couldn't visit each other, we occasionally talked through the fence when no superior was in the vicinity. We were not supposed to do that, but there wasn't any way to prevent it. Some men even had the nerve to have sex right through the fence at night. The girls would back up to the fence and the men would put their penis in from their side of the fence. It must not have been very comfortable, but some of the women were determined to get pregnant so they would be discharged from the Arbeitsdienst. This caused one hell of an outcry from the male and female leaders on both sides of the fence, and the participants were put in solitary confinement.

The ammunition we worked on was earmarked for the spring offensive at the eastern front. At the beginning of March 1942, when we had caught up with the orders, we were on the train back to Bomst. Berlin was under air attack again. When we arrived at the base camp, we were told that we would be released within the next few days.

The Hero catchers

During the last week in Bomst the recruiters from the services of the Wehrmacht and the SS came to the camp to look us over. These recruiters were referred to as hero-catchers. The SS was looking for tall men, so I was approached. Fortunately I could tell them that I had signed on with the Luftwaffe already. The SS officer made a belittling remark about that, but I could have cared less. Around March 25, I was on my way home to Landsberg and hoped for a few weeks of peace and quiet before being called up by the Luftwaffe.

Oh, did it feel good to be home again. To be able to sleep in a decent bed, not to be awakened rudely in the morning, to wear comfortable clothes, and to linger at breakfast as long as I wanted. What luxuries. Now I really appreciate that and told my mother so.

Of course I had to pay a visit to the rowing club and I even took the skiff out for a short row up the river. The weather was still cold, and being all by myself out there wasn't really that enjoyable. I missed my friends. They were in the armed forces, scattered all over Europe by now and one was under the sea in a submarine. I wondered how many of them would return home. I found my old girl friend Friedl, and we spent a few enjoyable hours shooting the breeze.

New Induction Papers

Several days later I got my induction orders to the Luftwaffe. On April 15, 1942 I was to report to the 15th Wireless Company of the Chief Commander of the Air Force. This assignment was unusual because it was one of the top staff units of the Luftwaffe, directly under Hermann Göring.

On my last weekend at home my father came from Berlin. We had long talks, and I was glad to be able to confide many things I couldn't talk about with other people. Father said that the location where I was to report was a top notch facility. Compared to what he had experienced in World War I it was a "luxury resort" he said, being familiar with his sarcastic sense of humor, I wasn't sure what to make of that remark. My father wouldn't give me any further information and just said, "You will find out." Well, I thought, it couldn't be much worse than the RAD camp in Bomst. I was going back to the city where I was born and was going to be stuffed into another uniform.

Hans, into the National Labor Service (RAD), 1941

Boot inspection in ten minutes, 1941.

Temporarily in civilian clothes, 1941.

*History: an account mostly false, of events unimportant, which are
brought about by rulers mostly knaves, and soldiers mostly fools.*
Ambrose Bierce

4
To Hermann Göring-Meier

On April 15, 1942 I boarded the train to Berlin. The unit I had to
report to was in Berlin-Kladow, an area that was at the southwestern
periphery of the city. The last leg of my trip was on the upper deck of
a double-decker bus. I sat on a first row seat with an unobstructed
view. The bus went through small villages or towns which had been
independent at one time and had been annexed by Berlin, the sprawl-
ing capital of Germany. Many of the small places still had a core of
very old buildings, around which more modern, and often high rise
buildings were erected. Finally the bus stopped right in front of the
entrance gate to a large military compound.

The "Hermann Göring Kaserne" was a huge complex of two-story
stone buildings, with beautifully landscaped streets and grounds. It
didn't look like a military facility at all. Even the new military compounds that I had seen in Landsberg couldn't match this one. Hermann Göring sure took care of his Luftwaffe personnel. If it weren't
for the military, one would like to live here. After showing my induction papers to the guard at the impressive cut stone entrance with a
huge wrought iron gate, I was directed to a building off the main boulevard. When I arrived at the building where the 15th Radio Communications Company was located, the usual routine of signing in,
filling out papers, and getting room assignments took place. After the
dreadful wooden barracks in the RAD, I was to share a room on the
first floor with only three other recruits. No bunk beds, and very large
lockers. Looking out of the window, I could see birch trees and lawn
with shrubs. Holy cow, it was almost civilized.

As always in the military, civility didn't last long, and the sergeants
saw to it that the new recruits were trained to toe the line. We recruits were issued full military gear, all new, from jack boots to steel
helmets, gas mask, the standard carbine 98k with ammunition, and
numerous other pieces, which all had to fit into the military rucksack.
The worst hassle was to get gear that fit and to keep track of it during
the training time.

In the first three weeks there was nothing but drills. Many recruits came directly from civilian lives, and there were quite a few university students and even an aspirant for a Ph.D. degree, who was in his thirties. To the men who had gone through the rigors of the RAD camps, the routines here were old hat, except that there was more emphasis on military drills, long marches, physical fitness, and weapons instruction.

After most of the "sharp corners had been ground off," radio communication instruction was phased in. Morse code and "Q" groups, encoding and decoding, radio operations protocols, radio gear setup, trouble shooting and maintenance, were interlaced with ten mile marches with full gear. One mile of the march was with gas masks on, and even singing under gas masks (very important under combat conditions) was a frequent routine. I didn't have too many problems with these physically demanding exercises, except that I perspired heavily in the heavy uniforms we had been issued. When I came home from these marches my underwear was always dripping wet.

There were other "humorous" exercises such as "masquerades", where we had to change from fatigues into full combat gear, then into sports gear, then change into standard uniforms, then into other gear, all within minutes of each other, at the whims of the sergeants. The first three men to reappear in the required gear were exempt from the rest of the circus. I was in that fast group every time. I was then excused from the rest of the hustle, and could go up to my room. Sometimes I helped my buddies to get dressed faster, and I could bring my locker up to snuff. Sure enough, at the end of the "masquerade", Maskenball as it was called in German, the sergeant announced, "Locker inspections in ten minutes."

The men had tossed everything into their lockers during these fast clothing changes, regardless of military locker protocols. It was hard to fake it, because the drill sergeant would ask for specific items, and they better came from the right place, or else. The "or else" was an assignment to clean toilets, or sidewalk scrubbing with a toothbrush, at the whim of the sergeant.

At the shooting range we recruits had to zero in our newly issued carbines. That took patience and hollering from the instructors at the range, because most of us had never handled a rifle before. They also instructed us on the use of the MP 38, a small sub-machine gun, that is mistakenly called a Schmeisser in the USA, the standard pistol 08/15 (parabellum), as well as the M.G. 15, which was an aircraft machine gun, although it was at times pressed into ground service.

To change the pace, there were gas mask tests inside a chamber filled with tear gas. We had to change our mask filter inside the chamber to show that we could do it without getting gas into our lungs. We had to learn to march in large formations, present arms, and even learn the goose step, all "important skills" to win a war.

Two recruits on the floor where I lived had come down with scarlet fever so they closed that whole floor off, and quarantined everyone. The door handles were wrapped with gauze and soaked with disinfectant. We could not work with the other soldiers, but had separate classes. A doctor visited every room daily and checked each man. I had gone through scarlet fever as a kid, but during the daily medical inspections I was found to have a higher than normal temperature so they send me into the hospital's isolation station to find out what was wrong. That's where I was at the time the goose stepping exercises were going on. From my window I could see the whole exercise area, glad that I didn't have to beat my feet onto the granite surface of the parade avenue. The doctors couldn't find anything wrong with me, but I had to stay in isolation in the hospital for two weeks. Boot camp was over when I came out.

After the basic training was finished, we were allowed an occasional furlough into Berlin. Since I didn't have any money, it wasn't much fun, but together with some buddies I sometimes ventured into the very active night life of Berlin. I remember going to the "Resi" a very large cabaret type establishment, where they had table telephones, with the number displayed above the table. One could talk to other guests sitting at these tables, and some of the guys were of course after girls at the other tables. A large well known band accompanied the stage shows.

Other times we just stayed out at Kladow, walked down to the beautiful Havel River and sat in one of the many restaurants to drink the weak beer which was common during the war. One Sunday we had an unexpected show. Nearby was the Air Force War Academy, where fighter pilots were trained. The initial training was done in Arado 96 aircraft. When I looked out over the Havel River where a few sailboats were tacking their course, I noticed two Arados coming over the area in a very low level flight. They couldn't have been more than 50 feet above the water. One of them pulled up right over a sailboat that was rounding a buoy and gunned his engine. The prop blast hit the sail just right and flipped the whole boat on it's side. The pilot flew a few acrobatic maneuvers as he climbed up and disappeared. The crew in the boat was in the ditch, and other boats tried to help them. Maybe the pilots were ticked off because they had to go to war, while others were still having fun on the water.

The technical end of wireless communication now received top priority. Back at Morse code keying I had one hell of a time bringing my speed up in both cipher and clear text. The minimum requirement was ninety words per minute, and one hundred-twenty words per minute, if I wanted to go on to airborne radio operator school. I just squeezed by the top number.

To Fly or Not to Fly

I was sent to the school for airborne radio operators. The pilots were having fun flying crazy maneuvers to shake the hell out of the new recruits. The radio operators were supposed to maintain proper radio communications, and practice radio navigation through these maneuvers. We had to go and fly in various types of aircraft because there were differences in their radio gear. In the Ju 87 (Stuka dive bomber) the radio operator/tail gunner sat facing the aircraft's tail when going down towards a target. Normally the pilot warned of the pending dive, and the radio operator turned halfway around in the seat, to go down sideways, which was more comfortable.

The pilots however had orders not to give warnings to the recruits, because the tail gunner/radio operator was supposed to guard against an attack from a fighter. During the dive I puked all over the radio gear and my flight suit, and the pilot was stinking mad at me and I had an argument with him after we landed. Since the pilot was an NCO, my argument was considered to be an insubordination. The training officer decided that I was not going to face a court-martial, but declared that I was physically unfit to fly, and transferred me back to my unit in Kladow. I wasn't embarrassed about that.

After boot camp, with my mother in Berlin, 1942.

Good bye Dad, going to the front in Russia 1942

Berlin, camouflage in front of the Brandenburg Gate

*I know I am among civilized men because
they are fighting so savagely.*
Voltaire

5
To Russia Without Love

In August of 1942 I got my transfer orders, to the Airfleet 1 in Riga, Latvia. Going to the "Worker's Paradise" didn't sound very interesting, but what could I do?

I found that almost my entire company was to be shipped to the eastern theater. The only exception was the Ph.D. aspirant, who was promoted right away and send to the Africa Corps, because he was a specialist on Egyptian economy. At the company go-away dinner he already appeared in his new uniform and ensign rank, and the sergeants who trained him had to salute him. I managed to get a few minutes of English conversation in with him. He wasn't happy with his assignment either, because he didn't believe that Rommel could make it to the Suez Canal.

The next day we boarded a regular passenger train to Allenstein, Eastern Prussia, where we transferred to a freight train equipped to run on the wider Russian rail tracks. We were issued food and additional ammunition for our carbines and told to be alert at all times. These transports had been attacked by Russian partisans, who blasted part of the rails to stop the train, and than attacked it from camouflaged positions along the tracks.

The weather was summery warm. We were still not accustomed to the fact that we were soldiers going to war. I was enjoying the beautiful countryside where the harvest was peacefully in full swing.

After two days the train reached Riga, the capital of Latvia. In Riga we would get our individual marching orders. My friend Kurt König (King) and I and several others, were assigned to the Luftwaffen Liaison Company 3/31 in Siverskaja (Russian spelling Ssiverskij) about 40 miles south of Leningrad (now again St. Petersburg). We were told that we would not be leaving until the next day, because there was quite a backlog.

Since we had time to kill, we left our rucksacks at the Riga military train station, and walked through the beautiful and historic old city, which had been founded in 1201 by the Teutonic Knights. Riga was a member of the Hanseatic League, and a major seaport of the Baltic Sea. The city had been occupied in July 1941 by the German Army Group North on their way to Leningrad. Except for the large number of military people present, the city looked normal, with hardly any destruction or damage.

In the late afternoon we walked back to the station to check the train schedules. While I was in one of the restrooms a woman came in to clean. She was wearing the yellow star of David, which all Jews had to wear. It was the first time I had seen anybody with the yellow star in the military operations area. I started a carefully concealed conversation with her, because according to the official rules, we were not allowed to speak to each other. She spoke German and also English. She was from Riga, and had been forced to work for the German military. It was difficult to carry on a conversation since there were other soldiers in the restroom. I managed to tell her that not all people in Germany were for Hitler, or condoned what he did to the Jewish people. I tried to encourage her to go underground, because I figured that would be easier up there in Latvia, but she said that wasn't possible. She then had to leave quickly, military police called Kettenhunde (chain-dogs) because they wore an engraved metal plate hanging from a chain above their chest, appeared to check soldiers for transport papers. They told me to get my ass up to platform two on the double, since the train was coming through in about 10 minutes.

King, I, and the other assigned soldiers continued our trip on a passenger train full of soldiers returning from furlough in Germany. The mood of some of the returning soldiers was somber, because they had found their homes destroyed and some had lost family members in air raids. The trip took us from Riga via Pleskau (Pskov) and Luga to Siverskaja. From the station we walked to the company headquarters, which looked like an old Russian resort camp. The staff sergeant we reported to at our arrival was a rude and unpleasant character. I guessed that he was an alcoholic. He showed us were we would be quartered, where the mess hall was, and told us that at 14:30 hour he wanted to see us all in front of the administration building, where the company chief would address us.

The Company's commander was Captain Herrgot, a dashing and a little too elegant man in his forties, who looked more like the CEO of a large company than a military man. He welcomed us and briefed us on the basic function of his unit. We were to be the communications link between the Luftwaffe (Air Force) and the Army. Unlike the US Army, the German army did not have their own air force. Communication groups of his company provided the liaison between the forward army commands with "Airfleet 1" in Riga. At times we would serve as forward air controllers when tactical aircraft attacked enemy positions, and directed or corrected the targeting. The company had two armored personnel carriers with special wireless equipment, and numerous other ordinary communication vans. Captain Herrgot told the staff sergeant his highest priority was to have us new men trained on the equipment and have us ready for action within two weeks.

From the company's headquarters, communication groups of one officer and six to eight men with a communications van were dispatched to army command posts. The officer was officially called "Flivo" (Flieger Verbindungs Officer), an acronym meaning Air Force Liaison Officer. Our communication groups could be stationed from 1/2 mile behind the front lines at Divisions headquarters, to 15 miles back at Army Corps headquarters. The liaison group's prime task was to inform the tactical air force units where our front lines were, and to inform the army what air force units were available for supportive action. Another task was to interpret aerial reconnaissance photographs for the Army's tactical and information officers. At times we also performed weather observation functions for the flying units.

The communication vans were two axle 5 ton Opel or Mercedes trucks, with dual rear tires, not an appropriate vehicle for the road conditions in Russia. Enemy action had destroyed all but two of the much better suited three axle, all-wheel drive vans, which had been standard in prewar years. Due to the high replacement cost and the scarcity of material, no replacements were available. In the next two weeks we were trained to operate the equipment that was in the vans. On top of the truck bed was a camper shell which looked very much like today's campers. Attached to each vehicle was a 45 feet high (when fully extended) telescoping mast for antennas. A gasoline powered 220 volt AC generator was in a pullout compartment.

The radio equipment was of two kinds. The older so called Fu.G.3 (Funk Gerät 3) and the much newer Fu.G.10. Both were aircraft receiver/transmitter type units. The older Fu.G.3 was big and had been designed for aircraft like the Junkers 52 transport, or the Junkers 86, while the much smaller Fu.G.10 was used in the Junkers 88, Heinkel 111, Focke Wulf 189 and many other aircraft. Since both were designed for aircraft, they ran on direct current (DC) from the aircraft's batteries. In the vans there was a big rectifier unit that converted the alternate current that the generator delivered to the DC requirement of the receiver/transmitter.

Since I was always interested in the technical end of the electronic equipment, I soon made the acquaintance of sergeant Baumgarten, who was in charge of the technical support group. Sergeant Baum-garten was a genuine Berliner, and had owned a radio store there. He was a quiet and pleasant fellow, and we soon had a personal relation-ship of mutual trust, which we established through carefully worded conversations. It turned out that we both didn't believe in the Nazi bullshit. Baumgarten had a rather distinctly looking Semitic nose, to put it mildly. When we were alone, I kiddingly asked him one day, if he had been able to provide an "Aryan certificate" for his nose. Baumgarten laughed and said, "Don't you know what your chief com-mander has said?" And of course I knew. Göring had stated publicly at one time, "I determine who is a Jew." No more had to be said about the subject, because we trusted each other, and I never tried to find out how Baumgarten managed to end up in the Luftwaffe.

Each liaison group also had a personnel carrier, like the military version of the Volkswagen, or a Kfz.15, similar to the American GI vehicle. After intensive training on all these pieces of equipment, I left with a group on September 10, 1942 for the 170th Infantry Divi-sion in Michalowka.

Into the Mud around "Lenin's Grad"

Michalowka was located about 18 miles east of Leningrad and about ten miles south of Lake Ladoga. I was in the area that was part of the German military encirclement of Leningrad. The encirclement started in the west, with the German navy blockading Leningrad from the Gulf of Finland, denying Russian ships access to the Baltic Sea. The Gulf was heavily mined and closed off by a huge underwater steel net to keep Russian submarines out of the Baltic Sea.

To the south and east the German army had dug in around Lenin-grad. To the north Finnish troops had cut off the city. The only open-ing in the siege of Leningrad was across Lake Ladoga which at times allowed them to connect with the rest of Russia.

Lake Ladoga is the largest lake in the European part of the USSR. It has a surface area of about 6,800 square miles (about 90% of Lake Ontario) and a maximum depth of 750 feet. It is fed by many rivers, has more than 600 islands, and drains via the Neva River into the Gulf of Finland. The river flows through Leningrad, and splits into several arms giving parts of the city the appearance of Venice. Lenin-grad is surrounded by flat land, and parts are densely forested with birch trees and other trees that are well suited for wetland areas. Many areas to the east, particularly along the Volkhov River, are enormous swamps during every spring thaw. The land is thinly populated and there are few major roads. To make these areas accessible, the German Army Corps of Engineers, with the help of Russian POWs and civilians, had built hundreds of miles of corduroy roads. Corduroy roads were made by transversely laying millions of tree trunks on the ground, and tying them with heavy wire or steel cables. These roads were strong enough to be used by supply trucks, artillery, and tanks.

We were dispatched to a very large peat bog area south of Lake Ladoga. In peacetime, the peat was used in the largest peat fired electric generating plant in the world. The peat had been harvested by work camps called poseloks, probably manned by political prisoners, and was loaded on cars of narrow gauge rail lines, which converged towards the now heavily damaged power plant located right at the Neva River. The plant had supplied approximately one third of the electricity for the city of Leningrad. The front line was going right through that plant.

The German army, when it occupied Michalowka and Mga, had sealed off the city's last rail lines to the east, and hence the rest of Russia. The Russian army had made an attempt to lift this siege of Leningrad by attacking from the Volkhov front in the east, to break through the bottleneck south of Lake Ladoga. The initial Russian penetration through the German lines had been sealed off, and we were now counterattacking to eliminate this Russian salient.

My group drove into Michalowka over muddy roads and moved into an earthen bunker. Because of the high groundwater level (2-3 feet below the surface) the bunker had only been dug 12 inches below the ground, and railroad ties filled with mud formed the bunker walls above the ground. The ceiling of the bunker was made of old railroad ties with soil on top for protection. We were located in the middle of German artillery positions, which fired at the encircled Russian forces north of us. Supposedly 100,000 Russians were trapped in the swampy area south of Lake Ladoga. It was a horrible terrain to fight a war in. The groundwater level was too high to dig any real foxholes, and in the air were trillions of mosquitoes. Many soldiers on both sides came down with mosquito born diseases, such as the deadly spotted fever.

Where Iron Flies

Since the communications bunker was only 2,000 yards behind the front lines, we were frequently subjected to Russian artillery shelling. The Russians aimed to eradicate the German artillery, located all around our bunker. Because of the frequent shelling, our communication group moved the radio receiver into the bunker, and parked the van with the transmitter about 100 feet away. The transmitter was remotely operated from the relative safety of the bunker. I had to go outside from time to time to refuel the generator, or change transmitter frequencies. As the new man in this group, I got the shitty jobs that the old-timers didn't like to do, but I didn't mind. This job was a thousand times better than that of an infantry man sitting in a wet fox hole, fighting the deadly battles of a senseless war. However when artillery shells came down near our bunker we too had to hustle to survive the hot iron flying around.

Survival is the Prime Objective

In a war one learns survival, and one had better learn quickly to distinguish between the sounds of incoming artillery shells that will land nearby, the ones that come down close by, or the ones that are too damn close. In the latter case one usually didn't need the information any more, because one was a basket case. As radio operators, we all had exceedingly well trained ears that helped us sort out incoming artillery rounds. But our hearing ability was constantly damaged by the incessant percussion of exploding shells, and the firings of our own artillery. Conducting critical radio communications by Morse code under these conditions was tough.

During the firing of salvos from the German artillery I observed a strange phenomenon in our transmitter. When the nearby 8,8 cm Flak guns fired, the transmitter went silent for a split second. We could never find out why this happened, but I guessed that the 8,8's high muzzle shock wave was vibrating the grids in the vacuum tubes in the transmitter. It was frustrating, because we lost parts of our transmission, and had to repeat some text groups. We didn't like to be on the air any longer than necessary because we didn't want the Russians to locate our transmitter and aim their artillery at us.

Our bunker was next to the railroad tracks that ran east from Leningrad via Mga to Tishvin. On the other side of the tracks were remnants of trees that had been mutilated by exploding shells. We used several of the tree trunks to construct an open air latrine, referred to as the "Donnerbalken" or thunderbeam, an appropriate name.

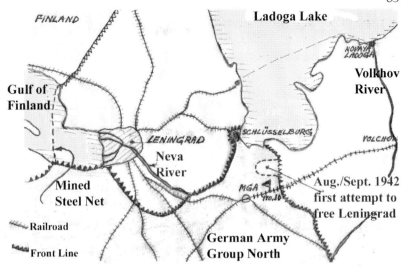

First Russian attempt to break the siege of Leningrad Aug./Sept. 1942,
which was repulsed.

One day I was sitting there fanning my rear end with reading material to keep the mosquitoes away, when "Ivan" decided to disturb my
meditation with rounds of his 3" guns. They were apparently aiming
at the railroad tracks. I estimated the impact points by the sounds of
the incoming artillery rounds. As they came closer I figured they would
soon to be in the category of "too damn close."

Despite unfinished business I beat a hasty retreat across the rails
towards the bunker, holding onto my pants. As I reached the wet and
slippery top step leading down into the bunker, a round exploded about
50 feet behind me on the other side of the tracks. The pressure from
the explosion threw me down the steps, and I crashed right through
the door into the bunker. I was still desperately holding my pants
with one hand, while trying to cushion my fall with the other. I cursed
like hell, while blood ran down my chin. "One cannot even shit in
peace in this goddamn war," I said. Everybody burst out laughing except the radio operator on duty. He frantically motioned to quiet down,
because he was right in the middle of receiving a message, and had
lost part of it because of the racket.

Apparently I had opened the bunker door with my mouth. I tried
to stop my bleeding and found that my teeth had cut into the upper
lip during the fall. From there on I was blessed with what the British
call "a stiff upper lip," if you will pardon the quip. After I had but-
toned my pants and regained my composure, I was the target of another barrage. But it was all good natured. They congratulated me for
having run the 100 meter dash in world record time, but remarked

that freestyle, with loose pants, was against the rule. After the shelling subsided, I tried to returned to the location across the tracks to finish my "business", however the "Donnerbalken" had been smashed to splinters. It had indeed been a too damn close one.

Human life and turnips remain cheap and plentyful.
Frank McKinney Hubbard

6
No Relief for Leningrad

The ring around the Russian troops was tightening in heavy fighting. Their fate was sealed since they were unable to break out of the encirclement. I heard the Russians had suffered 70,000 dead in their attempt to break the siege of Leningrad. Soon the old German front lines were reestablished and things quieted down. On October 18, 1942, our liaison group was recalled to Siverskaja. We were barely able to get all our gear in order when Captain Herrgot told us that a new attempt to take Leningrad was possible. Four days later we were sent off to a new assignment.

We arrived at the XXX. Army Corps headquarters in Uljanowka, about 20 km southeast of Leningrad, right on the "October" Highway between Leningrad and Moscow. We moved into an old farmhouse and set up our station behind the building. Soon we were on the air again. A few weeks later it started to snow, and another Russian winter was upon us. This time we had brand new winter clothing and the all important felt boots.

At nearby Pushkin, using a good set of binoculars I had a first look at Leningrad from Height 167. Height 167 was the highest point of terrain on the Dudergof ridge, overlooking an otherwise flat area. The elevation was about 450 feet. Visibility wasn't good that day, but I could see a few tall buildings and church towers. Back in Uljanowka, our liaison officer showed us a detailed panorama photo that had been shot from the Pushkin water tower with a 1000 mm Zeiss lens. It showed all the major buildings, and had labels with names over each outstanding feature. From the photo I could see that it was a beautiful city. What a shame to destroy it.

Rumors were soon circulating that Hitler's initial orders to level and take Leningrad had been superseded by an order to siege the city. Leningrad would be brought to its knees by hunger. These orders reclassified the area as a relatively "unimportant" front now.

One of the interesting things about the frontline southeast of Leningrad was that it was manned by the Spanish Blue Division, supposedly all volunteers. Their discipline was different from that of the

German army. For instance, they refashioned part of their gas masks into protective goggles by just cutting the mask apart. They said there was no use for the gas mask, so why lug it around. They carried their cigarettes or other important personal things in the gas mask containers. These troops had one hell of a reputation for man to man combat. The Russian patrols kept a safe distance from that front sector, because the Spaniards reportedly killed the Russians by slitting their throats.

First Furlough

On November 6, I was ordered to return to the company in Siverskaja. Arriving there, I was told to get ready on the double, because the next day I would be going on furlough. Some of my equipment had to be checked in, and I had to see the company physician. He looked me over for all sorts of diseases, and even inspected my penis to see if I had gonorrhea. I hadn't seen one female in the areas were I had been stationed. There was also a lot of paperwork to get the correct marching orders, and last but not least the ticket for the furlough train. This was the most crucial requirement, because no ticket, no admission to the train. There was only so much room on these trains, and each unit got a quota of tickets per month.

The trains were regular passenger trains that carried soldiers on furloughs only and they were usually late. I had to walk about three miles to the station in Siverskaja. It was winter and damn cold in the rail station, but the thought of going home kept me warm. The trains originated in Gatchina, only a short distance away, so there was plenty of room in the coaches. The rail route was via Luga, Pleskau (Pskov), Riga to Tauroggen (Taurage), where all passengers had to leave the train to go through a lengthy but well organized delousing process.

The Three-Ring Delousing Circus

The delousing was like a three ring circus in which all soldiers had to perform. The rumors was we had to turn our lice in marked with our dog tag number, but there weren't pencils sharp enough to mark the lice, so we were allowed to leave them in the clothes. Only kidding of course. Everybody had to take their clothes off, put them on hangers, label them with their names, and give them to a soldier, who would put them into a steam autoclave to be deloused. Next we filed into a huge room with hot showers. Large vats containing dark gooey stuff were everywhere in the shower hall. We were required to take that horrible smelling gunk and smear it over all hairy body areas. Head, armpits, legs, chest, pubic hair, all had to be "anointed" with that gunk. It was supposed to kill all the lice, fleas or whatever else one accommodated. Then the gunk was washed off in the showers.

Next we had to pass close muster by an inspector. He used a trouble light to illuminate all areas of the "hairy beast" to check if they were indeed free of "contaminants." The soldiers always said, "How would you like to have that job, looking at hairy apes for eight hours a day, maybe they should have hired pretty female employees for that job," said another guy. "That would never work," wisecracked another. "You guys couldn't get your pants back on again because of mass erections." Everybody burst out laughing and hurried to the clothes line, probably to hide the fact that this wisecrack had started their minds on a certain subject, and the result would be obvious pretty soon.

The clothes were usually a size smaller after delousing. For most soldiers that didn't matter, because the field uniforms were not tightly tailored. Officers usually fared much worse with their tightly fitting tunics. Many of them moved rather stiffly as if fitted into a tight corset when they came out of the "lousy circus". All that cleansing moved fast, it didn't take more than two hours.

We boarded the train again. The mood on the train improved considerably. We were rolling into Germany, East Prussia to be correct. Looking out the window we enjoyed the tidy farms, clean, small villages, and paved roads. Finally, early in the morning on November 10, 1942 the train rolled into Landsberg/Warthe, and I was home.

Since I had a lot of good stuff, saved from special frontline rations, such as Cognac and other liquors, cigarettes and tobacco, my luggage was heavy. It was too far to walk with the luggage to my parent's home, so I decided to check it in at the railroad station. Then I walked up to the end of Bahnhofstrasse, to report to the military police office. This was a strictly enforced rule, which had a number of reasons, most of them no good. It supposedly assured that one had arrived at the destination. At times furlough trains had been ambushed by Russian partisans, triggering exchanges of gunfire, and killing soldiers going on leave. When they didn't come back from their furloughs, their units didn't know what happened to them. They were then listed as AWOL, which triggered searches for them. The next reason was, that if there would be a major Russian offensive, they could recall soldiers to front line units immediately. The last reason was the only good one, everybody was issued ration tickets for the three week furlough.

I walked home and nothing had changed in the months that I had been away. When I arrived at the house, Mother and father were completely surprised. First I took off my uniform, put on civilian clothes, and then had a cup of coffee. Father and I then took the two bikes and went to get my precious cargo. Father was surprised when I told him what all I had in that rucksack. He said that I shouldn't have checked it in, because it might be stolen, but it was all there.

Mother had prepared a special meal, and we sat down and talked and talked, and had a good drink, and looked at the maps of the area around Leningrad, and a lot of photographs which I had taken.

In the afternoon I called Friedl at work and told her that I was home and to call me. Then I walked downtown and roamed the old stomping grounds. I saw familiar faces, but didn't meet old friends. Most of them were in the armed forces in various parts of Europe, and it was highly unlikely that their furlough would coincide with mine.

I got a newspaper and read the many obituaries of soldiers who had given their lives for "Führer und Vaterland". Fortunately none of my close friends were mentioned, but the old anger at Hitler and his idiotic war welled up again. It didn't matter whether or not I knew these fallen soldiers, they all had their dreams, loves and ambitions snuffed out, because of this insane politician trying to force his ideas on the rest of the world. I couldn't think of a more vicious crime. I also considered what all of this must mean to the parents who had worked, saved and worried to bring these young men up, just to see them killed for reasons not important to them. I was wondering too what was going on in the minds of the parents who had helped Hitler come to power, and who now saw their own kids being sacrificed at the altar of their "idol."

In antiquity religions had sacrificed their young to please their gods, and I couldn't help but draw parallels. Were Germans really that stupid, that they didn't see the similarity and blindly believed a politician who stepped on a podium and uttered political bullshit?

Fortunately, there was a flip side to all the war misery. The younger generation, still not in the armed forces, practiced limited liberty on their own. Benny Goodman was their idol and many of the popular American songs surfaced in Germany in 1942, often with lyrics that poked fun at the Nazi party, and their officials. Many of the German songs also ended up with anti-Nazi lyrics when sung in privacy. All this was the reaction to the increasingly depressed spirits of the people. Heavy air raids by the RAF all over Germany, and the nightmarish battle of Stalingrad, were beginning to give even the most optimistic Germans an inkling that God was not on our side contrary to the inappropriate "God with us" motto on every soldier's belt buckle. Of course the other side believed that God was on their side also, and I couldn't help but remember what Mark Twain had written about that subject under "From Europe and Elsewhere, The War prayer." How well he had expressed it.

Friedl and I went to the movies, sat around in cafés smoking cigarettes, and drank whatever was available. We had a good time, but we never discussed the future, because we didn't see any future. All too soon the three weeks were over. Before I left, my father gave me his 7.65 mm Mauser automatic pistol (M14), which he had worn during World War I and said, "I hope you'll never need it."

I arrived back in Siverskaja on December 3, 1942, around midnight. I had to go into the waiting room first, where everybody was briefed on the local situation. Apparently there had been night attacks on the Siverskaja airport by Russian partisans, and every unit now had sentries around their quarters. We were given the password, told to load our weapons, walk in groups of at least two and stay in the middle of the roads and streets. Wow, that certainly was a new situation. I cocked father's Mauser, and walked along the middle of the road as ordered, finger at the trigger. I was challenged several times by sentries, but reached the company's quarters safely.

Outbound with King

Three days later my friend Kurt König (King) and I were sent out to the XXVI Army Corps headquarters in Woitolowo, a typical small Russian village, south of Lake Ladoga. The XXVI. Army Corps was defending the east facing frontline of the ring around Leningrad. Everybody had dug in for another Russian winter. Our liaison group was quartered in a two story log house which had recently been built at the west end of the village. We had two rooms on the upper floor. One was a fairly large room with bunk beds, a table and chairs. The other room was the officers' room, which also served as the map room. Large maps on the wall showed the exact frontline positions. Since the fronts were reasonably quiet, so was the "Etappe" (meaning the rear sections behind the front).

We were in a comfortable location, since the headquarters of the commanding General was right next to us, and Generals usually surrounded themselves with the best available creature comfort available. Our group was determined to take advantage of that. The FLIVO was Oberleutnant Koiky, a tall, skinny and somewhat neurotic character. He was a reserve officer in his forties and a bank manager in civilian life. He was the uppity kind, but he took good care of his group, at least as far as food and supplies were concerned.

Germanski nix Cultura

Quite a few Russian civilians were still living in the village, mostly women and older men, who did various jobs for the military in exchange for food and money. To King's and my delight, we could use a newly built sauna nearby. Since the transmitter in our van was operated in shifts, it was easy to get in the sauna during our time off. King and I used it as often as we could, sometimes every day. It was near a large creek, which was frozen during this winter time. A square hole had been hacked through the ice, so when we came out of the sauna nude, hot, and dripping with perspiration, we would run out and jump in the creek for a few seconds to cool off. Russian women were usually nearby sawing wood for the sauna's stove, and when they saw us in the nude, they would always scream indignantly "Germanski nix cultura". The two of us laughed, rolled in the snow, threw a few snowballs at them, and quickly ran back into the sauna to get warm again. This drastic change of temperature felt invigorating. We were told that one would feel like a new born baby. However none of us could remember how we had felt right after birth.

Beethoven's Fifth, with a Fifth of Hennessy

On December 16, 1942, I celebrated my 19th birthday. King and I played chess until one o'clock in the morning, while listening to Beethoven's fifth symphony on the radio, and drinking a whole bottle of Hennessy cognac. I hoped that I would be able to celebrate my next birthday at home.

Since the liaison group was part of the General's staff we sometimes had to participate in military duties, such as sentry and guard duties. Once, I had to put in time as guard of the local POW camp. This was a small compound, where Russian POWs were kept temporarily until they were transferred to larger camps farther back from the front. The camp had a log house for the prisoners and an open yard with barbed wire around it. At one corner was a watch tower with a small guard shack which had a stove in it. It was pretty damn cold up there, so the fire never went out. When the guard needed more firewood, he called the Russian NCO who was in charge of the prisoners, and ask him to have one of his men bring up more wood. I always gave the POW who came up some of my cigarettes, even though the Russians didn't like the standard European cigarettes. I knew that they would use the tobacco, mix it with their own weird tobacco and then roll a "papyrossi" with it. Their smoking habits were something else. Their tobacco looked like tiny pieces of chopped wood, probably the ribs of the tobacco leaf, and they rolled it into a piece of newspaper. Both ends of that "cigarette" had to be twisted, so that the "tobacco" didn't fall out before they lit it.

One of the annoyances behind the Russian fronts was the night flights by weird Russian aircraft. These aircraft, which were officially designated as R-5 and U-2 aircraft, were originally training aircraft, and were often flown by Russian women. The planes were old-fashioned fabric covered two seat open biplanes, (similar to the Curtis Jenny). They were flown only at night and at low altitudes. Sometimes they dropped small bombs or hand grenades. Their only purpose seemed to be psychological warfare to harass the German troops.

On clear nights they also did reconnaissance, and they served as transport planes to partisan groups that operated in the back of the military occupied country. They were extremely difficult to shoot down, because their speed was too slow for the fire controls of the standard antiaircraft guns. In order to shoot them down with machine guns, they had to be illuminated by search lights, which the forward troops rarely had. Small caliber bullets merely put holes through the aircraft's canvas and they kept on flying.

We learned to live with them. I admired the adventurous pilots that flew them. One night I saw one explode in midair, which was highly unusual, and I went to the impact area to investigate. One crew member had bailed out and was captured and interrogated. As it turned out he had triggered a flare to illuminate the area below for photography and when he tried to throw it overboard, it slipped out of his hands and fell into the cockpit. He immediately jumped out and came down on his parachute. The other crew member didn't get out in time and burned with the aircraft.

Camouflage checks were frequently flown by us behind our own lines in the Fieseler "Storch" aircraft. This aircraft was a unique "Short Take Off and Landing" plane, which had remarkable capabilities. Its stall speed was about 25 M.P.H. I took part in one of the inspection flights, which showed that at low altitude and slow plane speed even the best camouflage could not hide a position, particularly in wintertime. We also discovered during night flights that there were landing strips in our rear area for the R-5 and U-2 aircraft mentioned above. These flights supplied the Russian guerrillas with explosives, food, medication and anything else they needed for their operations, and they sometimes flew out their wounded. They did this in a crude way by mounting large diameter, light weight tubes under each wing, and wrapping the injured person in blankets and tarps and stuffing them into the tubes, which then were closed at both ends. I could only guess what the survival rate among the evacuees was.

A White Christmas 1942 in Woitolowo

This was my second Christmas away from home and just as cold as the first one in the RAD camp. However it was a "wet" Christmas, because we had so much top quality liquor. There was the finest French cognac, champagne and wine, and we weren't sober most of the time. It was the only time in my life that I passed out from champagne. The next morning I had to face all sorts of accusations. They told me I had knocked over the Christmas tree and done other misdeeds. I couldn't defend myself, because I didn't know anything about it. It was a good lesson. I never ever got that drunk again.

There were rumors that the German Airfleet 1 in Riga would send a Junkers 52 transport aircraft clear to France to get more wine and cognac whenever we were dry. If true, it was amazing that some of it trickled down to near the front lines. Anyway, at times we could drown our worries about the damn war in alcohol.

Furlough from Russia, 1943

Furlough from Russia, 1943

Russia is a riddle wrapped in a mystery inside an enigma.
Winston Churchill

7
Russian Army Turns the Tide

Late in December and through the first week of January 1943 we received alarming aerial surveillance photographs from high flying Junkers 88 aircraft. Every day we scrutinized the new photos and watched an enormous buildup of artillery positions on the Russian side. When our officer presented this information at the meetings of the general staff of the XXVI A.K. he was ridiculed. We couldn't believe the general's staff attitude. Koiky finally gave up trying to convince them and we said we will see what is going to happen.

A similar buildup of artillery positions had been seen on aerial photographs on other sections of the front and precautions had been taken on the German side to prevent any Russian advance. However, it turned out that the Russians had built fake artillery positions with painted telephone poles looking like heavy artillery pieces. That had not been detectable in the photos taken at 26,000 feet by the Junkers 88 aircraft. The Russians had always been very good at what they called "maskirovka" or deception of their opponents. Koiky couldn't convince Generalleutnant Grasser, the commanding general, that what we saw was real.

This was a critical time in Germany's ill-conceived attack on the Soviet Union. The Russians, after enormous losses during the opening of operation Barbarossa were now getting organized, and quickly threw well equipped reserves into the battle fields. They always had more manpower and equipment than the German side.

The Russian Army was fighting their way back into Stalingrad with fresh new troops. These troops were winter-hardened units, from Mongolia, well equipped to oust the German Army from their positions. I formed my opinion from illegal listening on our excellent radio receivers, but that was strictly forbidden by law. I could be court-martialed and if found guilty, I could face the firing squad. I could listen only during the night shift, when I was alone, and I had to keep my mouth shut tightly, which was damn hard at times.

To give the reader an account of the activities of the communication liaison group, I will outline a typical message flow. The liaison officer was present during the daily situation meetings held by the commanding general of the Armee Corps. At these situation meetings, there might be a request for aerial reconnaissance over a sector of the front that had unusual activities, or a request for targeting of certain Russian strong points. The liaison officer would give the request in writing to us, his communications group. The request then was encoded on the "Enigma" machine.

This machine was like a typewriter, but above the keyboard were the 26 letters of the alphabet, each with an electric light bulb underneath. At the very top of the machine were three vertical wheels, each with 26 short, removable, connector cables. The cables in each wheel were used to program each cylinder according to a master code calendar. Each program was valid for a 24 hour day, however every 8 hours the positions of the three vertical wheels were changed. For instance, the center roll was moved to the right position, and the left roll to the center position, and so on. The text was typed slowly into the keyboard by one man, while a second man would read the resulting letters which appeared on top of the machine and write them down, or call them out to a third man if they were in a hurry.

The resulting letters were written in groups of five and together with a complex top line which identified the encoding key, formed the outgoing radio message. After contact with the central radio station was established, the text was transmitted in Morse code. Each liaison group had their own call letters which were changed regularly.

When a message was received, we would set the machine according to the code key in the top line of the transmission, and would then key in each of the received text letters. The resulting letters appearing on the upper part of the machine showed the uncoded text.

The End of the Siege

Around January 9, 1943, our predictions of a pending Russian offensive came true. A Russian artillery barrage of unprecedented intensity started at the Volkhov front, and continued uninterrupted for three days. When the Russian troops started to advance, they didn't find much resistance, because few German soldiers had survived. The Russians claimed they had fired over 500,000 shells at the German lines during these three days. They broke through the German lines and advanced in the direction of Schlisselburg, towards Leningrad, along the southern shore of Lake Ladoga. Heavy fighting took place all along a ten mile wide corridor south of Lake Ladoga. German forces tried, as before, to pinch off the advancing Russian troops.

This time, however, the Russians hung on to the narrow corridor against the fierce attacks and artillery barrages from the German forces. Around January 18, 1943, the Russians used the narrow corridor to get through to the beleaguered city on a land route for the first time and ended the 503 day siege of Leningrad. This is in contrast to the false report of 600 or even 900 days of siege. The Russians very quickly built a rail line through that corridor to Schlisselburg and a pontoon bridge was built across the Neva to connect to the rail lines around Leningrad.

The ten mile wide supply corridor was under fire from German artillery for almost another year, and was called the death corridor by the Russians, but supplies did get through.

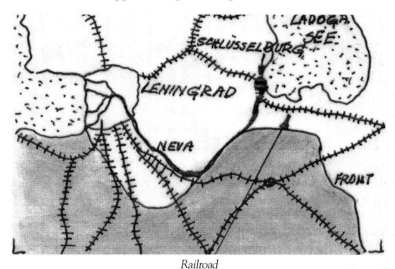

Railroad

January 27, 1943, after 500 days, the Russians are successful in breaking the German siege of Leningrad (now St. Petersburg).

An A-20 Short of Fuel

On April 6, 1943 I was called back to the Company in Siverskaja, and stayed there for two months. During that time, a Russian twin engine aircraft made an emergency landing on a field southwest of Mga and the pilot was captured. I drove to the location with an interpreter. The pilot had made a forced landing with landing gear up and the aircraft was damaged but in reasonably good shape. According to the pilot, he was shot down, but when I examined the fuselage of the airplane, I couldn't find any damage. The type of aircraft surprised me, it was an American made twin engine A-20 bomber, and had the complete operations and maintenance manuals on board. There was also a container with an emergency food supply, including some Hershey chocolate syrup and canned goods.

I wrote down the aircraft's serial numbers and labels, and also tried to pry out some of the radios They were bolted and I finally gave up. To get to the things we were interested in, I had to use my rifle butt to pound away some of the twisted sheet metal. We checked the fuel tanks and it was obvious why the pilot had landed, he was out of fuel. Apparently he was a transfer pilot who had tried to deliver this aircraft to Leningrad. We confronted him and he was ashamed to say that he had run out of fuel 15 miles short of the Leningrad airport.

Back again at my unit I took my carbine out of the personnel carrier and went inside the building to unload it. I laid the carbine on a table, with the muzzle facing the window. When I unsafe'd it to open the breach to extract the ammunition, the gun went off without me touching the trigger. Of course the shot inflicted the maximum damage by blowing out about 16 window panes of the large double-paned windows. Fortunately nobody was hit. Then came the difficult task of explaining to the staff sergeant what happened. He ordered me to show my rifle to the weapons master immediately. The weapons master said, "What the hell did you do with this gun?", showing me that the gun stock was cracked. To my embarrassment, I had not even noticed that. The stocks of the war issue 98k carbines were made from multilayered plywood, and practically indestructible. I got a new gun, but I had to promise not to break the gun stock over someone's head again. The weapons sergeant couldn't refrain from cracking that joke.

I used the Hershey chocolate syrup to upgrade the Russian Vodka. It helped, but still didn't get rid of the potato-cellar taste.

A few days later the staff sergeant questioned me about the type of radio equipment I had been trained on in the airborne radio operator school.

An Unexpected Transfer

Later in the week I was transferred to an aerial reconnaissance group at the Siverskaja airport, because they were short of radio operators for the FW 189 aircraft. I was surprised, and not very happy about it.

Within a few hours I was briefed in their radio procedures, received a flight suit and went on the first mission. This group flew short range daytime reconnaissance at between 10,000 and 20,000 feet, and so they were very vulnerable to flak and fighter harassment. The area under surveillance was the rear of the Russian frontline to a depth of up to 100 miles. The observations were primarily visual, rarely backed by photography. When observations were of particular significance, a brief written report was often dropped to the ground directly at the requesting army unit. This meant a very low level fly-by, and the drop of a smoke cartridge with the message inside.

Usually a man from the liaison crew would lay out a white canvas cross on the ground for the drop. Radio traffic was avoided, since the Russians listened in and usually had a "reception committee" waiting. The aircraft, although exceptionally well suited for aerial observations with an extensively glazed crew nacelle, was a sluggish performer. Its maximum speed was about 220 M.P.H. in level flight, a sitting duck for any fighter plane. I flew only four half way "normal" missions with the aircraft. On the fifth mission we were intercepted by a Yak-2 fighter plane. He attacked from a 4 o'clock position, and I opened fire with the top turret. The Yak fired into our starboard engine, which started to burn.

Our pilot put the aircraft into a steep dive, apparently hoping to get the fire out and go down on the deck and back over the German lines. The Russian fighter flew a wide circle to the left and attacked again, this time from nearly a 12 o'clock position. Our Focke Wulf 189 copilot opened fire with the 20 mm guns that were in the leading edge of the wing. But since our aircraft had a nose down attitude, its guns were also pointing down, and didn't reach the Russian. The Russian had miscalculated too and overshot us at high speed without being able to hit us again. By that time we were only about 1000 feet above the ground, and the next Russian attack had to come from above since we were going down rapidly on one engine. In all that excitement I couldn't tell where our own front-lines were. Our pilot was aiming for a small forest clearing, and I protected myself as well as I could for the impact.

Thank God the plane hit the ground at a shallow angle with landing gear up, and plowed right into a big tree stump, kicking up the tail end of the aircraft. I was thrown up into the top of the cockpit, and sustained a deep cut on my forehead. I freed myself and looked to see if the two pilots had survived. The aircraft had the whole front of the cockpit smashed in, and pilot and copilot had been slammed into the debris of the cockpit. The aircraft was practically standing on its nose. As I tried to get out of the aircraft I heard the engine of the Yak, and saw it firing with all guns at our downed aircraft. Sonofabitch, I thought, that guy is really angry. None of his bullets hit me, and I ran for cover under some trees.

The Russian fighter came down again and fired. The Focke Wulf exploded from the fuel that had leaked out around it. I was afraid of exploding ammunition in the aircraft and ran away from the aircraft.

My face was full of blood and I couldn't see out of my right eye. I had no survival gear, it had burned with the aircraft. I took off my undershirt rolled it and wound it tightly around my forehead and knotting it at the back. I thought that the Russian fighter wouldn't have tried so fiercely to destroy us if we had landed behind the Russian lines. POWs come in handy for information, and ground troops would certainly take care of any survivors. I concluded I was already somewhere behind the German lines.

I dozed off because of the shock and blood loss. Motor noise woke me up, but it was hard to judge how close it was. At least I could sense the general direction. After what I thought was at least an hour of walking, I saw a typical rollbahn (corrugated road) and some German vehicles. Another half hour and I was close enough to waved the next vehicle down and got help to patch up my bleeding forehead.

They took me to headquarters of an infantry unit. I reported to the officer there, who connected me to my squadron by telephone. Three hours later a vehicle finally showed up. I was weak and dizzy, and just hoped that we wouldn't fall into the hands of partisans on the way back to the airport. When we reached my squadron I tried to get out of the vehicle but I collapsed. When I came to, I was in a hospital bed. The nurse told me that I had a bad concussion and heavy blood loss, and that the doctor had to stitch up the cut in my forehead.

A week later I returned to the squadron and was interrogated about the crash. Then I requested and was granted a return to my original unit in Siverskaia.

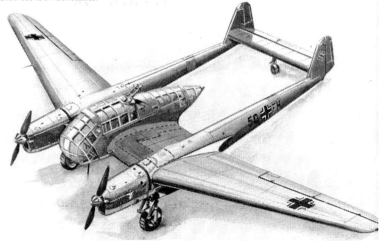

This plane is similar to the type of airplane I flew in.

Silence is golden, speech is Dachau.
German proverb in Nazi times

8
Another Furlough

Back at my Liaison Company, I had a pleasant surprise, I could go on furlough again. Maybe the company chief felt that after my crash I deserved a rest. On June 10, I arrived in Landsberg/Warthe and surprised my mother, who was working in the garden. That evening I called my father in Berlin, who promised to come home as soon as he could. This time the weather was perfect, warm and summery. I put on shorts and soaked up the sun.

A few days later I went down to the boathouse, and pulled out the old skiff with the funny name of "Jung Häschen" (young hare) for a solitary excursion upstream. I was uneasy in the beginning, because perfect rowing coordination is essential to keep a single racing shell from capsizing. After getting away from the pier, I didn't have any problems at all.

I visited Friedl, several times, but she still didn't want to go to bed with me and I finally lost interest in her. I went to see my father in Berlin, and a girl with whom I had corresponded. She had been one of those "write to a soldier pen pals" which were common in Germany during the war.

Berlin is a Mess

In Berlin I saw the extensive damage done by British and American bombings.

I stayed with my godmother, Else Gottschalk, who was still in the millinery business. Due to war shortages in material she now primarily did alterations of lady's hats. There were shortages everywhere, because after the declaration of "Total War" earlier in 1943 all "nonessential" businesses had been closed. Even the best restaurants had only one or two meals on the menu. Often they served only "field kitchen meals" which was a stew of potatoes, cabbage and here and there bits of most likely horse meat.

Father had gotten me tickets for a stage show, and I invited my pen pal Ingrid to join me. She was attractive, reasonably intelligent, and neat, but she couldn't have been more than 5'-1" tall. To me, at 6'-1", that was too much of a mismatch.

I went home to Landsberg thinking I had lost the ability to enjoy life and have a good time. I was overweight, because of the high carbohydrate diet of potatoes and cabbage with little meat or fat.

When back in Siverskaja, I was surprised that the Company's name had been changed to Liaison Comp. z.b.V.1, meaning "Air force liaison company for special assignments". The new name was more appropriate for what we were doing, but the abbreviation "z.b.V." had a special meaning in German military parlance. It was given primarily to penal units, which were always assigned to the most hazardous battle situations. They performed tasks that were called "Himmelfahrts-kommandos", or suicide missions. I was never able to find out if the renaming was a clever camouflage to prevent the company from being integrated into a Luftwaffen Field Division (LwFD).

Decades later I found out that in 1943 the Luftnachrichten Regiment 31 was reorganized and renamed. Those Luftwaffen Field Divisions, mentioned above, were the catch basins for nonessential air force personnel. They had a poor reputation because of their lack of infantry training, lack of combat experience in ground warfare, and officers who didn't know their ass from a hole in the ground during front line actions. The whole northern front had been jeopardized by one of these Luftwaffen Field Divisions in the frontline between the Army Group North and the Army Group Center.

A Weak Sector Breakthrough

The Russians, who were always probing for weak sections in German front lines, found it in the area south of Kholm. That was where the 2. Luftwaffen Field Division was entrenched. The Russians attacked in a narrow sector there, and broke through the lines with several T-34 tanks, because the Luftwaffen soldiers had no antitank weapons. Encouraged by their initial success the Russians penetrated deeper, took the town of Nevel and tried to penetrate further towards the Baltic Sea. They hoped to encircle the entire northern front, and cut it off from the adjacent central front.

On July 5, 1943, my liaison group was ordered to report to Army Corps II, about 18 miles southwest of Kholm. This was the southernmost section of the German Army Group North, where that breakthrough had occurred. We got off to a bad start. I was sitting in the communication van and was trying to get more information about the military situation at our destination. As I looked out of the window on the left, a loose wheel sped by, passing the van and going in the same direction. As I wondered where the hell that came from, a second wheel zoomed by, and the whole truck started to tilt, making godawful grinding noises.

The driver stopped the vehicle and we all got out to look at the damage. We retrieved the lost wheels, but could only find two wheel nuts. The group cracked all sorts of jokes about the incident, but it was not funny. The van could have tipped over on its side because it was top heavy. We had been lucky, we were going only at about 30 MPH when it happened. The Noncom was furious, and when the officer who was in the lead car stopped and came back, he immediately set off towards the next telephone to tell the company chief what had happened. Within an hour a vehicle from the company was on location with the maintenance supervisor and the mechanic who had serviced the truck before we left. The poor guy got shit from everybody, but fortunately he had been smart enough to bring tools plus wheel nuts along, to try and fix the problem right there. We were lucky that none of the threads on the wheel bolts had been damaged by the escaping wheels or by the road surface. We continued south via Luga and Nikolayevo and then over bad corduroy roads to the area near Porchov. We were now about 10 miles from our destination.

To Wade Through Knee-Deep Mud

The road to our destination was under knee-deep mud, so we had to wait for a vehicle to tow us. Finally a large half-track vehicle normally used to move heavy artillery pieces pulled our Volkswagen, the communications van, plus several other waiting vehicles, for at least 10 miles through the worst muck. The communication van was top heavy and not very stable. We all felt seasick during the ordeal. I was responsible for the vehicle and its functionality, and I visualized it being tipped over or torn apart. The wheel incident was on my mind too, but we made it through to the II. Army Corps headquarters in one piece. The HQ was located in the undamaged small village of Gorki with Russian civilians still living there. We parked the van next to a house, which was going to be our quarters, while the officer moved into an earthen bunker up a shallow hill from the house. We set up the station and acquainted ourselves with the tactical situation of this section of the front. We were about 40 miles north of Nevel.

Another Stalingrad in the Making?

The II. Army Corps was at the northern flank of the Russian break-through, and in heavy fighting had brought the Russians to a halt. The initial Russian success had gotten the attention of the generals of the 18th Army, the northernmost frontline contingent, still en-trenched south of Lake Ladoga, about 300 miles farther north. If they didn't make plans for a fast withdrawal, the whole German "Army Group North" would face a fate like Paulus' Army in Stalingrad.

On our maps we apprehensively tracked the evolving strategy of the Russian forces. The Russians had gained the initiative after their breakthrough at the central fronts, and were moving rapidly and steadily towards the west and now north, to encircle the Army Group North by cutting through to the Baltic Sea. The northern front was still solid, but was several hundred miles farther east than the central frontline, and in danger of being separated and encircled. At our lo-cation in Gorki, we were in the middle of nowhere. Access to retreat routes was limited by the terrible road situation and visibility of the overall tactical situation was not much better.

Forward Comrades, We are Retreating

Retreat was now the only action possible on the German side de-spite Hitler's "No retreat orders". In retrospect I say that the Generals of the Northern Front made far more sensible decisions than those of the central and southern fronts. The German Army Group North had hardly any reserves, but they manipulated the few available re-serve units so quickly and strategically correctly, that the Russians, despite their enormous manpower advantage, did not succeed in en-circling the 18th and 16th Army during their retreat. It was often at the last minute that we were able to avert a major catastrophe through heavy rear guard fighting. About 900,000 German soldiers had to be moved from the Leningrad fronts and brought back to the Baltic States. On no other fronts was the situation so well under control.

Trouble was brewing all through July of 1943. The allied forces landed in Sicily, and the Italians where so shocked, that a palace revo-lution took place, and Mussolini was ousted. In August the Allied forces finished the occupation of Sicily, and the Italians started armi-stice negotiations with them. On the 8th of September, Italy surren-dered, after British forces had landed in the south of Calabria. Every-body said, "With friends like that who needs enemies." A few days later the Americans landed near Salerno. The German forces in Italy,

Albania and Greece now had to fight the Italians, as well as the Allied forces in the Mediterranean theater.

Along the central eastern front the Russians took Kharkov and advanced on a broad front. On the Northern Front the advancing Russian forces, which had reached Nevel on October 7, 1943 as part of their goal to reach the Baltic sea, were finally stopped.

My liaison group, in the meantime, was sitting tight in this little village, hoping that we would get out before it was too late. Some Russian women were cleaning house for us, which was always a suspicious activity, because we couldn't watch them constantly. To a trained eye one glance at a map or a frequency chart would be enough to gain important facts. These women were assigned by the village commandant and our group didn't have any say in the matter. The commandant also rounded up women for work assignments in Germany. One young woman who could speak some German and who lived in the adjacent house came crying, and told me that she had to go to Germany. She wanted to know what to do. I told her to disappear, go underground, because the war was not going to last much longer. She gave me a surprised look. I didn't find out whether she actually went to Germany.

On the 2nd of November I was called back to the company in Siverskaja. That was traveling in the wrong direction, because the frontline was getting close to that town. I reached Siverskaja and was immediately turned around going west to the company's "advance" group, in Aluksne, Latvia. Rumor had it that this was in preparation for the withdrawal of all German forces from northern Russia towards the Baltic countries. I helped to set up the central transmitter, which enabled the company headquarters to keep in touch with all the liaison troops. I also met and worked again with my old friend Baumgarten, the company's electronic expert.

News from a Mysterious Source

The company chief, Captain Herrgot, had somehow acquired brand-new super fancy 20 tube Telefunken receivers, which were in a class by themselves. I enjoyed using them for all sorts of legal, and illegal, information gathering purposes.

I could, for the first time, hear the best source of allied propaganda, the "Soldatensender West", camouflaged as a legitimate German Armed Forces radio station. I eagerly listened to their clever and intelligent program. The Russian propaganda, where the most despicable character Ilja Ehrenburg urged the Russian troops to rape and

plunder, was far worse than Joseph Goebbels. Ehrenburg actually reinforced the Nazi's opinion that all Jews were deplorable criminals,
who must be killed. Although I understood the Russian's hatred of
the Germans for invading Russia, Ilja Ehrenburg's propaganda did a
disservice to the Jewish people, as well as the Communism that Russia wanted to sell to the Europeans. In retrospect I think he should
have been on the defendant bench in the Nürnberg Trials and should
have been hung like the German war criminals.

I was in for a furlough, and wondered what connections Captain
Herrgot had that gave our company so many furlough tickets. The
next surprise was that my best friend King had a furlough too.

We left on December 30, 1943 by train to Gulbene, and then to
Riga. Here we went aboard the "furlough express". We had to have
our weapons ready at all times. The locomotive of the train pushed
three flatcars loaded with sandbags ahead in case the railroad tracks
were mined by partisans. We saw two blown-up trains along the route,
evidence of increased partisan activities. Between Riga and Tauroggen
we celebrated New Year's Eve on the train, drinking whatever we had
brought along. Since we never before had the luck to go on furlough
together, King and I decided to spend a couple of days together at
home. King lived in Guben and had to return via my hometown Lands-
berg/Warthe, and he would arrive two days ahead of our return journey to stay with me.

I arrived at Landsberg on Sunday, January 2, and called home from
the railroad station. My father came down by bike and we walked
home together. I asked my father how things looked in Berlin, and he
said, "pretty grim." He said that during one of the air raids he had
been at grandmother's place. Incendiary bombs had crashed through
the roof and landed in the staircase of the four story apartment block.
He checked for problems after the all clear sirens sounded, and found
several bombs still burning in the staircase. He used a shovel to toss
them out of a window and saved the whole apartment block from
going up in flames. Eighty families would have lost their homes if he
hadn't been there.

The British had come up with a new trick in these incendiaries.
Normally they didn't do much harm because all the uppermost floors
in large buildings in Germany had a layer of sand on the floor, to
prevent ignition of the wood. Now the bombs drilled themselves
through the sand layer. Another example of men's misguided intelligence, channeled into mutual destruction rather than mutual welfare. Small wonder Nietzsche said, " War is the father of all things."

I had brought enough liquor to be able to celebrate a second New Year's Eve at home. Father went out in the garden and butchered a chicken and we had a real old fashioned noontime meal. I opened a bottle of the wine I had brought and we celebrated the beginning of 1944. We talked all afternoon, unfortunately without a decent cup of coffee, but with a reasonably good carrot cake that mother had baked.

A Sarcastic "Happy New Year"

Later on I called Friedl, Inge Bergner and neighbors and wished them a happy and successful 1944. Had I told them the truth, they wouldn't have believed it and I would have been arrested. I was determined to live it up according to a newly surfaced saying, "Enjoy the war, the peace is going to be horrible!"

I dated Friedl a couple of times and told her that my friend King was coming and I was trying to set him up with a date. She promised to ask her girl friend Helga. Several days later Helga called and asked about King. She also asked me how I was getting along with Friedl. I told her that we get along fine, except that we couldn't agree as far as sex was concerned. Helga told me that Friedl had talked to her about it, but that she was afraid. Helga promised to talk to her again and invited me over to her parents place. As I was on my way, another air raid alarm sounded off. Damn, was I pissed! I decided to go home. I was even more ticked off the next day when I called Helga to apologize. She told me I should have come anyway, because they habitually ignored the alarms.

When King arrived he went out with Helga and they had sex on a park bench, while I didn't get anywhere with Friedl. I knew that King, like myself, had never done it before. Now he had beat me with a date that I had set up for him. We stayed good friends anyway.

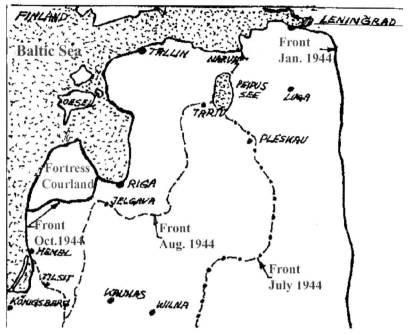

The 1944 retreat of the 16 and 18 German Armies from the Leningrad front into the Baltic states. Finally, into the Fortress Courland.

Fighting the Russian mud 1944

One should not fight dictators, one should ridicule them.
Bertold Brecht

9
The Beginning of the End

King and I went back to our unit, and arrived on January 27, 1944 in Aluksne, Latvia.

In February, while I was on duty at the central wireless receiving station, I left the receiver for no more than one minute to get some cigarettes next door. Captain Herrgot walked in and found the receiver unmanned and chewed me out right on the spot. He said that it was guard duty negligence, and I would have to face disciplinary action.

In the Clink with "Mein Kampf"

I was sentenced to five days of solitary confinement with bread and water. Per regulation they could have court-martialed me if I had endangered the security of the troops. As was military custom in those days I was allowed to take one of two books with me, either the Bible, or Hitler's "Mein Kampf". Since I had never read "Mein Krampf", as it was secretly referred to (meaning "my cramp" instead of "my fight"), I opted for that. My opinion had always been that Hitler's Kampf was my Krampf.

When I got into the cell I counted the number of pages, and divided them by five to determine how many pages of that "Krampf" I had to read every day. The company chief might question me about it, so I had to be careful.

When I came out of confinement I knew for sure that the Austrian paintbrush swinger (Hitler), by underground propaganda often referred to as "Painter Schickelgruber", that was the maiden name of his mother, was a psychotic maniac. Hitler was an illegitimate child, who was adopted when his mother married a man by the name of Hitler. His book was the worst trash I had ever read. Thank God nobody questioned me about it.

On February 26, 1944, I was sent out to join Oberleutnant Koiky's group again, which was at the Army Group Narva in Jöhvi, Estonia.

That assignment didn't last long, and the group moved to the 270th Infantry Division in Mereäre, Estonia. Then we joined the battle group Berlin for the battle around the town of Narva. We moved into a log house village that housed the staff of this battle group, comprised of several divisions.

We set up our communications van inside the circle of buildings, to remotely operate the transmitter for the two-way voice communication with Ju 87 Stukas, which were on their way to bomb a Russian bridgehead across the Narva River.

Instant Trouble, Just a Malfunction Away

Gerhard and I heard the aircraft formation approach, and I tried to activate our transmitter. The aircraft couldn't hear us, but we could hear the aircraft. It took a few minutes to realize that there was something wrong with our transmitter. I climbed on the roof of the van, and held a small neon bulb next to the transmitter antenna. The bulb glowed, indicating the antenna radiated the carrier frequency. That was strange, because the transmitter radiated even though we had not activated the mike button at the end of the remote cable.

I told Gerhard to shut the transmitter off immediately, because our constant transmission disturbed the frequency of the Stukas overhead. Gerhard did that, and was just coming out of the van, when a Russian shell exploded about 20 feet away, right inside the circle of blockhouses. I had heard it coming and like a Pavlovian dog I had ducked between the full gasoline canisters on top of the van. I could hear the shrapnel pieces whistling by. Luck had it that none went through me or the gasoline canisters and I was off that roof in seconds. I saw Gerhard collapsed and groaning on the ground in front of the van. Alfred, the driver of the van came running and together we carried Gerhard inside the blockhouse. A few more rounds landed nearby, and we all went to the floor. We checked Gerhard's wound, and could see that a shrapnel piece went sideways through his abdomen. Within 15 minutes an ambulance was there, apparently one of the generals had called them.

I was ordered to take over the van, and I quickly rolled up the coaxial cable we used to remote the transmitter with. After the coaxial cable was disconnected, everything went back to normal. So the cable must have been the problem. As I examined it inch by inch over the 30 foot length, I discovered that a tiny shrapnel piece had embedded itself in the cable. It shorted the cable and activated the transmitter. The short in the cable had the same effect as if the microphone button had been pushed to activate the transmitter.

It was clear that the constant transmitter output had provided an ideal target for Russian surveillance receivers to pinpoint the position of our transmitter. That was pretty basic, but that they had been able to direct their artillery fire so quickly and precisely surprised us. We never gave the Russians much credit for electronics warfare, but this proved us wrong. I realized that the same thing might have happened during the battle south of Lake Ladoga, when we got plastered by Russian artillery rounds.

On March 27, the group transferred again, to the XLIII Army Corps, located first in Kohtla-Järve, and later in Kahala. Here we moved in with an Estonian farm family. It was almost peaceful.

Woyli and his wife Ursula had a baby, and an attractive niece about 14 years old. Woyli farmed, and we helped him when we had time. In return we got milk and occasionally eggs and a chicken. The van was parked parallel and about two feet away from their house wall, partially camouflaged by big trees in the yard. The weather was getting better and spring was around the corner, but there was still snow on the ground. We were quite a distance from the Army Corps headquarters, got along well with our Estonian hosts, and officer Koiky was stationed far away. We hardly saw him, and we did our work as we saw fit. The war seemed far away.

We were sitting outside one day soaking up the sun when we heard an airplane high overhead. The 8,8 cm flak, which was at a nearby airport, opened fire immediately, which was unusual. We stayed in our folding chairs and watched. The flak failed to shoot him down. The plane disappeared and the scene turned tranquil again. Suddenly I noticed a persistent sound, at an unaccustomed frequency. I told Walter to shut up, and we both listened intensely. I got up with a strange, uneasy feeling. The sound persisted and gradually increased in volume. I walked up to the van entrance, and Walter followed me. The sound was now much louder and the pitch much lower. I recognized now what it was and dove under the van and yelled at Walter to duck too. A split second later we heard the impact of a large piece of metal hitting the ground, where Walter had stood just a second ago. It was a hot and smoking jagged piece of steel torn from the 8,8 flak shells that had been fired at the Russian aircraft. Walter took the piece for a souvenir, and said, "Thanks Hans, you saved my life."

The next night we heard low level aircraft noise, and a string of heavy explosions moving in our direction. We ran to the doorway with our Estonian hosts. The last of several bombs fell about 100 feet from our van on the other side and shook the whole house. What looked like a twin engine bomber pulled up above us finishing his low level bombing run. Most of the bombs had fallen on the airfield and caused considerable damage. We checked our van and found shrapnel holes in the side that faced the nearest bomb crater.

The Beginning of the End?

During the night shifts when I was alone, I scanned other frequencies when not busy on our frequency. I came upon a very strong transmission in Morse code. Encoded messages are in equally long groups, this one wasn't. The strange call letters were "abc", followed by the customary string of Vs, and it was machine keyed at a high speed, at least 140 words per minute. I had one hell of a time following and writing it. I realized it was clear text, but in English. I wrote as fast as I could, but lost words and sentences here and there. When it ended, it was repeated and I filled in most gaps. After working at it for a while, it became clear what it was. A press release about the landings of allied troops in Normandy, France. The date was June 7, 1944!

The next morning I told the men that I had "accidentally" picked up a message and didn't know what to do with it. When I told them what the message said, it hit like a bomb. Should I tell Oberleutnant Koiky and face a possible court marshal? I couldn't make up my mind. Then I thought of some bullshit I was going to give him. We had a spare receiver in the van, and I set it up and tuned in the frequency that I had heard the signal on. I wasn't successful, but after stringing a better antenna, the signal was readable. Now they couldn't get me for taking the main receiver off the network during my shift. I then went on the field telephone and told Koiky that I had heard a clear text message close to our own frequency and what it said. For a moment there was silence at the other end which made me damn nervous, but then Koiky said, "Oh my God, that is the beginning of the end." I only said, " Yes, sir." Koiky passed the information on to the commanding general, who had not heard of any landings. Two hours later it was confirmed over the radio by the German High Command.

On July 19 we left this idyllic location for a new assignment and soon rolled towards an area west of Daugavpils in Latvia. The Russians were trying to cut us off again. They tried to break through to the Baltic Sea.

For the next four to five weeks we changed location every few days, sometimes daily. The Russian's forward momentum encouraged the partisans to step up their activities too. Our group adhered strictly to the rule that everyone had to knock on the door of the van, wait for the crew on duty to lift the drawn curtains, look out, and identify the person. Inside the van weapons were at the ready. One day the dumbbell driver opened the door suddenly and found himself looking at the muzzle of my automatic, with my finger on the trigger. That really shook the driver up. Had I been a split second slower in recognizing him, he would have been dead, and that taught everybody a lesson.

At our next stop, again quartered on a farm, the farmer told us that he had evidence of partisan activity in the vicinity of his property. Koiky sent me and two other men out to investigate. That was stupid, because it could have been a setup for an ambush. We went out armed with submachine guns and took the farmer with us, to preclude possible surprises. The farmer led us on a narrow path through a wooded area with heavy underbrush on either side. Suddenly there was noise in the underbrush. "Who's there?" I hollered, and got no answer, then heard more rustling in the underbrush. I fired a series of shots from my MP38 in that general direction. The answer now came loud and clear, and it sounded "Moooooh". I had shot a cow hidden in the brush that happened to belong to the farmer walking with us. He had hidden his livestock in the forest, to keep it from being confiscated by the German army. One of my shots went right through the cow's neck. A damn good aim without actually seeing the target. I was embarrassed because I was so quick on the trigger, but we were all up tight in situations like that. The cow was gushing blood. The farmer took the cow home immediately, and it survived.

The group then proceeded alone to see what evidence of partisan activity we could find. We found a fairly recent cross on what looked like a grave. We could not tell if this was real, or had other meaning.

Another Plot Bungled

The German westward retreat continued, and things got pretty congested at times, because of the masses of equipment and people that threaded west through a narrow passage around Riga. When my van stopped along a highway near Riga, I heard via radio about the assassination attempt on Hitler. This news spread like wildfire through the troops who were making a fast, and orderly westward retreat out of Estonia. I remember a senior army colonel coming to the open door of my van and asking if the assassination attempt he had heard was true. I confirmed the rumor, and handed him headphones so he could listen to the radio. He was sitting by the door, while I was sitting in front of the electronic panels with the receivers and transmitters. I was watching his facial expressions, trying to determine how he felt. His face remained expressionless throughout the entire broadcast. Who knows, he could have been an officer who was involved in the plot. I couldn't understand why the assassination was unsuccessful. All these upper echelon guys in the military were totally incompetent. They couldn't even kill Hitler at point blank range. It was unbelievable.

The Russians had almost broken through to the Baltic Sea west of Riga near Tukkums. A successful breakthrough would have meant encirclement for about half a million (my guess) German soldiers still in Estonia. However the Russians couldn't hang on to their gains. They were driven back far enough to allow a continuing fast German retreat westward, into Latvia and possibly into Eastern Prussia.

During July the top commander of the German Northern front, General Lindemann, was replaced by General Friessner, who was then replaced by Field Marshal Schörner.

We soon called Schörner the "Polit-Commissar," for his Russian style leadership. He showed up everywhere, demoting incompetent officers, or even having them executed on the spot. His driver, the saying went, always had two uniforms with him. One with the rank insignia of a corporal, and the other one with the insignia of a master sergeant, because he was constantly demoted and promoted.

Hitler had rounded up all the old professional Army Generals and everyone else who had possibly been involved in the conspiracy and the assassination attempt. We never heard an exact number, but the BBC broadcasts mentioned that several thousand had been rounded up and executed. Many of the well-known Generals, such as Rommel and von Kluge, committed suicide.

On July 24, 1944 the order came to no longer give the military salute, but to give the Nazi salute, and say, "Heil Hitler", as an expression of loyalty to the Führer.

Ursus Ante Portas

By the end of July 1944 the Russian troops were approaching the old German border in East Prussia, while the German 16th and 18th Armies were still hanging on to Latvia. Finally about the 7th of August there was a stabilization of the German forces along the entire northern Front. The Russians had made so much headway that they couldn't supply their frontline troops. They were consolidating their lines, while the Germans were pressing them hard, to keep them out of Lithuania, Latvia and western Estonia.

Then there was more bad news. On the 4th of September Finland ceased military activities against Russia, opening up the Baltic Sea to the Russian navy. In the west the American forces also reached the German border.

In the next few weeks the entire 16th and 18th German armies, about 300,000 men, including my unit, retreated southwest past the city of Riga. The 13th Russian Army of the Leningrad front tried again and again to break through to the Baltic Sea to encircle parts of us. The area around Riga had been fortified, and after the bulk of the German armies had retreated past Riga, heavy rear guard fighting took place there.

Besieged in Courland

On the 10th of October, the Russians finally succeeded in breaking through to the Baltic Sea, but about 150 miles farther west than expected, near the city of Memel. This sealed off the land bridge to Germany for the 16th and 18th Armies. Irony of ironies, we now had moved from the siege of Leningrad to being besieged in Courland, a province of Latvia.

About 300,000 German soldiers were trapped in northern Latvia even though a breakthrough to the west would have been possible, Hitler's lunatic orders to hold the present position at any price, forced Schörner to order a defense in Courland and prepare for a hole-up effort there. If Schörner would have had any guts, he could have overruled Hitler's order and ordered the Army Group North to continue westward into Eastern Prussia. Hitler wasn't in any position to prevent that and couldn't have done anything to stop such a move. The whole eastern front was already in a state of collapse, but Hitler refused to believe it.

Courland situation at May 8, 1945

Communications van with crew? 1944.

Man is the reasoning animal. Such is the claim. I think it is open to dispute. Indeed, my experiments have proven to me that he is the unreasoning animal. Note his history . . .
Mark Twain

10
Courland, Latvia

Courland is a province of Latvia, jutting like a large peninsula into the Baltic Sea. It was the area into which the 16th and 18th Army had retreated, after being forced out of the Leningrad and northern Baltic fronts. Hitler claimed our position there was essential as a jump-off point for a future flank attack on the advancing Russian armies. He ignored that the manpower ratio was now about 7:1 in favor of the Russians, and the tank and artillery ratios about 20:1. This Courland defense looked like the making of another Stalingrad.

By the end of October 1944 my liaison group had moved into Lubezeres, a little town in northern Courland, and stayed there until the end of February 1945. We really lucked out.

Lubezeres was a pleasant little agricultural town, bypassed by the war and it would have been nice to live there. The liaison group was quartered in a half-timbered farm house, surrounded by large trees. An elderly couple owned the farm, and had an older female farm helper who also lived at the house. Our group respected their property and their right to certain privacy, realizing that it was an inconvenience for them to have six men living with them. The communication van was set up in front of the house under the trees and we guys strung an extra long, extra high receiving antenna between the trees. We would need good reception, in order to be well informed about what was going on in Germany and Europe.

In town a large plant manufactured high grade alcohol from potatoes and sugar beets. When the first German troops had come in, they had gotten their hands on some of that 80% "Schnaps", and went on a drunken spree. Two soldiers died of alcohol poisoning. The commanding general put a stop to that, and the alcohol was now used as an additive to the meager gasoline supply to stretch it. We had to be almost completely self sufficient in the "Fortress Courland" as it was now called. The German navy could still supply us with certain provisions, and take back the wounded soldiers, but with the Russian Navy now on the loose in the Baltic Sea, supplies were questionable.

Fortunately the fairly orderly retreat from the Russian northern front sector had made it possible to salvage substantial amounts of equipment and material. Before the military mail connection with the rest of Germany was broken, I had sent my father a letter and told him in a round-about-way where I was. I told him that I would try to get back, by "playing the partisan game" provided I got stuck in Courland to the end. Father's answer was that he was very much concerned and didn't think I would be able to pull that off. He urged me to be extremely careful. That was the last mail I received.

My super antenna enabled us to keep an ear on the rest of the world. The situation for the German Armed Forces on all other European fronts deteriorated by the day. The Latvian population was hungry for information too, because they worried about their own safety and future. Quite often we had several young women come to visit us to find out what was happening at the Courland front. One good looking girl had her husband at the Latvian SS division in action there.

Courland and the War Situation

The Courland peninsula roughly resembles a triangle, with one leg facing the Baltic Sea, and the other leg facing the Bay of Riga. Along the hypotenuse of this triangle was the front line, where about 30 relatively well equipped, battle hardened German divisions had dug in. German troops where also still holding part of the island of Saaremaa, in the Bay of Riga. Officially there were eight major Russian offenses to smash the defenders of Fortress Courland, but I counted a total of 23 attacks, all unsuccessful. The front troops had dug in, and whenever the Russians gained some advantage they were beaten back in counterattacks. The few Panzer units that were still on our side were now partially equipped with Russian T-34 tanks which had been salvaged from the battle fields. At least spare parts were available for those tanks from salvage operations in the no-man's-land between the front lines.

Jokes about Fortress Courland

Many jokes were cracked about the war situation during these successful defenses. The jokes went, "Paris has surrendered to the Americans, Fortress Courland is holding." "The Russians have marched into Budapest, Fortress Courland is holding" etc. One day I overheard a tank commander holler to another soldier, "We lost the last war, why shouldn't we win this one?"

All these wisecracks were grim humor, since the war situation in Courland had no meaning with respect to the outcome of the war. The Russians obviously did not have their crack troops at our front, but they figured sooner or later we would run out of ammunition, fuel, food etc. and be forced to surrender. We were however able to defend ourselves successfully until the end of the war.

To bolster moral, front line troops received an embroidered stripe for their uniforms saying "Festung Kurland" for winning these defensive battles. The wisecrackers said that the stripes for noncombat soldiers were given only to those who had seen the white in Field Marshal Schörner's eyes ten times.

My private news gathering service learned about the latest developments via my favorite radio station, the "Soldaten Sender West" (Soldier's Radio West). It had comprehensive news from all military fronts. Sometimes curious happenings at the home front were reported in detail. Since they also gave the official daily report of the OKW (High Command of all German Armed Forces), the station sounded legitimate. However, reading between the lines, it was obvious that it came from "the other side". They had an incredibly well informed news service with pointed sarcasm mixed in, and were always ahead of the OKW's admittance regarding losses.

On December 16, 1944, I celebrated my 21st birthday, which finally made me an Adult according to the German law. Shortly after my birthday I was promoted to corporal, but under the circumstances it didn't mean a damn thing.

On the same day I heard of the big German counter offensive in the Ardennes. It didn't stop the Allies. After 5½ years of war Germany was exhausted, no matter what the stupid Nazi propaganda machine blared.

Christmas 1944

We had a depressing Christmas, even though we had been supplied with excellent liquor and food. Our Latvian hostess even baked traditional cakes and cookies for us, and we sang some Christmas songs together. I celebrated New Year's Eve with a bottle of genuine "Black & White Scotch Whiskey." It was the first Scotch I had ever seen or tried, and I was surprised about the taste. We all hoped that the goddamn war would be finished in the coming year. We celebrated heartily, reminding ourselves again of the current saying, " Enjoy the war, the peace will be terrible."

Russians Take Landsberg

On January 30, 1945, I heard that the Russians had taken my hometown, Landsberg/Warthe. What an irony, it was on the very same day that Hitler had come to power 12 years earlier. It happened to a city that also shared the name with the Landsberg/Lech city, where Hitler had been imprisoned back in 1923. If the Bavarians had only kept him there. I hoped that my mother and our friends had gotten out before the Russians came in.

Later on I told Oberleutnant Koiky that there was heavy fighting around Königsberg, and he just about had a nervous breakdown. Koiky was crying when he said he hoped his wife and children had safely gotten out of the city before the Russians came. At the end of February our group drove back to the company headquarters, somewhere east of Liepaja and I was assigned to Oberleutnant von Collins' group.

We were sent to the XXXVIII Army Corps on March 5, 1945. From that date on the group was constantly on the move. It was obvious we were no longer needed anywhere. There wasn't much of a Luftwaffe left in Courland. Reconnaissance was flown by Focke Wulf 190 or Messerschmitt 109 fighter planes, and they reported verbally in clear text to the liaison group if something important was observed.

Then the rumors started that the Navy was going to evacuate everyone. I thought that would have been unfair, since only the rearward troops could have been evacuated, and the fighting men at the frontline would have been left behind. General Hilpert, who had taken over from General Rendulic, who had taken over from Field Marshal Schörner, canceled the effort. That was probably just as well, since a Russian submarine had already torpedoed the large German Hospital ship the "Wilhelm Gustloff", with thousands of wounded soldiers and refugee civilians from Königsberg on board. The Titanic catastrophe was a minor accident compared to this tragedy in which approximately 7,000 people vanished.

Bones Stronger than a Truck

While we were making another location change the van got stuck in snow. All men had to lend a hand to get the damn truck out, and then try and catch up with it and jump on the side board. That was a dangerous game with all the snow and ice on the road. I missed the step, fell to the ground, and got my left foot run over by the truck's rear wheels. God, that scared the daylights out of me, because I was sure my foot was broken. However I managed to hobble after the van and catch up with it. I took my heavy felt boot off and nothing was broken, but I had one hell of a contusion above my ankle. Apparently my foot had gotten into the gap between the dual tires, and only the outer tire had rolled over my lower leg, which was protected by a heavy felt boot, and cushioned by the snow underneath. For a week I could hardly walk. After three weeks my leg, gradually going through the colors of the rainbow, came back to normal.

We moved from the VI. SS Corps, to the Tank Hunter Group of the 24th Infantry Division. Here we met with another group of our company where my friend Kurt König (King) was. I hadn't seen King in a long time. We stayed with that group for five days, waiting for further orders to proceed to an assigned army unit. This gave me an opportunity to have a long conversations with King regarding what we should do to get ourselves out of this goddamn predicament. It was obvious that it was just minutes before "zero hour", and that we would all march into POW camps, probably somewhere in Siberia.

A Flight to Sweden?

During those five days, we considered stealing a Fieseler Stork (a small liaison airplane) that was parked nearby, and try to fly it across the Baltic to Sweden. The closest Swedish territory was the large island in the Baltic by the name of Gotland, which was about 200 Km (125 miles) away, well within the capabilities of that aircraft. We debated that for hours and finally decided against it, because we could not give the plane a check out to determine if it was operational, without arousing suspicion. Even if it was operational we didn't know how much fuel was in the tanks, where the pilot was, and we would have to fly it out at night. That was beyond my capability.

It turned out to be a wise decision, because I found out after the war that the Swedish Government had turned all German internees over to the Russians. That was not in compliance with the Geneva convention, but the Swedes had indirectly supported the Germans so were apparently scared shitless of the Russians. I found out decades later that they had about 6,500 German internees in Sweden whom they sent to Russia and of those only about 1,650 returned from Russian POW camps.

I told King that I had decided to hike back to Germany. I told him what I considered to be essential for my hike. Maps, compass, food etc. and we parted with heavy hearts, since we wouldn't be able to pull it off together. We exchanged home addresses, hoped that both of us would survive and said an emotional Good Bye to each other!

Not in my wildest imagination would I have thought that from that point on our lives would proceed in totally different directions.

Finally on March 12, 1945, we got our orders to proceed to what was left of the 12th Panzer Division. On March 13, or 14, we heard on the radio that President Roosevelt had died, but hardly anybody attached any importance to that, except some super optimistic characters, who thought the USA would pull out under a new president.

Hitler's Last Order

A few days later the Russian armies attacked Berlin, and Hitler gave his last order to the Eastern Front, "Whoever gives the order to retreat is to be shot on the spot." It was clear now that he had flipped his lid. The damn corps of German officers had sworn an oath of allegiance to this madman, and still felt obligated to honor that oath. It was incomprehensible to me that nobody in the upper echelons of the armed forces was willing to put a bullet through Hitler's head. I considered them all traitors to the German Nation.

Courland Undefeated to the End

During the last days of April 1945 I heard over the shortwave that the American troops had met with Russian troops at the Elbe river near Torgau, and that Zhuikov's army was in the center of Berlin. The newest version of our old joke was now, "Germany defeated, Fortress Courland stands victorious." It was not even a joke anymore, since Germany had been totally defeated and many areas completely destroyed. A march into a POW camp for us, but where, and for how long, that was the question. Would it be Siberia, Murmansk, or Wladiwostok?

I was determined to go in the opposite direction, back to Germany. I told King that I was going to hike back to Germany. We hugged, said good-bye and had tears in our eyes.

A Death 12 Years Too Late

On the evening of May 1, 1945 I heard the news that I would have loved to hear 12 years earlier. Hitler was dead! The Nazi propaganda machine had the audacity to announce that Hitler had died in Berlin while fighting for Germany. I was outraged, Hitler had never fought for Germany, he had destroyed it.

I made a show announcing Hitler's death to my wireless group by reenacting a secret joke, a Flüsterwitz, that had circulated in Berlin during Hitler's reign. I stood up, banged my headphones on the table and hollered "Achtung" to get everybody's attention. As they stared at me I said, "Good evening gentlemen" and sat down again.

Puzzled silence fell over my wireless group and they probably guessed why I all of a sudden didn't have all cups in the cupboard anymore. After a moment another Berliner remembered the joke and asked, "What do you mean, is he dead?" and I, waiting for that question replied, "Yes guys, the Gröfaz is dead." Gröfaz was the name given Hitler by nonbelievers and stood for "Grösster Feldherr aller Zeiten" in English:" Greatest Strategist of all Times".

Gradually an expression of disbelief appeared on several faces. They gathered around me to hear the details. I told them that Admiral Dönitz had been designated as Hitler's successor.

Within minutes we found our officer, Oberleutnant von Collins. He brought some staff officers of the 12th Panzer Division with him. All had grave expressions on their faces. Up here in Courland (Latvia) were two German armies, the 16th and the 18th, with about 200,000 soldiers, that had been totally encircled by the Russians in the "Festung Courland". It was anybody's guess what would happen to us up here 600 miles northeast of Berlin.

We manned our shortwave receiver 24 hours again. Military radio traffic wasn't important any more, but hard news about Germany was.

A few days later, on May 5, 1945 we heard that Admiral Dönitz had ordered some of the German forces to cease fighting. On May 7th we heard that Germany had signed an unconditional surrender of all forces at Eisenhower's headquarters in Rheims. However there was no specific mention of the troops in Courland. On May 8th 1945 our entire Division staff was called together in a forest clearing. A staff officer of the 12th Panzer Division announced that the remains of the Army Group Courland had surrendered and one minute after midnight on May 9th 1945 the most devastating war of all times had finally ended.

It was the day all soldiers had been waiting for. For many of them it wasn't the way they expected it to be. Due to my involvement in communications I was well informed and had long ago come to the conclusion that Germany had lost the war.

Peace by persuasion has a pleasant sound, but I think we should not be able to work it. We should have to tame the human race first, and history seems to show that that cannot be done.
Mark Twain

11
The End is Here

Coming back from the announcement my group of seven sat around a table and contemplated what to do. We were independent of the 12th Panzer Division which we were assigned to, so we could return to the company headquarters, or go home on our own, if we thought we could pull that off.

I listened to the Allied radio stations since there wasn't anyone to stop me. To my surprise I could not raise "Soldaten Sender West" and was beginning to doubt that it was a British station. Why would a British station go off the air at the end of the war? Who was really behind "Soldaten Sender West" if it ceased to broadcast at the end of the war? I will elaborate on this extraordinary radio station later in my book.

I had privately talked with Oberleutnant Sepp von Collins. We conversed in English, as to not arouse any anxiety in the rest of the group. I had dropped a bomb by declaring that, if the Russians wanted me for their Gulags, they had better catch me first. I was going to try to "hike" home to Germany.

During the past month I had laid the groundwork and was going ahead as planned. It was the first time I made such an important decision on my own, and finally freed myself of the straightjacket that the decisions of others had always put me to.

I had planned a route, collected maps of the areas to be traversed, had a good compass, dehydrated food, extra clothing, tobacco and cigarettes etc. and other paraphernalia I deemed necessary, including my small Mauser automatic. I also took my little Agfa camera along.

When I told the other men of my plan, I was surprised when they said they wanted to come along with me. I said that a group of seven people was too big, and that we would have to split into two independent groups to have any chance of success.

We would have to travel through 600 miles of Russian occupied territory, without any certainty of food or support from the local population. The group agreed to try my plan after much unrealistic discussion. They figured they would have a few more days to prepare, before the Russian side would come and take charge of the situation and tell them what to do. We sat down in the old farmhouse and drank whatever alcoholic beverages we could muster to drown our concerns. On my suggestion we all fantasized aloud where we wanted be in 1950, 1955, 1960. Nineteen-sixty was as far as anybody was willing to think ahead. Sepp von Collins, who was from an old, aristocratic Austrian family, said he hoped that Austria would be independent again. He invited all of the guys to come and live in Austria. Hannes Rhode, a professional soldier with the rank of sergeant major, had been wounded five times, had fought with the Legion Condor in the Spanish Civil War and had been in all the major war theaters including the war against Russia from the beginning. He could not imagine what he was going to do. I stated that by 1960 I would be out of Europe.

Professional soldiers never gave much thought to what would happen if the other side won the war. What did the victorious Allies plan on doing with Germany? We assumed that there would be occupation, but for how long? The idea that some of us would not have a town anymore to go home to, because certain areas of eastern Germany had been given to Poland and Russia, never entered our minds.

The next morning we packed everything into our communication van, and slowly rolled east towards the former front lines near Tukkums. We disabled the transmitter and threw the radio tubes out of the window. We were still laboring under the illusion that these items were classified as "secret" and should not fall into enemy hands. We stopped in a forest and burned our station documents, log books and took a big hammer to the "Enigma" encoding machine making sure it was totally unusable.

Next, we destroyed some of our personal belongings. I saved a few pictures of my girl friends. Then we removed all rank insignia and decorations from our uniforms. I told my buddies, if you get caught by the Russians tell them you were in a penal unit and had deserted. These units were not allowed to show any rank insignia.

We got into a traffic jam of military vehicles. Suddenly I saw a Russian Yak-2 fighter plane swooping down for an attack and shouted to get under cover. The Yak-2 came down and strafed the stalled military vehicles. I had dashed into a nearby house. When I heard the plane circling for another attack, somebody outside opened fire on the Yak-2 with a quad-barreled light antiaircraft gun mounted on one of the vehicles. The gunner was apparently an experienced man and the Yak-2 went off trailing smoke. What a jerk, I thought, here the damn war was finally ended and this Russian clown starts his own, and probably got killed, because I didn't see anyone bail out. What a shame. Everybody congratulated the gunner and we all hoped the other side had heard that the war was over.

Our group continued driving towards the east end of the former front line. That might sound strange, but I had reasoned that it would be easiest to cross the frontline there. I thought the Russians would think no German soldiers would escape in that direction.

In the late afternoon we drove into an encampment of an infantry unit and parked our vehicles. The unit was a Saxonian infantry regiment, probably from the 24th Infantry Division. The officers of the unit tried to persuade us not to go through with our plan, and offered us new army uniforms, and new identification papers, if we needed them. That was strange, but they might have thought that the seven of us were from a penal unit, who wanted to get our asses out of Courland. They also offered some provisions, which were gladly accepted. When it was dark, we packed our rucksacks, thanked the friendly Saxonians, said good-bye to each other and exchanged some home addresses. Then we started our Odyssey back to Germany, which we named, **"Our journey of no return."**

Clark's second law...The only way to discover the limits of the possible is to go beyond them into the impossible.

12
Hike West, Young Man

My plan was to hike during the night and hide during the day in the extensive forests of the Baltic states. Hannes Rhode, Herbert Kauerhof and I were in one group. Sepp von Collins, Alfred Sopart, Siegfried Penzel and Karl Niemitz were in the other group.

First one chickens out

Hannes, I and Herbert crossed the now deserted former front line. We came to a river, with the remnants of a blown up stone bridge partially submerged in the swiftly running water. The night was dark except for an occasional flare fired on the other side of the river. We could hear drunken Russian soldiers, firing their guns at random, and singing to celebrate their victory. We started across the river on the broken and crazily pitched bridge spans, moving with extreme caution so as to not arouse any attention. In the middle of the bridge Hannes and I stopped to let Herbert catch up with us, however we could neither see nor hear him. We assumed he had chickened out, had decided to leave our venture and return to the shore and we would proceeded without him. We figured the smaller the group, the better. It took us a long time to reach the opposite bank.

It must have been around 4:00 am as daylight started to creep up from the east. We trudged right into a row of rickety wooden buildings occupied by Russian soldiers who were soundly asleep, saturated with vodka. Occasionally a body moved and fired a six-shooter. We managed to squeeze through their camp without being detected. I had to admire Hannes for having the nerve to take his Steyer submachine gun with him, which he carried casually over his shoulder, as if he was going to a duck hunt.

We walked towards a forested area, and noticed a string of Russian sentries sitting by campfires, paying no attention to the area around them. Why should they? The war was over, and they had won. Their fires made them highly visible and gave me and Hannes a chance to circumvent them. We were able to maneuver easily through that line, which was probably set up to prevent just what we were trying to do.

It was amazing what one can detect at a distance, even in the middle of the night, just by listening and surprisingly also by smelling. At first I was at a disadvantage since I didn't have any direct frontline experience with Russian fighting troops. Hannes, however, had that "nose" for their actions. He had been a forward aircraft controller during the early days of "Barbarossa" (the German advance into Russia), and knew their modus operandi.

We spent the first day in a deserted earthen bunker, probably part of an earlier front line. After nightfall we continued on our journey, crossing more former frontline trenches. Hannes almost stepped on a body that nobody had bothered to bury. It was too dark to determine what nationality he was. That gave me the creeps and we increased our pace to get the hell out of that area. Being in a former frontline we were very much afraid of buried mines, so we decided to hike along a road. It started to rain, so we hung a camouflage tarp over our bodies and rucksack, and went on. The rain was welcome at night, because nobody likes to walk around in the rain unless they have to, that decreased the chance of being detected.

Now that we were through the former front lines we steadily advanced in a southwesterly direction. We saw fewer and fewer Russian military installations and personnel. We settled into a daily routine of hiking at night and sleeping during the day. I navigated by maps made by our own Luftwaffe, derived from aerial photographs. They were very accurate, but the scale was 1:300,000 (similar to the US aeronautical maps) which was difficult to walk by at night.

Occasionally we found an exceptionally good hiding place, and cooked a meal from dehydrated food which I had brought along. I had a small foldable stove, made of three pieces of hinged sheet metal. It opened up into a U-shaped stand to hold a cooking pot with room underneath for the fuel. The fuel was in tablet form and fairly long burning. Since we didn't have a pot, we used our mess kit. The dehydrated food was a mix of vegetables and potatoes and tasted like a wet piece of cardboard, but it was badly needed calories. If we stretched our food supply we could sustain ourselves for three weeks.

One night we walked into a strange swamp. There were islands or clumps of what looked like pampas grass, widely spaced, with knee-deep water between. We got our German army boots full of water and were cursing while jumping from clump to clump back in the direction we had come from. We couldn't walk far with boots filled with water, which would cause blisters on our feet. This would be a serious problem, since we still had hundreds of miles to walk and only a minimum of first aid supplies.

When back on dry land again, I checked the map by flashlight, and sure enough the swamp was right on the map. We had lost valuable time towards our planned ten mile hike per night. The walking time was getting shorter every night, because the summer solstice was getting closer. We now had only 4 hours of true darkness. Our location was about 57° north latitude (equivalent to Sitka, Alaska).

Some necessary dry-out

We found an abandoned camp, with several earthen bunkers with wooden bunks and an old iron stove. No personal belongings of any kind were around, but I was scared about this creepy facility. Old Hannes wasn't bothered by such considerations and to my surprise, he started a fire in the bunker's stove. He took his wet boots and socks off and told me to do likewise, which I reluctantly did. I checked outside from time to time to see if anybody was attracted by the smoke from the chimney. While our equipment dried, we ate one slice of bread and a piece of beef jerky, our daily ration. Soon our walking gear was reasonably dry and we packed and moved out.

It was daylight and we could see the size of this installation. It must have been at least an army corps headquarter, because there were numerous other bunkers and even some barracks.

Suddenly there was a movement in an opening of the forest. A group of civilian characters were assembled as if for a roll call and they appeared to be unarmed. However they must have noticed Hannes's submachine gun. They hesitated for a moment, which gave me and Hannes a chance to disappear into the underbrush. We put our guns into firing mode. The Russians, or Latvian guerrillas or whoever else they were, seemed to spread out to a search action. We heard the men walking around us in all directions, communicating with each other by whistling varied tunes. This intrigued me, because in my family we had a tune which we whistled to give our location when in crowds. Their search (or escape) was rapid, and they moved away, Hannes and I got out of the area quickly.

When we were a safe distance away I raked Hannes over the coals for being so damn careless just because we had wet feet. Hannes shrugged it off and said, "Well what do you want, we came out all right." I was annoyed about Hannes' nonchalance which I felt we couldn't afford in our situation.

We came across a functioning railroad line and decided to walk along the tracks to speed up our progress and to eliminate navigational errors. We played with the idea of hitching a ride on one of the freight trains running in a westerly direction. With the little food we had, we couldn't afford to burn many calories. We thought that the Russians needed to run loaded freight trains west into Germany to supply their occupational troops. We totally misjudged them. All westbound trains were empty and going at top speed, with little chance to jump aboard and catch a ride.

Several nights later we were walking towards one of the railroad trestles when we scared a guard standing in the middle of the bridge. He fired his rifle in the air, giving his presence away. We concluded that the reason for the guard was that the Latvian resistance was harassing the Russians now, just as they had harassed us when we were the occupational force.

On May 23, 1945, we had been on the go for almost two weeks. We were living on less than 500 calories per day. The water that we collected along creeks or ditches as drinking water was not the best for human consumption. Although both of us had a good fat reserve when we started, we felt that our bodies were using up these reserves. But we were in good spirits.

Disaster strikes

Around midnight, walking along a small road, under a full moon, we came to a house with no light to indicate it was occupied. For a moment we stood at the edge of the forest clearly visible in the moonlight, listening for any activity and checking the map.

Suddenly the door of the house opened and a soldier with a submachine gun appeared and said something in Russian, most likely asking for the password. Hannes answered, but what he said did not please the Russian, and I was horrified that Hannes even tried. One doesn't argue with an armed guard. When I saw the Russian raise his gun into firing position I dashed left with top speed. The Russian fired a volley of at least 10 shots in the direction where we had stood. I couldn't see what Hannes did because my back was turned as I was running away. A few moments went by and the Russian went back into the house.

I crept back and looked around and found Hannes breathing hard. He probably must have turned just 180° and ran back under the trees. He told me that he was hit in the chest. He was bleeding back and front, where a bullet had gone clear through his lung. I helped him take his rucksack off and sat him against a tree with his blanket pressed against the entry wound. I found two military type gauze pads in my rucksack, which I put over the front and rear wound to stop the bleeding. That was all I could do for him.

As an experienced soldier who had been wounded five times, Hannes told me that he better stay put, or he would bleed to death. He told me that the wounds would eventually plug up and prevent too much blood loss if he didn't move. We were sure that the Russians would comb the area in the morning.

Hannes told me to get the hell out of the area. I knew he was right, but I didn't want to just leave him there. We discussed what else I could do. Should I just shoot the house up with Hannes' submachine gun? That didn't make any sense, because I didn't know how many Russians were in the house, or how heavily armed they were. I told Hannes that I would put his Steyer gun into a cocked, single shot mode, and put it next to him. I asked him to give me five minutes to get away, and then he should fire the Steyer at regular intervals to attract attention. He knew there was a chance that he would make it through his ordeal.

Five minutes out I discovered that I had lost my maps and I had to backtrack in the forest to find them. Moonlight breaking through the trees helped me find the maps again, and I considered that a sign of providence, which encouraged me to continue on my way.

I doubled back to the railroad right of way and followed along the tracks for several miles, until I saw a small building ahead in the moonlight. Having just had the horrible experience with Hannes, I was very nervous and super careful. I laid down behind a stack of wooden railroad ties along the embankment, to observe what was going on and had one of my slices of bread with some water. I heard steps along the tracks and soft voices and I huddled closer to the ground. Two men walked by, about six feet away. They continued towards the small building ahead. Suddenly someone near the structure raised a gun and fired a shot into the air. I could now make out that structure was another railroad trestle, which had the customary guard shack right in the middle of the trestle.

I crept forward to check out the terrain, and followed a foot path down into a valley underneath the trestle. I needed a safe hiding place for the day and found it farther down the valley in an area of deciduous trees. I crawled into dense underbrush and covered myself with my camouflage tarp. Rain woke me up early in the afternoon. I set up my tarp as a roof over my head to keep dry.

I had to analyze the events of the last night and assess my solitary situation. I studied my map and tried to lock my compass on a distinct feature of the area which would coincide with a feature on the map, but couldn't find any. It was going to be navigation by intuition. I walked into open rolling farm land now where hiding for the daytime would be considerably more difficult.

In the late afternoon I continued walking in southwesterly direction. I was hungry and had to find someone who was willing to accept some of my cigarettes for bread or other edibles. I approached the edge of a small forested area with several farmhouses but kept at a distance to see what was going on. There were young women and children walking around one house and their door was open.

After a lengthy observation I finally dared to walk up to and knock at the open door. A woman came to the door, and I showed her some cigarettes and tobacco and indicated that I would like to exchange them for bread. She invited me in. The women in the room were not intimidated or hostile. In the course of our broken language conversation I found that they had mistaken me for a Russian NKVD man, because they had noticed me watching the area. It finally dawned on me now that in rural areas there is no way to walk around undetected, because everybody knows everybody else, and any unfamiliar person obviously sticks out.

When I told them I was German they gave me some soup to eat. They expressed to be "sympatico," as they phrased it in broken German. They gave me some bread for my cigarettes. We were just finished with our barter when I heard a horse-drawn cart pull up right in front of the entrance door. Damn it, just what I needed, another surprise. The women quickly went out to the man and welcomed him and distracted his attention. I seized the opportunity and casually walked out the front door right by him, hoping he would not level his gun at me. I heard him ask the girls who I was, but I couldn't hear their answer. They quickly ushered him into the house, and I disappeared. The terrain, with many patches of trees, was well suited for a hasty retreat. When I was out of sight I sat down, badly shaken. Wow! I thought, survived another close one. I really felt like a fugitive on the run now, but I had at least food for another couple of days.

Thoughts while being on the run

After dark I consulted my map using my fading flashlight. I had crossed the former Latvian/Lithuanian border into Lithuania. It was May 27, 1945 and I had been on the run for almost three weeks. I was getting weaker, because I had so little to eat, and was exposed to wind and weather 24 hours a day. The area where I was hiking was pleasant with well maintained forests. I wished that I could live in a similarly nice area without the constant threat of being shot or arrested. Sometimes I just sat down in the middle of the forest and looked up at the tall trees, listened to the birds, and observed the ground flora. It was very much like back home in Germany, and I fantasized being there and being free. I wished I could make myself invisible and just walk through the country observing its beauty without being threatened.

Free milk in the middle of nowhere

The next morning, walking through a densely forested area, I came upon a small clearing, where to my total surprise a woman was milking a cow. A man next to her holding a pail was waiting for her to finish the milking. They were as surprised as I was, but since I didn't look threatening, they offered me some fresh cow-warm milk. I was a bit skeptical when I saw the color of the milk. It looked like café au lait, light brown in color. I had never seen milk like that. The wartime milk ration in Germany which was ironically referred to as bluemilk and looked that way, with only 0.5 percent butterfat. This milk must have had at least 25% butterfat. The milk tasted incredibly good. I gave the farmer some of the tobacco I had, and he rolled himself a cigarette right away and smoked it. He probably hadn't seen any real tobacco for a long time. I asked them in German if they knew of anybody who would swap some bread for tobacco and they said something in Lithuanian that I didn't understand. By using sign language they told me to come to their house later in the day.

That was a suspicious suggestion and warranted extreme caution. These people were under the guns of the Russians. Some of them had experienced unpleasant contacts with the German occupational forces and might have thoughts of an acts of revenge. I could not blame them, but I always had to anticipate a trap. In this case I was willing to take a chance. I knew that these farmers made every effort to hide their farm animals from an occupational force. This setup sure looked like it. Several cows in the middle of a dense forest, well out of sight.

I disappeared into the woods again, and zigzagged in random fashion through the area, so that the couple could not see me. I found a house that was probably theirs, and selected a hidden vantage point to observe the house. I watched for several hours, I memorized the surrounding area and checked for suspicious activities or Russian soldiers. I paid particular attention to the edge of the forest near the house, from where there could be an ambush. Finally the couple who had given me the milk arrived at the house, and performed the usual farm tasks. Since I couldn't observe activities behind the house, I decided to check that area too.

I quietly moved through the underbrush, resting every few minutes to scan the area farther ahead. An older man walked up to the house. He could be an NKVD man, but he looked too old for that. Finally I took a chance and approached the house, and offered the old man a cigarette. The man said that he would take me to his neighbor, a woman who could speak German. We walked through the forest on a barely visible trail. After an hour we took a rest, and I offered him another cigarette and had one myself. I very casually opened my jacket just enough so that the man could see my sidearm in the holster. I knew damn well he had observed that. I did that to tell him he better not betray me to the Russians.

When we were near some railroad tracks, he motioned me to stop. He checked to see if the tracks were clear of people, then motioned me to follow him across the tracks and into another patch of forest. From there I could see a small farmhouse and a big barn. My guide motioned me to stop, while he went ahead and knocked at the door. An older woman talked to him and he waved at me to come too. I put my Mauser into my pants pocket, de-safe'd it and then, carefully looking around, walked up to where the two were talking.

A Lithuanian who speaks German

The woman greeted me in perfect German. I was surprised and relieved, and thanked my guide by giving him some more of my tobacco. He disappeared the way we had come.

The woman invited me in, and introduced herself as Sophie Grizius and her younger sister as Elsa. Sophie had worked in a German field hospital during the end of World War I. As was customary in all the Baltic states, professional people had to be fluent in the German language to have access to technical publications in their respective fields, since the market in their own countries was too small for translations of important textbooks.

I told her where I came from, and what I had in mind to do. She said that I could stay for the summer, which made me suspicious, but I figured I would soon find out why she made the offer. I had no intention to be there for any length of time. She told me that there was some straw out in the barn where I could sleep. I was still suspicious, but happy to be able to talk German with somebody. Sophie gave me something to eat, and then took me to the big barn, where I made myself comfortable.

The next morning I had terrible diarrhea, probably because of the fat milk I drank the day before. My body wasn't used to anything that resembled normal food. From inside the barn I watched the outside world through gaps between the siding boards. In the distance to the north I could see railroad tracks, which probably lead to Palanga at the Baltic coast. To the east was the edge of a forested area, to the west an additional smaller barn and to the south the farm garden and the house in which the women lived. Unless something unforeseen happened, I could rest up and recover. I was worried that Russian soldiers would raid the place.

When I mentioned that I was afraid that my looks would be conspicuous, Sophie gave me a pair of khaki colored Russian jodhpurs that I could wear with my jackboots, plus a civilian jacket and a black cap, often worn by Russians. These drab looking clothes made me look more like a native. At least I wasn't immediately identifiable from a distance. I buried my Luftwaffen uniform in the backwoods.

A few days later Elsa brought a newspaper from the next village and Sophie translated it for me. I learned for the first time what was happening back in Germany. A map showed the four occupational zones and I was puzzled that there were four. I couldn't believe the Allies would give France a piece of the action. There was an article of a planned Nürnberg trial. When I read the names of the defendants I felt that all deserved to be executed. I thought that all the top Allies leaders like Stalin, Churchill and all their Generals should be on the defendant benches too. I felt that all of them committed hideous crimes against humanity too, just like the Nazis. I felt that if the Allies beat the Germans in the same beastly ways that Hitler used, then they were not one iota better than Hitler.

The allied carpet bombings killed millions of women and children indiscriminately in Europe and that was not any different than Nazis killing them in concentration camps. When I discussed this with my Lithuanian hostess she agreed with me totally, because they had also suffered severely from Russian persecutions and thousands had died in Russian concentration camps and gulags.

We talked about the risks for them if I stayed. I was sure they would be severely punished if the Russians detected me. I didn't want to offend her by turning her down right away, but I had 20/20 tunnel vision and a one track mind to get back to Germany as soon as possible, but they couldn't understand my hurry.

One morning Elsa brought some breakfast over to the barn. She was in her late twenties or early thirties, attractive, and often came to the barn dressed so that her cleavage discreetly showed when she sat down near me. I could see that her breasts were fairly small and firm. Under different circumstances I would have succumbed to her lure, but I could not see myself being tied down by being her lover and fathering a child. We couldn't even communicate with each other, she didn't speak German or English.

I didn't realize then that these women were trying hard to secure a man of their own, and have children. Sophie was in her early fifties and probably past menopause, so she was willing to leave me to her younger sister. It probably wouldn't have bothered them if I had left after I had fathered a child. I knew that Lithuania's younger male population was practically wiped out in World War II and so their desire was genuine. Later on I thought about my naiveté with regards to the situation there. I had not been brought up to be nonchalant about generating children.

In the distance I could see numerous trains with Russian troops and equipment. I was wondering, were they completing their occupation, or were they demobilizing? What caught my eyes were the trucks that I saw on the flatbed railroad cars. They didn't look like Russian made trucks to me. I found out much later that they were Studebaker trucks, made in the USA.

One day Sophie came over to the barn, and told me that they had been surprised by a Russian soldier coming up to their door. He wanted to buy food, but they told him that they didn't have anything to eat themselves, and he left. What she said concerned me, because I had not seen or heard anybody walk or drive by the barn. Did Sophie just tell me that she wanted me to leave? Had the Russians already been tipped off about my stay, or were they snooping to find evidence of my presence? All these thoughts raced through my mind.

A couple of days later when I was talking to Sophie out in the garden, somebody drove up in a horse drawn wagon. I quickly flattened myself to the ground behind a hedge, while Sophie talked to the man. He turned out to be her neighbor. Since the conversation was in Lithuanian, I couldn't understand a word they said which made me feel insecure. After the neighbor left, Sophie told me that he had lived in the USA and in 1939 had decided to come back to Lithuania.

After my diarrhea got better, I told Sophie that I should leave, and thanked her for what she had done for me. I asked her to contact her neighbor, to see if he would be willing to guide me to the nearest railway station. He agreed and was going to pick me up in the early evening, and take me over to his house. I said good bye to Sophie and Elsa and gave them a big kiss. Elsa was in tears, and so was I.

At the neighbor's house, I was introduced to his three daughters, one of whom had just come back from Germany. She had been forced to work in Berlin, and could talk a pretty good German. When I mentioned that I was born there, she gave me an account of her experiences in Berlin, most of them good. She was an attractive woman in her early twenties. When I asked her if she would go back there, she said yes she would. I thought to myself I would not mind getting married to her, because I could communicate with her in English or German, and I liked her very much. But I didn't dare bring up that subject, because of the uncertainties connected to the Russian occupation. They were catholic, which didn't bother me, but to get married I would need identification papers!

Her father and I talked in English, and he was still optimistic that things would turn out OK in Lithuania. I admired his optimism. He invited me to have dinner with them and we had a pleasant evening. In retrospect I realize that the family had welcomed me in a typical American way.

Later that night he told me that he would take me to the rail line that ran through Kelme to Taurage, and which I thought, continued on into former East Prussia. From there I would be on my own. We went off shortly before midnight, and hiked at a very brisk pace along narrow trails for quite a distance. My attire was native and even my air force blue rucksack was now camouflaged by an old flower sack so I felt relatively safe.

It was June 22, the summer solstice, and nights at that latitude (about 56 ° North), were not dark. It was 44 days after I had left my unit in Courland. It was around 4 am when we reached the railroad northeast of Taurage. He pointed out the rail line and the station to me and we said good bye. These people had all been so wonderful to me, and I couldn't do anything to repay them for their help.

Any mistake in any planning will be in the direction of most harm.
Old engineering wisdom

13
I Am a Hobo

I observed the periphery of the railway station to look for a place to hide and observe the rail traffic, the schedule of trains, and passenger mannerisms. Near the station was a building that had been damaged in the war. I found a relatively safe spot on the upper floor that gave me a good view of the area. I sat there all day long, just watching, and even had the audacity to take pictures with the little Agfa Carat camera that I still had along. Late in the afternoon an empty freight train pulled into the station and I noticed a few civilians and soldiers hitch a ride on it. I ran downstairs and jumped into one of the empty cars.

I had hiked about 150 miles through Latvian and Lithuanian forests from the former Courland front to Kelme, carefully avoiding any contact with Russian troops. Now I was a hobo, trying to ride an empty freight train towards the old Fatherland Germany. I wanted to get home from the damn war.

It felt good to move again after all that sitting around. I watched the scenery and the other "hobos" carefully, and noticed that there were Russian guards on the train and at every railroad trestle. That indicated in all likelihood there was still Lithuanian partisan activity in the area. That was bad news, because the Russians would be suspicious and alert. Finally at about 11 pm the train rolled into Taurage and stopped right at the station. Shit, what now? I saw all the people leave the train and was contemplating whether I should do the same. I decided to take a chance and see what would happen. I sat in one corner of the rail car and pretended to be asleep, figuring it would be an excuse for not getting off, if the guards found me.

At the old delousing station, once more

I was stuck here in this bloody old railroad station in Taurage, as I had been before, when this was the delousing station for going home on furlough.

Russian guards were searching the empty train, car by car, even checking under each car for stowaways. When a guard checked the car I was in, I quietly released the safety catch on my loaded Mauser without removing it from my pocket. I was ready to pump a bullet into this guard, when the guard motioned me to get off the train I saw additional guards standing below on the station platform. That changed the odds for winning considerably, and I safe'd my gun and left it in my pocket. The guards tried to talk to me, but since I didn't speak Russian, they couldn't figure out who I was, and what business I had on this train. They took me to the guard station for interrogation.

An older Russian officer tried to talk to me in Russian, Lithuanian and then Polish. Finally I had to admit being German and they immediately frisked me. When they found my Mauser, every soldier in the room leveled their gun at me. Good grief, I thought, the Russians are still scared shitless of the Germans. Next they found my diary, maps, compass, my German Luftwaffe papers and photographs and the 35 mm camera that had accompanied me throughout the war. The commandant hollered for an interpreter to come on the double. A seedy looking character in dirty fatigues came running in. He tried to talk to me in a godawful German.

I told him that I was coming from the Courland front and was a former German soldier. I said that a Russian officer had told us after the capitulation, "The war is over for you, go home," and that was what I was trying to do. After the interpreter translated, the Russians put their guns away. They offered me something to eat and drink, then put me in a holding cell underneath the station building.

The cell had a window below ground level, with steel bars nailed to the wooden window frame, but no window in it. Outside of the window was a concrete casement with an iron grate up on top. Blast it, I thought, trapped again and I resolved to escape, and went into action as soon as the guard left.

I took a wooden board from the bunk bed and used it as a lever to bend the bars back and forth, applying a shearing force to the nail heads holding the bars in place. Eventually one of the nail heads popped off. Then I heard the guard come back to check on me through the window in the door. The guard would come back every hour to check on me, so I had to time my work to coincide with the guards absence. I figured if I could get one more nail head to break, I would only have to lift the grate, and I would be free. At daylight, I ceased my activity. I very carefully placed the broken nail head back on top of the nail. I would break out during the next night.

I laid down and must have fallen asleep. I dreamed that I was a tiny kid again enclosed by a play pen, and imprisoned by the bars of its railing. I couldn't get out until I had learned a couple of tricks to deceive my mother, who was holding me captive.

I remembered standing up in that dreadful cage they called a crib. After several unsuccessful schemes I finally learned how to tip the whole crib on its side rail. If I kept quiet enough so mother wouldn't notice, I could get a long way from that crib.

I woke up when a guard came in to bring some food. It was a thick soup of questionable ingredients, with dark bread and water. The food was terrible, but I was hungry and ate it. I was led to another interrogation. This time a nurse was the interpreter. She was good looking and spoke German fluently. When I asked her at the end of the interrogation what would happen next, she translated that to the commandant and he replied that I would be shipped back to a jail in Schaulen, the direction I had come from. An armed guard was assigned to escort me on the next train that entered the station from the west.

We stepped up to a freight car that was filled with demobilized Russian soldiers coming back from Germany. I noticed that all the freight cars had bicycles piled high on their roofs. Obviously that was loot the soldiers had stolen in Germany, and were taking home with them. After the guard and I were in the car, the station commandant stepped up to the car too, and announced to the soldiers that I was a German soldier and warned them not to harm me in any way. The train started rolling back in the direction I had come from.

The soldiers in the train were in a boisterous mood, they had won the war, had survived and were going home. When they found out that I was from Berlin, they told me that they had been in the battle of Berlin, that the city had been completely destroyed by their artillery bombardments, and that they had fucked the hell out of all the women. This information did not cheer me up, but I pretended indifference so that they didn't get any satisfaction out of their psychological warfare. What surprised me was that not one soldier was armed. I concluded that Josef Stalin was indeed a very smart man. These soldiers had seen with their own eyes how people in the capitalistic world lived, and I was sure they would compare that to what they were going to see at home. They could now form their own opinion about the accomplishments of their communist regime.

I suffered an hour of their psychological warfare, then the train stopped at Siauliai (Schaulen). We got off the train as it was getting dark and I sized up my guard to see if I could get rid of him somehow. He was an older militia (reserve) type character. We walked along a deserted street and I was getting ready for a judo chop against his

144 / From Bär to Bear

throat. Before I could execute it, some soldiers appeared from around a street corner, and that saved the guard, and possibly me.

When we reached the jail, I was marched into a cell with several other prisoners. There were Russians, Lithuanians and Poles, and now there was also a German in the cell. Since nobody could, or wanted to speak German, there was no communication. Some of these cell mates seemed like ordinary criminals, who obviously had lots of experience in the life behind bars.

The next day a new man, better looking and better dressed, came into the cell. After several attempts to communicate, we discovered that we both had a fairly good command of the English language. He told me that he was a lawyer who was accused of collaborating with the Germans during the German occupation. That sounded fishy, because he claimed not to be able to speak German. He asked me if I was armed when I was arrested. When I told him that I was, he casually mentioned that being in possession of a firearm carried a 15 year jail term under Russian law. That came as quite a shock, but I thought, we'll have to see if my gun will make it to a court hearing.

The next day an armed guard took me by train to Kaunas, the former capital of Lithuania, and I was bureaucratically booked into jail there. This included fingerprinting and the confiscation of all pieces of clothing that could be instrumental in a suicide. At least a dozen other prisoners were in the cell I was led to. They were all Russian soldiers and the atmosphere here was different. Some of the prisoners were playing chess with figures which they had manufactured from the soggy bread that was common in Russia. I played some games with them and won a game. Some of the men even smoked self-rolled cigarettes.

Who me, a British spy?

When I was led to an interrogation, I immediately sensed that I was up against a different game. A civilized looking Russian army officer in his early 30s questioned me. He wore an immaculately tailored uniform and expensive riding boots. His manners were impeccable. I judged his army rank to be at least that of a captain if not higher. The interpreter was again a very good looking woman in a nurse uniform. The officer offered me a manufactured Russian papyrossi cigarette out of a silver cigarette case. From past observances of the German interrogation procedures this friendly gesture put me immediately on alert. I was obviously dealing with a top notch intelligence officer. The officer then sat on top of his desk, so as to elevate himself above me, and opened the interrogation with, "We know now where you came from, Gans." Since there is no H in the Russian language they always called me Gans, which in German means goose. The officer then paused menacingly, and took a drag on his cigarette. The suspense was "killing" me. The officer continued in a deliberately slow and arrogant pace, "Gans, you are a British spy, who was dropped by parachute to make contact with the Lithuanian underground organization!"

That accusation was certainly unexpected and an outrageously ridiculous fabrication. I almost broke out laughing. I had read enough about Russian tribunal cases to not laugh at his nonsensical accusation. In a subconscious compulsion of self-defense, I made a facial expression of absolute wonder, and replied that I was puzzled, not only by this accusation against me personally, but that the British would find a need for espionage against their Russian Allies. This statement seemed to surprise the officer, because I had intuitively elevated the conversation to a political level, which was not the subject of this interrogation. I sensed that the officer was stuck now, and could not continue the interrogation. I concluded from his reaction that he was surprised that his broadside had not devastated me, but that I had taken the wind out of his sails.

After that flash of verbal fencing, the officer sat down behind his desk and questioned me on details of my hike from Courland. He wanted to know why it had taken me so long to get to Taurage. I, encouraged by my initial success, now did something that startled both the officer and the interpreter, and could only be defined by the Jewish word chutzpah. I took my right jackboot off and rolled my pant leg up to show the nurse/interpreter the enormous scar on my right leg. I explained that it was a war injury. The nurse/interpreter was very interested and obviously surprised about my use of proper medical terms in my explanations. She accepted my condition as an explanation for why it had taken me so long to walk that distance.

As I explained my leg problem, a new idea hit me like lightning. Coming back to the officer's original accusation, I told the nurse that I didn't think the British would be so stupid as to send a crippled man like me on such an important mission. My leg injury would have made it very difficult to successfully land after a parachute jump. The nurse had some difficulty suppressing a laugh as she translated what I had said. I sensed that I had gone to the limit of what I could say, because if I ridiculed the officer directly, I was in deep shit and that was very dangerous with a Russian in a power position.

The officer hid his disappointment very well. I was sure that he didn't expect that kind of a reply from a 21 year old Luftwaffen corporal. He then questioned me about Courland defense details, probably in the hope of tripping me with some inconsistency. I gave him the information he wanted, since the war was over. The officer showed his manners when he thanked me and released me to my cell.

The next day I was taken by train southeast to a new location. The name on the destination railway station told me that I was in Vilnius, the capital of Lithuania.

The personal property, taken away from me as evidence, was always carried by my guards, and it got less and less with each transfer. After the arrest in Taurage my Mauser automatic had found a new owner, some of the other evidence such as maps, compass, etc. had vanished in Schaulen. That didn't bother me, since these items could have hurt my defense. I was surprised however, when the guard asked me if he could buy the little 35 mm Agfa camera. Stupidly I said no. It might have been a good idea to get rid of that evidence too. The previous investigators had taken the film out of the camera and held it up to the light to see what was on it. They did a good job of eliminating suspicious evidence. The same happened with my roll of bulk film that I carried with me. My case seemingly began to look better. However to anybody knowing the Russian justice system, my idea of relief was overly optimistic if not totally unjustified.

The better part of valor is discretion.
Shakespeare

14
NKVD Commissar Krapnikov

In Vilnius I was taken to the headquarters of the NKVD for Lithuania. The guard who took me there broke out in a cold sweat when he telephoned from the outside of the building to gain entrance. We were checked in by an armed sentry at the entrance. I was frisked and even my boots were closely examined and my guard had to deposit his gun at the entrance. They sure had tight security here. We were directed to what appeared to be an admission room, where there was a small crowd of people with gravely concerned faces. Some seemed to be close to a nervous breakdown. Two bureaucrats doing the booking were standing behind a counter. An additional armed guard was inside the door into the room.

When I sat down on an old decrepit sofa, in a rather casual manner, with one leg over the other, I immediately caught shit from the guard. He motioned me to get up, move to a chair, and sit in a proper subservient attitude. The sofa must have been for the upper echelons only, and the guard tolerated no deviation from the norm. None of the other people sat down. I realized now that I was at the "Russian Gestapo" headquarters for Lithuanian.

The bureaucrat checked me in and took almost everything from me, including my belt, suspenders and my glasses. Next they gave me a haircut, right down to the skin. The Russians did it with hand clippers, making their jokes as they cut once lengthwise and once crosswise over my head, then the rest. Next came my beard and then the joker asked me if I wanted to keep my mustache. I told him yes, and he obliged. Actually I should have been grateful for the haircut, because my last haircut had been three months back by a German army barber. However, after I saw myself in the mirror I was really outraged. Now I looked like a Russian criminal. The guy who clipped my hair made his joke and said I looked like a bulldog now.

I was marched off to a jail cell and again, there were at least 15 men in the cell already. The guard assigned me a bunk, and I was so tired that I had to lie down and dozed off. I was awakened by a guard and led upstairs to a room with several desks and finally I could see what time it was, 11:45 pm. That gave me the creeps, because I had read of the Russian tactic to jerk prisoners out of their sleep and interrogate them at all hours of the night. A Russian officer of apparent Jewish ethnic background appeared. I instantly knew that I was in for a tough interrogation. Since the Russians never introduced themselves or had name signs on their desks, I baptized him "Commissar Krapnikov."

Krapnikov sat down at a desk and told me in good German to sit down. He made the usual inquiries about family name, age, etc. The next question was, "What party were you a member of?" It struck me as an incredibly stupid question, because just like in Russia, there had been only one party in Germany. I said that I didn't understand. The Commissar barked at me "Were you, or were you not, a member of the Nazi Party?" I said that I was not and Krapnikov wanted to know why. I told him that by German law, active members of the Armed Forces could not join the Nazi Party. That apparently puzzled Krapnikov. I also mentioned that the Nazi Party would not have accepted me if I had applied for membership. The commissar wanted to know why. I told him that I had Jewish relatives. That cracked the commissar up, especially when I told him that the relatives had left Germany for the United States of America.

Then the commissar looked into the diary I had kept. He said that he could not read what I had written. I asked him why not and he answered that he was not familiar with that kind of German writing style. I had written in the old Sütterlin alphabet, which was certainly different from the modern Latin alphabet. The commissar asked me to read from my diary and reminded me that by Russian law it was a punishable offense to lie. I thought to myself, "You'd better tell that to the editors of the "Pravda" newspaper, but kept my mouth shut. The commissar pointed to a page in my diary and asked, "What did you say here on this page?" I read it to him and he seemed satisfied. That made me suspicious. Maybe he was just testing me and had been capable of reading my handwriting and it was just another interrogation trick.

In the next few days I was interrogated several times. Krapnikov went through a variety of subjects, with a repetition of some of the earlier ones, to test my previous stories. This was boring, but I could not deviate from my previous testimony, or I would have been in deep shit. One day the subject was the pictures of my girl friends. He wanted to know who these girls were and where I had met them. All the pictures in my possession were German girls from Landsberg, my hometown. I had deliberately destroyed all others before I left Courland. Commissar Krapnikov wanted to know if any Russian or Baltic women had fraternized and collaborated with me. I absolutely could not reveal that I had stayed at Sophie and Elsa Grizius' place in Lithuania, or they would have been deported to Siberia immediately. The commissar was probing that point again and again, to find any contacts or help given to me by the local population. I told him that my unit didn't like help from the Russians, because they spied on everything we were doing. Krapnikov got very angry after my statement and told me that Russians would never spy. I concluded that the NKVD's prime goal was to find and eliminate all the people who had helped Germans during our occupation.

One day Krapnikov was so upset about not getting any "correct" answers from me that he threatened to shoot me. To emphasized that point, he put his old six shooter on the desk with the muzzle pointing at me. I said that I never doubted that the "Herr" Commissar could shoot me, but added that millions of good people had been shot senselessly in this stupid war, and it wouldn't matter if there was one more casualty. I was fed up with the commissar's bullshit and really didn't care at that moment if he pulled the trigger. Krapnikov ended the interrogation abruptly and I was taken back to my cell.

It was a good thing that I couldn't communicate with the other cell mates. I was pissed off to the hilt, and would have given anybody a piece of my mind and my fist about this goddamn bloody Soviet communist system. An outburst like that could have been my death knell, since the NKVD had stool pigeons in every cell.

Signing my death sentence?

The next day I was called out for another interview. I was surprised that it was during daytime. Since all holding cells were below the ground, I couldn't tell what time of the day it was. The same commissar Krapnikov talked to me some more, and then pushed a stack of papers across the desk and said, "Here, sign these at the bottom of the page." I looked at the papers, but everything was in Russian and I had no idea what it said. I looked at the Commissar and said, "I can't read what is in these papers. How can I sign them? I could be signing my own death sentence!" Krapnikov replied, "Never mind, just sign them!" I thought about it for a few seconds and since I really had no choice, I signed them, but above my signature I wrote, "Without knowledge of contents", and then gave it back to him.* The commissar read my note and said, "Well, aren't you a "Schlaukopf" (a clever guy)" So he obviously could read German after all !

See note at end of chapter. *

That was the end of that session, and the question was what would happen next? I was very much on edge, because they could ship me to Siberia or shoot me.

The next morning a prison guard came in and motioned to me to follow him and to bring everything with me. That was the biggest joke, since there wasn't much but a wooden spoon, a tin can with a piece of wire for a handle and an empty bag. The guard led me to the same room where they had booked me in and confiscated my paltry possessions. Another young man was in the room and he was also getting some of his belongings back. One of the guards motioned to me that I was allowed to talk to this man, which was unusual since communications between prisoners had always been discouraged.

He turned out to be another German ex-soldier who had some command of the Russian language. He was upset and argued with one of the employees over missing belongings. I was sure one of the Russians had stolen whatever it was that was missing. I didn't get any of my papers back either, not even my military pass. Only some clothing and a belt and suspenders were returned. When I asked the other man where we would be taken, I was told to the nearest prisoner of war camp. I replied that I was skeptical about that and if true, I would feel like having won the lottery. The other guy gave me a disagreeing look and said that he wasn't happy about that at all. I couldn't fathom what he expected, a free train ticket back to Germany?

* Solzhenitsyn's said in one of his books that the NKVD interrogators were promoted by how many "confessions" they extracted from their prisoners. Krapnikov must have gotten some brownie point for my signature, because I didn't know what I was signing.

The NKVD prison is now a Lithuanian museum and when I read a story about it in *US News and World Report*, I saw that Menachem Begin, later the prime minister of Israel, had been in the same prison after the Russians occupied Lithuania in 1939. I wrote to the Curator of the museum to find out whether papers of my case were still in existence, but I never received an answer. The US Embassy in Vilnius wasn't interested in helping me either.

The Lithuanian government searched for two Jewish commissars that had shipped thousands of Lithuanians to Siberia. One is living in Israel now and the other one in Bonn, Germany. Extradition attempts were not successful.

Marching to where?

When everything was in order an older armed guard took us out the front door and marched us through the old downtown area of Vilnius. It was a beautiful warm, sunny, summer day. As we walked, I talked to the other German soldier and found out that he was a deserter who had sneaked off into the Baltic forests two years before the end of the war. He said he had survived there all by himself. If true, a remarkable feat.

This day was July 9, 1945. I had been in custody for 16 days. Ten days in the horrible NKVD prison in downtown Vilnius.

Years later, after reading "The Gulag Archipelago" by Solzhenitsyn, I began to understand why Krapnikov hadn't known how to deal with me. He had never faced anyone who had not been completely intimidated by the Soviet system already. I did not feel that I had been defeated or intimidated by their armed forces nor that I was responsible for the damn war, or any atrocities committed by the Germans. Even though Germany had been defeated, the Fortress Courland where I had been was literally undefeated. It sure made a difference in my attitude and morale. The commissar had not been able to intimidate me.

The sunrise never failed us yet.
Celia Thaxter

15
Even the Sun Dimmed

As we two prisoners were escorted along the streets at about 2 pm, the sky and the surrounding areas turned darker and darker. When we arrived at the gate of POW camp Number 195, it was almost completely dark. Everybody was looking at the sun through blackened pieces of glass or projected the eclipse through pinholes onto walls or pieces of paper. I was both depressed and elated about these unusual activities.

Depressed, because the darkness seemed a bad omen for the next stage of my existence. When I walked through the gate however I remembered the Latin saying "Per aspera ad astra" and hoped that it would apply here and guide me back to a normal life.

I was elated, because the people at the camp were intelligent enough to find ways to safely observe a rare total sun eclipse and they all spoke German. I could communicate with them. What a relief. When the sun began to illuminate the area again, we were checked into the camp. I was issued a shabby old green German army uniform because I was in civilian clothing, which was not allowed in a POW camp. My old German military boots were in relatively good condition and I was allowed to keep them. We were then told that we had to go through a three week quarantine. Only after the work commandos had left the camp in the morning would we be allowed to walk around in the yard. Sanitary conditions were bad and maybe that was the reason for the quarantine. We shared the room with several other POWs who had come back from hospital stays outside the camp. They too had to go through a three week quarantine.

Several old-timer POWs taught me the camp's modus operandi. I listened attentively, and kept my mouth shut. An older, sick looking Berliner took a liking to me. I called him "Orje" which was a typical Berliner slang expression for George. He told me that he had been in Stalingrad and had been a POW for three years. Orje had been in many other POW camps and I figured if he had survived that long, he certainly had learned a lot and was a good person to know. Orje struck me as a typical blue collar proletarian, working in the factories in

Berlin, not an intellectual, but street smart. From his worn uniform I could not tell what rank he had held, most likely an NCO. I was sure he was close to twice my age. At first I didn't trust him, because he struck me as a dyed in the wool, communist.

This POW camp No. 195 complex was out of the ordinary in every respect. It was in the former Slupka Palais, probably built in the 18th or 19th century by a Polish count and situated right by the Wilija River. The complex consisted of two story brick buildings and was surrounded by a concrete wall at least 10 feet high. Until 1941 it had been a Lithuanian penitentiary. During the German occupation it served as camp for Russian POWs and under the Russian occupation it served as a German POWs. What if these walls could talk?

The four corners of the concrete wall surrounding the compound had wooden guard towers occupied by armed Russian guards . When I walked around the camp for the first time, the first thing I noticed was a big Russian propaganda sign. It was a satirical reference to "Painter Schickelgruber's genius". "Schickelgruber" had often been used to describe Hitler in Russian radio propaganda. I had rarely listened to it, because whatever they said was exaggerated and was often not factual.

As I continued on my walk I heard music and a choir singing and I suddenly recognized the music as Johann Strauss's "Blue Danube Waltz." It was so unexpected that tears came to my eyes. The next surprise was a sign on a door advertising, "Swing Music of Glenn Miller, played by the Wilija People's Jazz Group." I went back to Orje and reported what I had seen and heard and asked, "What the hell is going on?" Orje told me that this camp had several artistic "kollektives" (groups), who were probably rehearsing for the next variety show. They had to work eight hours a day like everybody else

I replied, "Variety show? You are kidding me, Orje." "No," he said, "These POWs are operating in the camp under an Austrian music director and he has to come up with a different show every month. The entire Russian camp staff with wives and kids come to see the performance. Since Russians are great lovers of music, they appreciate these musicals. The rest of the POW work groups will see the show later."

I was thinking of my dreadful experience with the NKVD and guessed that this was one of their dirty propaganda tricks to show foreign correspondents how well they treated the damn Germans. * See footnote.

I asked Orje about a job opportunity that I had seen on the bulletin board. The Russians were looking for optics experts. Since I had been educated in that field I thought that might be an interesting job. Orje took me aside, and after carefully checking all around, quietly said to me, "Don't be crazy Hans, they are looking for people who will re-erect the optical factories which the Russians have dismantled in Germany and which are now being unloaded east of Moscow. They will keep you for years, don't fall for that trick." He told me that he had been in a POW camp east of Moscow, where they had built the factory buildings to house that equipment from Germany. This had happened long before the war was over!

The camp had six barbers taking care of the approximately 1,500 POWs. There was an infirmary with a female Russian doctor, a Russian nurse, and a German military doctor, complete with juicy rumors about their relationship.

Everyone had to work in this camp. There was an "Invalid Company" (IC) where soldiers who had been badly wounded, like the several amputees in the camp, could work. The largest percentage of POWs was working outside the compound. They cleared the rubble left by the war, repaired the vehicles of the NKVD, rebuilt the city's generating plant, and felled trees in the nearby forest.

While I was in quarantine Orje asked me, "What is the matter with your right leg?" When I told him, he said, "You go to the dispensary immediately and get yourself a cane. I never want to see you walk without that cane, and that is an order. Try and get into the IC group." I never walked without the cane again. That whole incident got me to think that one never knows how a dreadful physical disadvantage can turn into an advantage later on.

My mind wandered back to what had happened to me during my first year in school. When I started school in Düsseldorf in 1930, I was injured in physical education, during the high jump exercise.

My grandpa in Berlin found out that the chief physician of the Charitè Clinic in Berlin, Professor Dr. Bier, was the foremost authority in bone surgery, and my mother took me there. The next day I was prepared for surgery and was wheeled into a large auditorium. I could hear Professor Bier talk about my case to a number of students. Two days later the assistant surgeon reported that my peroneus (motoric) nerve unfortunately had "jumped over the surgeon's scalpel" meaning that Professor Bier had accidentally cut the nerve. He said that I would not be able to lift the tip of my right foot any more, because there was no way that the severed peroneus nerve could be sutured and made to function again.

That dreadful injury might just get me into the Invalid Company (IC). Orje himself was in that company. He was just skin and bones, and I guessed that he was suffering from tuberculosis and probably had other serious health problems. After three years in Russian POW camps it was surprising he was still alive.

The members of the IC had to do light work inside the compound, such as making wooden shoes, weaving baskets, helping the cooks and other general cleanup duties. Orje told me that even though the food ration was lower for IC duties, he felt they were better off than the outside work crews, who often had physically demanding jobs.

When we "quarantinees" went through a physical checkup before being released to the work units, I requested to be transferred to IC, and was told that I qualified, but it would take a few days for the camp administration to make the transfer. Meanwhile, I had to go out with the work crews. The unit I was in had the job of clearing the rubble at the local power generating plant, on the other side of the Wilija River. The next morning, using my cane as ordered, I marched out of the camp with an 80 man work detachment to help restore what had been destroyed during the war. It was hard work moving big chunks of concrete. I had lost about 40 pounds, had a greatly weakened phy-sique, and was exhausted all the time. The other POWs were in simi-lar conditions and worked with minimum effort to preserve precious body strength. I think we subsisted on less than 800 calories a day.

While on work assignment, I had an interesting conversation with a young Russian lieutenant, who was an engineer and spoke German fluently. I didn't know what branch of the military he was in, he could have been with the NKVD. He said that Stalin had made a big mis-take by stopping his troops at the Elbe River, because he should have conquered Europe all the way to Portugal. I was appalled about his naiveté, because he seemed to believe that the western allies would have just given up Europe to the Russians.

Another day I asked him about that big peat fired electric plant near Leningrad. He gave me some impressive figures about it. He was obviously an electrical engineer specializing in power generation, which made his presence at this job in Vilnius logical. He mentioned that soon there would be better ways to generate electricity, using methods the American "Manhattan project" was developing. I didn't know what he was talking about. Many years later when I did know about the Manhattan program, I was even more surprised that the guy knew about it in 1945!

After several days on the outside work commando, I was transferred to the IC and got a job in the basket workshop. Here several men were weaving strips of wet wood into rectangular market baskets. It was reasonably light work in a small, quiet basement shop. We had a quota of so many baskets per day, and didn't have much of a problem to meet that, except if we didn't get the necessary material in time.

* The Russians said the Americans let tens of thousands of their POWs die in Germany. I didn't believe it, but I know better now, because it was factual and is pointed out in the book "Other Losses" by James Bacque. My friend Dietrich (Dee), who was a POW in one of those camps verified that. However, compared to the death rate in Russian POW camps (one third of the several million POWs died there), it was "insignificant."

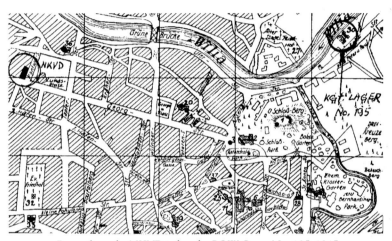

Route from the NKVD jail to the POW Camp No. 195, 1945

In 1945 POW camp No. 195

125. Das Slupka-Palais an der Wilija im früheren Zustande
Rechts die Peterpaulskirche — Zeichnung von Smuglewicz vor 18

Old photograph of the Slupka Palais, later POW Camp No. 195

Things are seldom what they seem, skim milk masquerades as cream.
W. S. Gilbert

16
Food, the Lack of It

Food was the most important subject in the POW camp. There was never enough of it and what there was wasn't nutritious. The work crews received 400 grams of bread a day, while the IC got only 300 grams. Once a day there was soup consisting primarily of water, cabbage and potatoes. Sometimes we got some jam, and some Sundays even "kasha", kind of a millet gruel. My military canteen had been stolen by some employees in the jail, so I had to eat out of an old tin can with a piece of wire attached for a handle. My only eating implement was a hand-carved wooden spoon that I had gotten in jail in exchange for cigarettes. There were no tables to eat at, we sat wherever we could find a spot.

With the quality of Russian bread, heavy with water, the daily ration was a slice of bread approximately one and a half inches thick. The Russian bread was in a "special quality" class. There was so much water in the dough that the loaves had to be baked in metal forms. Fast distribution was a must for the finished product, because if given a chance to dry out, the weight would have been reduced drastically. The camp was allotted so many kilograms per day. The bread loaves without any packaging were transported into camp on open trucks. The loading (after weighing) at the factory and the unloading inside the camp was done by POWs.

The bread hauling process was a constant battle of wits between the POWs and the Russian men and women at the government owned bread factory. Speed and diversionary tactics were necessary to tip the scales in favor of the POW camp. Rigging scales to show less weight, calculating faster than the Russians could comprehend, and other more or less crooked methods were applied. There was a limit to what could be done, but every additional loaf of bread was a lifesaver. The men employed for this job were a permanent crew, had a reasonable amount of success in this racket, and were trusted by the POWs. I wondered how many of them had been CEO's in their civilian life. Each member of the bread crew was given an extra loaf of bread for that battle against the bread factory. Everything in the "worker's paradise" was based on hook or crook.

For the bread distribution inside the camp, each group had their own scale, and everybody would sit around watching the man working the scale to make sure he was doing it right. A beastly job that I turned down.

We took the bread and either ate it right away or put it away. Saving it was dangerous, because it could be stolen. Since four other man and I worked in a workshop by ourselves, we could store our bread there because we trusted each other. In the dorm stored bread would disappear overnight. In general there was good discipline, because if a man got caught he'd be beaten up by the other POWs. In camp No. 195 things were well organized, probably because it had been in existence for a long time. The camp commandant was a racketeer, who organized the work of the POWs so that he could make some profit.

During the monotony of POW life, one of the highlights was the kitchen duty (KP) chore. Every guy hoped they could get extra food this way. One day it was my turn with some other men to help prepare a truckload of cabbage for the kitchen. When I arrived at about noon for KP we were face to face with a huge pile of cabbage heads piled in one corner of the kitchen. We had to chop the cabbage with a cleaver, the only way to process that amount of cabbage fast enough to feed 1,500 POWs.

We had to be very careful not to chop our fingertips off, so we each developed our own chopping techniques. When the man next to me found a fat maggot in the first cabbage head he attacked, he asked one of the cooks what to do. The cook stared at him, then laughed. The other soldiers laughed too and told him, "Hey man, chop it, chop it, where do you think we're getting our protein from? Chop it, we're in a hurry here. What do you think is going to happen to the cook if the soup isn't ready when the work commandos come back to camp?" So, we didn't pay any more attention to the extra meat in the cabbage, and consoled ourselves with the fact that it would be cooked by the time the soup was finished. I snatched a piece of raw cabbage trunk once in a while, just to get an extra bit of carbohydrates and something to chew on.

The chopped cabbage was pushed into big buckets, which were then emptied into one of the big cooking kettles. At the other tables fresh fish were cleaned, and they were added to the kettles, bones and all. I, who had always been a finicky eater, had to turn my mind off completely about this whole unappetizing mess in the kitchen, or I would have thrown up right into the cabbage. After the maggot experience

I scrutinized my soup more carefully, and sure enough found a couple of green caterpillars in it. I offered them to any taker, but there were no offers, so I used my spoon as a catapult and flicked them out the window.

The great patriotic bedbug caper

One of the biggest problems in the camp was the infestation with bedbugs. This caused a lot of sickness and many lost working hours and consequently pissed the Russian camp commandant off, because there was a never ending stream of complaints from the working group captains.

One Saturday, Commandant Shlitzki decided to take "great patriotic bedbug action." He called all the POWs to a rally and through the interpreter let it be known that tomorrow, on Sunday, a bedbug extermination campaign was to be launched. This action would consist of the following: Room by room all bunks were to be dismantled and carried down to the yard, where another group of POWs were to wash every wooden board with a strong lye solution. After that, all the bunks were to be reassembled and the action continued until the entire camp had been cleaned. From my own childhood experience with these nasty pests, I knew that this action would be totally ineffective. First, the bedbugs were in the walls and floor and relatively few in the bunks, and the lye solution didn't bother the bugs at all. They probably would laugh all the way to the next victim. Shlitzki made it quite clear that, after this action was finished, no more complains were permissible, and no more sick calls would be accepted. I thought, if that's the way the Russkis solve problems, maybe I ought to attend their political schooling and learn more about that system.

Since I was very sensitive to bedbug bites, I had already devised my own remedy, which was ninety percent successful. I had fashioned a sleeping bag out of my blanket. It had an upper flap long enough to cover my head while I was in it. I slept right on the floor in the middle of the room under a light that was on all night. That helped, but occasionally I still got big welts from their stings. The bedbug misery brought back a memory of my childhood.

In 1927 my parents had moved to Breslau and into a very large apartment. When the place was redecorated the painters had nonchalantly painted over some bedbugs on the wall. When the bugs crawled away later, the original paint color underneath them showed through. It was an interesting color effect and absolutely infuriated my mother. She called the painters damn pigs, and called the building manager and gave him a piece of her mind, pointing out the stippled wall. He in turn called an exterminator, but even his first attack was unsuccessful and had to be repeated to get rid of the pest. In light of that experience the "great patriotic bedbug hunt" was laughable.

Better Groucho than Karl Marx

The camp had political schooling and I was curious to see what the guys with the other red flag, the one with hammer and sickle instead of a swastika, had to say about solving problems. Maybe I would be able to use some of their methods in my future life. I took a course in Dialectic Materialism. After listening for three evenings, I decided that what the communists were preaching was far worse than anything I had ever heard. Worse even than Goebbels' "fairy tales". On the fourth evening I fell asleep during the lecture and canceled my subsequent classes, because I thought my falling asleep might net me some re-schooling in Siberia. I could not understand how anybody with that kind of a convoluted philosophy could win a war. When I had enrolled in the course the other POWs immediately picked at me, saying I was obviously one of those guys who always turned my flag into the wind, as the saying goes in Germany. Orje came right away to my defense and stated that as a young man, I was certainly entitled to at least hear what the other political philosophies were.

I have to admit that many years later, after reading the book "Stalin's War" by Ernst Topitsch, I finally understood what the Russians and Stalin specifically meant by "dialectic". It certainly wasn't what Aristotle and Plato had in mind. That is also the reason why in debates with communists one never receives an answer to a question, but a diversion to another subject. It equates with Murphy's Law which states, "Dazzle them with your brilliance or baffle them with your bullshit." The Russians were masters of the latter.

The Swedes to the rescue

One day there was a notice on the bulletin board that a Swedish Red Cross Commission was going to visit the camp. Their physicians would examine POWs who were sick and/or amputees, for possible early discharge. Anyone who felt qualified could put their name on the list. Both Orje and I submitted our names. I had come down with pleurisy, and a heart murmur had been detected. The German camp doctor had no medication to combat it. He gave me a tincture of natural digitalis, because he hoped that it would help with my heart problem. He told me to try and keep my chest warm. The only thing I could do was to trade some bread for a strip of material from an overcoat. I cut a hole in the middle for my head to poke through, folded the two ends over my chest and back, and tucked the ends into the pants. At least my chest was warm.

At the end of July, 1945, the Red Cross Commission finally arrived and spent two days examining about 300 to 400 POWs. There were two Swedish doctors and two Russian doctors, as well as the two camp doctors. If a name was put on their list, it meant that an early discharge was likely. Thank God I qualified, the pleurisy, my heart and leg problems must have helped! However, when we would be discharged was another question. We were told it might be several months before railroad cars would be available. So it was back to the old army routine, "hurry up and wait."

About ten days later, on August 8, 1945, the camp was called together in the evening and the camp interpreter climbed on a box and told everybody that he was authorized to tell us some news. That was highly unusual, since the war in Europe had ended four months ago. He told us that the Soviet Union had declared war on Japan and that the Americans had dropped a new super bomb which they had perfected from a German design. My first thought was, oh shit, this means we are not going to be released because the Russkis will again need all their rolling stock for troop transports to Siberia. Many of my friends said, "So there really was a super weapon that we had always been promised. Why didn't we get it in time to use against the Russians and England?"

I was more concerned about a postponed discharge than this super bomb. I didn't think I could survive the coming winter.

Shortly after that announcement all of us on the release list were called together, and we were told that the first transport would be put together within the next two weeks. Then the names of those on the first transport were read. My name was not on that list. By the end of August the first contingent of POWs left Camp No. 195 for home, and we gave them addresses and notes to relatives back in Germany. And of course we were envious. We didn't trust the Russians, and wondered if there would be another release transport.

Several days later the camp gate opened and in came a company of well dressed, disciplined German army soldiers, properly marching to orders of a noncom officer. Everybody was stunned, we hadn't seen anything like that since the war. They even wore all their war decorations and had most of their equipment except weapons. It turned out that the unit came from Courland. How they got to the camp without being frisked and stripped of their belongings was a mystery. When the tired work commandos came back in the evening they keeled over laughing when they saw those men. Whenever they encountered one of these new POWs still wearing their Iron Cross decorations, they called out loud, "Attention, Iron Cross bearer from the left or right etc." Well, it wasn't long and these new arrivals looked just like the rest of us.

Then around the middle of September, 1945, we were told that the war in the Pacific was finished and that Japan had surrendered. I said to one of my IC buddies, "Very interesting, but where is the train to get me home?"

The weather had turned cooler, and fall was unmistakably in the air. The self-made calendar showed the end of September and we still hadn't heard when the next group would be going to Germany. I visited the camp doctor regularly and my pleurisy caused me pain. It was fortunately a dry pleurisy and according to the physician it was not getting any worse.

"Home" had now become questionable, for me, because we had finally gotten a big map, drawn by a POW, that showed the outline of the occupational zones in Germany. To my dismay I found that the town my parents and I had lived in for the last ten years, Landsberg, was now under Polish administration.

Why should the Poles get this huge area that had been part of Germany for several hundred years? I was really incensed and I remembered what had happened after World War I. Due to the many territories that Germany lost in the Versailles treaty, World War II had started. Did the Allies think it would be any different this time? Or were they deliberately sowing the seeds for the next World War? Let a bunch of idiot politicians decide the fate of nations, no matter where, and they will fuck it up.

In the meantime the guy whom I had met at the NKVD headquarters, and who had told me when we walked into No. 195 that he would try to escape at the earliest opportunity, did exactly that. He had managed to get assigned to a lumber work crew, which was felling trees somewhere in the forests around Vilnius. One day he vanished. I could not find out how and what happened, because that work commando did not return to the camp every day as all the other ones did.

Soon, another POW got acute barbed wire syndrome and scaled the high concrete wall one night. He climbed over the barbed wires on top of the wall and, while the guards fired numerous shots at him, escaped right down the other side and ran to the Wilija River. He must have known that a rowboat was tied up in the reeds along the shore. He got into it and skillfully maneuvered it into the fast running river and disappeared. The next morning he was a distance from Vilnius. He rowed to the river bank and continued on foot, but he walked right into one of the POW lumber detachments, where they greeted him like a long lost friend and recaptured him. Back at the camp he got five days of solitary confinement at water and bread.

He who does not feel his friends to be the world to him,
does not deserve that the world should hear of him.
Johann Wolfgang von Goethe

17
Back in the Same Cattle Car

It was early October 1945, nighttime temperatures started to dropped to the freezing point and it rained on and off. Finally on the 13th of October the rest of the Invalid Company men were called together and names were read again from a list. Every man they called had to step to the right and Orje had also stepped out. I didn't hear my name and at the end I was the only one left. I walked up to the guard and interpreter and gave my name, saying that I did not hear them read it. They checked one more time and discovered that my name was misspelled. I told them I didn't give a damn what they called me as long as I was released. They laughed and I was to be shipped out.

We were told to assemble Sunday at noon for the final frisking. The following clothing items were not allowed to go with us: woolen sweaters, blankets, overcoats or leather boots. Those items would be desperately needed by the remaining POWs during the next winter. It gave me the creeps, thinking that these men would have to endure another winter. During a man to man frisking by Russian guards the next day, I had to open my army jacket. The guard pulled at my chest-warmer, which fortunately came out of my pants under the guard's grip, so it wasn't considered as a sweater, and they let me keep it. I am positive that this unique piece of clothing prevented me from getting pneumonia, which could have meant certain death on the long way back to Germany.

While everything was being squared away by the guards, it started to rain. Late Sunday afternoon we finally formed a marching group of four abreast and slowly walked out of the gate, accompanied by the best wishes of all those remaining behind. I could not figure out why the releases always took place on Sundays. The Russians wanted the working crews to see that they actually released some of the men. They figured that it would improve the moral of the remaining soldiers. Our group walked in the rain to the rail yard and by the time we were in the empty boxcars our clothes were soaked. I saw that there were six boxcars with 30 POWs per car, a passenger car for the guards and the "nurse", some kind of a baggage car for the food, and a caboose with an elevated brakeman's seat for the armed guard on duty. I was in the same type of boxcar in which I had been arrested 114 days earlier. I prayed that this time the journey would get me to Germany. The boxcars contained nothing that would have made our stay in them comfortable. They were bare.

Since our clothes were wet and it was quite chilly, we decided the only way to keep warm was to give the Soviet's "collective" system a try and sit on the floor close to each other and dry the clothes through our combined body heat. This wasn't comfortable, the collective body temperature was barely sufficient, and like the real Russian collective system, it stank. We had to change our seating positions several times during the night, so the outside men could get warm. We couldn't sleep, so we told old jokes. Then one guy said, "Gentlemen, permit me to remind you, that we thank our Führer for this comfortable situation. Without him we would be sitting comfortably at home and being bored." That caused a tumultuous reaction, until I finally said, "We should have called him "Fuhrmann" (teamster) instead of "Führer", because he drove all of Germany into a pile of shit." There was an "Amen" from several sides, and it became very quiet after that.

Suddenly somebody said, "Gee, this stink is terrible, what did you eat yesterday Karl?" It wasn't more than a second before Karl replied, "As hors d'oeuvres I had Russian eggs with lobster mayonnaise and caviar, after that filled Hungarian peppers with capers, and as the main course I had larded tenderloin of venison with red cabbage and caramelized potatoes, accompanied by a bottle of 1943 Alsatian Gewürztraminer, and as dessert, puff pastry filled with raspberry mouse, and a cup of mocha." This almost uninterrupted gourmet dinner menu was accompanied by ahhs and oohs, with instant silence at the end. Then somebody piped up, "But Karl, that was the wrong wine with the venison," and another answered, "Karl always had bad taste," and still another, "Small wonder it stinks here." Which was accompanied by a roar of laughter.

Early in the morning of October 14, 1945, our cars were finally connected to a train and we slowly rolled out of Vilnius. Exactly on that day in 1941 I had left home to report for duty at the National Labor Force (RAD). I could not escape two facts. First, that I had wasted four years of my life in this incomprehensibly idiotic war, created by one asshole politician who called himself "Führer." Secondly, that I had signed up for four years of service and had now fulfilled my contract.

Everybody milled around in the boxcar and looked out the open door on one side, while everybody took turns to relieve themselves through the partially opened door on the other side. The German POWs had impressed the camp commandant with their ability to make their lives more comfortable. I must admit that as a man who had only served at high Wehrmacht commando posts, I was an inexperienced "acquisitioner". Most of the men in my car had been frontline soldiers and knew how to make something out of nothing.

Orje, my mentor in the camp, took command of our boxcar. He assigned certain responsibilities to each man. He never gave unnecessary orders or advice, and yet remained in control of any situation. This man, a POW for three years, amazed and impressed me every day. I thought every man in that car owed Orje a lot for his leadership in this unusual situation.

Four men were assigned to fetch the meager food rations from the guard car when the freight train was stopped, because there was no other way to move between cars. The food for the entire trip was bread, some jam and dried fish. There was no refrigeration, so dried and salted fish was the only thing that survived in edible condition.

All rail lines in eastern countries were single track so the train stopped frequently on a spur to wait for an oncoming train. Since there were no toilets on board our train, except in the guard car and the caboose, we also had to use these stops for toilet purposes. What a way to travel, but man, we didn't mind, we were going west.

Soon the train took us into parts of former German East Prussia, which had been primarily an agricultural area. Here we saw more sad consequences of the war. The large farms in the area had been abandoned by the German owners ahead of the advancing Russian armies. Most of their farm equipment had been rounded up by the Russians and stored in open fields for transport to Russia. We found that abandoned houses often still contained personal belongings. This was either because nobody knew the houses had not been stripped, or because they were so far from main roads along the rail lines that they were ignored. The important thing to us was the food stored in field pits, underneath layers of straw, covered on top by a layer of earth. These storage pits (Mieten) contained primarily potatoes, but also grain, turnips, carrots and beets. They provided a welcome addition to our meager rations. There were also potbelly stoves left in some of the abandoned houses as well as pots and pans and all sorts of other goodies. In order not to let those valuable things go to waste, we quickly organized bucket brigades back to our boxcar to "upgrade" our rolling quarters.

Soon we had straw on the floor to sleep on, a potbelly stove with stovepipe, and cooking utensils to cook the vegetables we had harvested from the pits. There was firewood, a couple of benches to sit on, and wardrobe hooks on the walls. Our life was getting a little easier and better organized with every day of our journey west.

The lookout men had to make darn sure that the requisition guys didn't miss the train. They had to give a loud whistle before the train started to roll again. This was not too difficult when we were on a spur in wide open country, because the scenery in East Prussia was pretty flat and we could see the oncoming train for miles. The guards were very lax, because none of us would escape, but they were responsible for X number of POWs whom they had to deliver at the release camp. When the train stopped at a station, the POWs were not allowed out of the cars, because then the guards themselves were watched by whatever Russian officers were at that station. All POWs understood that and cooperated.

As our train progressed further into former German territory, the scenery began to look familiar. I was finally convinced that we were going towards Germany and not in the opposite direction, as I had before. We were into the eighth day of our journey, a journey that under normal circumstances would have taken no longer than 20 hours. This was caused by the incredible chaos caused by the war.

So close and yet so far

Two POWs had died on our train. We didn't know this right away, since we could not talk with men in the other cars while the train was in motion. A number of men were quite sick when they boarded the boxcars at Vilnius. Of course there was only the most basic first aid supply with the nurse on this train, and no medication or physician was available. The dead men were put in body bags and stored in the caboose, because the guards had to account for all of the POWs, dead or alive. Such were the Russian rules.

The rest of the POWs were beginning to have problems too. We could not wash or bathe, and only had one set of underwear and clothing. We all stank and were infested with lice. The lice deposited eggs in the seams of our clothing and they hatched under the body heat. During the four years in the war, I never had any problems with lice.

Soon we heard about the third death, and we thought, "Who is next?" Some of the dead guys might have been POWs for a long time and now that the end of their misery was near, they kicked the bucket so close to home, how utterly tragic.

The train rolled into the northeastern corner of the province of Brandenburg and my knowledge of the area and the rail lines told me we would be passing through my former hometown, Landsberg/Warthe. I was apprehensive about what I would find there. Observations along our rail tour did not give me much hope. The train rolled into Zantoch around midnight, and stopped for several hours.

Zantoch was situated at the confluence of the rivers Netze and Warthe and I had been there many times with the rowing club. A freight train pulled into the rail yard from the opposite direction and stopped next to our train. The train had "interesting" cargo. The open freight cars were filled to the brim with potatoes. Of course that put everybody on the alert. We always needed more food. The entire food supply on our train had been used up, the trip had taken so long.

This potato train was guarded by an armed Polish militia man, who was sleeping on top of one car. To acquisition from this train was taking a chance, because he would fire at the POWs if they tried to steal any potatoes. That would awaken our Russian guards too. The first thing the guys had to do was to disarm the guardsman. Orje huddled with some of the guys, and made up a plan of attack. Several POWs climbed on the guard's car from opposite sides, confiscated the gun that he had rested next to him and threw it under one of the railroad cars. That woke him up, but since several POWs stood above him he didn't have much of a chance. He didn't know what hit him and tried to raise a ruckus. To shut him up the POWs quickly wrapped him into the tarp he was sleeping on, and several of them sat on him. In the meantime others started to unload the potatoes. This all happened so fast that the Russian guards and most of the other POWs didn't realize what was taking place.

Trauma of seeing the hometown again

Hours later we rolled into Landsberg/Warthe, the town that I had left four years ago when I was drafted. I had spent my teenage years here, and I loved this country. I had many friends here with whom I had shared the joys and pains of growing up. I didn't know if my mother was still there, or if she had fled before the Russians had occupied it on January 30, 1945. Even that date had its own sadistic significance. Twelve years earlier, in 1933, on that very day, Hitler had become Reichskanzler. What he "accomplished" was right before my own eyes now. How could this insane man devastate this beautiful country without anybody stopping him?

When the train slowly rolled through the town on the elevated tracks, I could look onto the Marienplatz at the center of Landsberg. I saw many burned out buildings. I knew there had not been any fighting to gain this town. The town had been surrendered by the mayor. To my surprise the train stopped just west of the railway station near the city's gas plant, and I found out that we would be delayed for about two hours.

Orje and I got off the train to look around. We met some Polish residents who spoke some German, and they told us that the Russians had deliberately burned down almost the entire center of the town and that there were very few Germans left, most of them had been deported. Everywhere I looked, buildings were in a state of disrepair and destruction. There was a feeling of anger and hopelessness even by the Polish people. Overhead wires of the streetcar system were hanging down on the sidewalk in Friedrichstadt. When I looked into some of the buildings of the gas plant, I noticed that even light switches and conduits had been stripped and none of the buildings had windows or doors. Polish people told me that the Russians had done all this, before turning this area over to the Polish administration. Here I was, a 21 year old man, realizing that I was homeless. I lost my remaining faith in humanity and it would never be fully restored.

I decided to say a last good-bye to the Warthe river which had so enjoyably enhanced my life as a young man. I walked through an underpass down to the edge of the river, dipped my foot into the water and thanked the river for all the good things it had given me. Then with a heavy heart I walked back to the train. My life would never be the same, but it went on, and I had to try and make a new start someplace else.

The train was moving again and when we passed the places I knew well, I drank the scenery in one last time. We passed through Küstrin which was completely destroyed, and then continued towards Berlin. The train should have turned south in Küstrin, to get to Frankfurt/ Oder, but apparently the direct rail lines were still interrupted or destroyed. This was not surprising since the heaviest fighting took place here before the Russians advanced on Berlin. There were still pieces of destroyed war machinery sitting everywhere along the railroad tracks. Whenever we saw a destroyed Russian T-34 tank or some other Russian equipment, a loud "hurrah" went up. The POWs' spirit was starting to recover.

Our cars were uncoupled from the train and put on a spur. We could not leave the car because of the curfew. Early the next morning I thought I was seeing some familiar sights and figured they we were somewhere east of Berlin. Then we were hitched to a locomotive and moved in an easterly direction.

End of the journey

Finally after ten days and nights, on October 25 1945, we were pushed into a switching yard near Frankfurt/Oder. Here we disembarked. God, what a relief to finally have reached our destination, Rest-Germany! It was sad to see three dead buddies being unloaded from our train. Orje said, "Who knows, they might be better off than we are. None of us knows what horrors might lie ahead of us." When we marched from the rail yard, we saw some high ranking Russian officers walk along our vacated boxcars, pointing to the "luxurious" interior and shaking their heads with unsmiling faces. On a parallel track other POWs were coming off their train.

We were taken to a former German Panzer compound with buildings in very good condition compared to what we had seen during our trip. German employees were running the paperwork here and the really sick soldiers received medical help. The most exciting feature was the halfway decent food with genuine German Kommissbrot (standard German military style bread). The next day was spent filling out forms, taking a first shower, washing some underwear and finally getting the Russian release paper, called a sprawka. They briefed us on the rules of the Russian occupation zone. The city of Frankfurt/Oder was off limits to all POWs. Anybody caught there would be arrested and taken to jail. I was very disappointed, because I knew the Master Optician in Frankfurt/Oder and had hoped to get a duplicate of my technical education papers from him.

On the next day we were each given one loaf of Kommissbrot, were told that we are on our own from here on, and that there were no scheduled trains running yet. We were practically chased out of the compound, and I, as sarcastically as always, remembered what Kaiser Wilhelm II had said to his troops leaving for World War One, "Der Dank des Vaterlandes ist euch gewiss," meaning, "Be assured, the Fatherland will thank you."

Orje, who always focussed on necessities, rather than emotions said, "Let's get going right away, maybe we will be lucky and find a train or locomotive to hitch a ride on." Two other Berliners joined us.

Berlin, about 50 miles west of Frankfurt/Oder, the city I was born in, was going to be our destination. If all else failed, we would walk there. Most of the other released POWs also had to go to or through Berlin since all roads lead to Berlin, to re-coin an old Roman phrase.

Just outside the switch yard we talked to a German railroad engineer who had his engine under steam and was obviously ready to pull out. He told us that he was only going as far as Fürstenwalde, but he would let us ride on the tender at our own risk. The four of us climbed on. Orje suggested that we each give him a thick slice of our bread, and he gratefully accepted the precious food.

It was late in the afternoon when we arrived at Fürstenwalde and the engineer warned us about the curfew restrictions. Even though I had been here before, I didn't recognize the area around the switch yard. The four of us decided to use an empty old barn as our home for the night. There was straw in the corners of the barn and we heaped up a small pile to sleep on. We decided to take turns sleeping in order to preclude any surprises from Russian soldiers. We talked in a whispering voice so as to not attract any attention. We ate quite a bit of our Kommissbrot, because we hadn't tasted any decent bread for such a long time. I asked Orje what he was going to do when he was back in Berlin, and to my total surprise Orje said he would get himself a few "race horses." I didn't understand the meaning, but the other guys explained to me that it meant he was going to have some prostitutes working for him. I was sure he was not kidding.

Next morning we eyed the area through gaps in the barn's siding and decided that curfew was over, because we could see people walking around in the distance.

We talked to a switch yard worker, who gave us a hint as to when an empty freight train would be leaving for Berlin. This time we were lucky and ended up in an empty boxcar (déjà vue) in a freight train. The trip to Berlin used to take an hour during normal times. The war destruction and the dismantling of many rails for reparations by the Russians would lengthen our trip.

At about midnight we finally ended up at Rummelsburg in Berlin, a large switch yard in the eastern part of the city. It was north of the river Spree on the other side from where I had lived and gone to school. We could not leave the train because of the enforced curfew. A yard worker happened to walk by and we asked him if the train we were on would leave during the night. He didn't know. So it was just wait and see what happened. At the first movement we would have to abandon the train, and hide some place until the curfew was over. So it was another night in a damn freight car. The train didn't move overnight and a sunny morning dawned. On the other side of the river Spree I could see the Plänterwald.

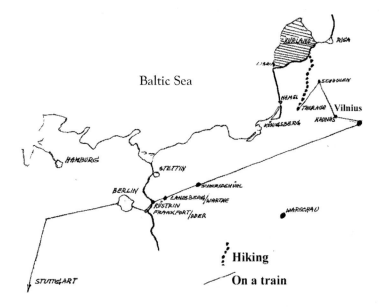

Baltic Sea

The long way home,

... . *hike from Courland, approximately 150 miles*

Total distance traveled, approximately 1250 miles from Courland to Stuttgart.

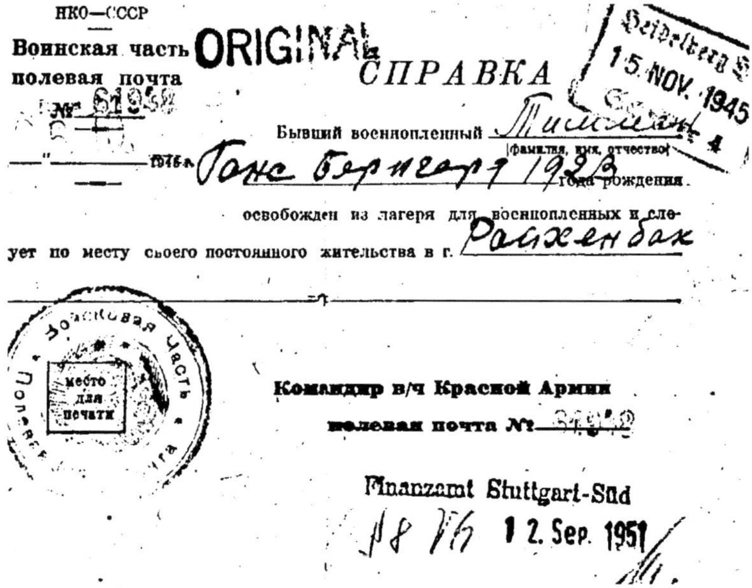

НКО—СССР

Воинская часть **ORIGINAL** СПРАВКА
полевая почта
№ 61954

Бывший военнопленный _Тиллман_
(фамилия, имя, отчество)
1916 г. _Ганс Бернард_ 1923 года рождения.

освобожден из лагеря для военнопленных и следует по месту своего постоянного жительства в г. _Райхенбах_

Командир в/ч Красной Армии

полевая почта №

Finanzamt Stuttgart-Süd

1 2. Sep. 1951

Release paper from the Russian POW system, 1945

What experience and history teach is this: that people and governments never have learned anything from history, or acted on principles deduced from it.
Georg Wilhelm Hegel

18
The Colors Never Change

Vae Victis (Woe to the Vanquished)

It was a beautiful fall day with a slight haze or fog over the Spree river and the trees showed their best fall colors on the other side of the river in the Plänterwald. It was time for me to set out on my own. I emotionally said good-by to Orje, who had done so much for me. Without his fatherly advice I would have never made it back to Berlin that quickly. It didn't occur to me to exchange addresses to be able to stay in touch with each other, but we didn't have anything to write with. I hugged Orje for a long moment and stammered a tearful thanks for all he had done for me. Then we all shook hands and hugged again with tears just running down our cheeks and wished each other good luck for our uncertain future.

My mind was still in the survival mode. I had survived 1475 days as a soldier, 170 days from Courland back to Berlin, including 16 days in jail, and 98 days in a POW camp and I couldn't quite comprehend that it was all over.

Then, crossing many tracks, I made off to the nearest street along the yard, waved back to my fellow ex-POWs and walked westerly along Köpenicker Chaussee towards railroad station Ostkreuz, which I could see in the distance. I figured that it would get me to the Stralauer Bridge and across the Spree river into the suburb of Treptow, where my maternal grandmother had lived. It was a reassuring feeling to still know my way around the big city, even though I had been away for almost ten years.

The Stralauer bridge, even though it had been blasted, was usable and I ended up in the Treptow Park area. I was appalled at the huge Soviet War Memorial that was being built in the park. It was monstrously overdone in the usual bombastic Stalinistic style, and lacked taste and dignity. It reminded me of similar Nazi abominations. Finally I walked along Neue Krugallee where both grandmothers, my parents and I had lived, until we moved to Landsberg in 1936. Damage in this area was minimal, and when I finally turned the last corner, I could see that the apartment block where grandma lived was still the way I knew it.

I did not know that returning POWs were still an uncommon sight. It was October 31, 1945, and everywhere I walked people stared at me, and asked questions. Where did I come from and what happened to all the other soldiers etc. This was understandable, since every family had men in the war. There were still no German radio stations with factual information. The postal service wasn't working, I had seen no newspapers, so people were almost totally in the dark about what was going on in Germany. What they heard were rumors interlaced with Russian propaganda.

To the people I came in contact with, I must have been the manifestation of Germany's total defeat. I was certainly a sorry sight. Limping, walking with a cane, in a dirty, ragged old army uniform with a "woyna pleny" arm patch (POW in Russian), disintegrating wooden shoes on my feet, long unkempt hair, unshaven and with an empty tin can hanging from a rope around my waist. I wished somebody could have taken a picture of me for posterity, but who still had a camera in Berlin in those days? They had all been stolen by Russian soldiers.

When I walked up to Grandma's apartment door, the neighbors had already spotted me and came out to see who I was. When I told them that I was Hans Thielemann, they were shocked. They said that my Grandma was presently queuing at a grocery store over on Köpenicker Landstrasse for available food. They said that my mother was living with her. Wow, I just couldn't believe my luck. My mother was working at a construction site at the corner Köpenicker Landstrasse and Baumschulen Strasse. I was puzzled, my mother at a construction site? Since I was familiar with all these locations from my childhood, I set out to surprise them both.

As a kid I did grocery shopping for my mother at the store I was heading for now. Things had not changed much. This area was loosely crisscrossed by large apartment complexes, most of which had been built in the late 1920s and early 1930s by labor union credit institutions. The buildings were modern for the times, with large areas of greenery between each complex and garden plots for the ground floor units. They were four stories tall and each apartment had a balcony.

When I arrived at the grocery store, I recognized Grandma right away. She had never been my favorite grandmother, because she had always played the "grand dame." She had supported Hitler and for that reason had been at odds with most of the family. She was overweight as far back as I could remember, but was considerably thinner now, and she looked good. She was surprised that I was back from the war already. As always she bitched about the living conditions, her health, and about that idiot Hitler, whom she had idolized just a few years ago. She had not changed one iota. I exchanged a few pleasantries with the other people standing in line and then walked off to find my mother.

My mother cleaning bricks?

The building at the corner site the neighbors had directed me to was heavily damaged, and was in the process of being torn down. As in every other bombed out place in Germany, the bricks of these buildings were either crushed, and converted to new building blocks, or they were recycled. At the site, I asked a foreman about my mother. When he heard who I was, he immediately went to get her. She was cleaning bricks in the inner yard of the building. She was appalled about my condition, but surprised and relieved to see me back from the war in one piece. Her supervisor gave her the rest of the day off.

As we walked home she told me that she had not been able to save anything in Landsberg. She hadn't been home when the Russians came in, and when she finally returned home, all valuable things had been stolen. The Russian soldiers had chopped up the bedroom furniture for firewood and camped in the house. She had been taken in by Hildegard who lived upstairs. Hildegard was shacking up with a Russian engineer, and he protected both of them. Mother was deported by the Polish administration, and had been given 20 minutes to leave. After seeing my attire she was particularly distressed that she hadn't been able to save any of my clothes.

When we arrived at Grandma's place I was astonished to find it the way I remembered it. Nothing seemed to be missing and it sure felt good, but unreal, to be back in civilization again. Grandma's first question was, "Do you have lice." After my affirmative answer, she said "Go out on the balcony and take all your clothes off and leave them there." She had a little coal and wood stove for cooking out on her balcony, because neither city gas, or electricity had been restored. She filled the biggest pot she had with water, and brought it to a boil and then put all of my underwear into it. I washed myself from top to toe with the miserable wartime soap that was still common, but it felt good to be reasonably clean again. There was even an old razor and I was able to chop off my long whiskers. When I felt halfway civilized again, and it was time to sit down for a long talk.

They had a difficult time dealing with the miserable living conditions in Berlin. No gas, no heat, only part-time electricity and for months hardly any food. Shelter, food and utilities were the biggest problem everywhere in Germany. However, unlike most Berliners, they still had a roof over their heads.

I finally conked out and had the first decent sleep in months. The next morning we had "breakfast", consisting of a slice of bread and fake coffee. Mother, who had to go back to cleaning bricks, urged me to go to the district's administration office immediately, to get food ration tickets. She said, that as a returning POW, I was entitled to ten days worth of food tickets, but after that, I would have to go to work to get any food tickets at all.

Wherever I showed up, I was bombarded with questions. The hunger for information was every bit as large as the hunger for food. After I had taken care of the tickets, I went back to visit my mother at the construction site and let her know that I had something to eat, at least on paper.

Checking up on the relatives

When Mother came home from work, she told me that my cousin Wolfgang had come home even earlier than I did, and that surprised me. He had been with the Waffen SS, but had apparently left his unit near Magdeburg and walked home to Berlin. He had a badly wounded leg and knee, from stepping on a mine earlier in the war, and he walked with a cane, limping badly. Mother told me, that through an incredible stroke of luck, Wolfgang's family had not lost any of their possessions, except the things that they had evacuated to Landsberg. They were still living in the same apartment in the Berlin city center near Bahnhof Friedrichstrasse.

A pile of rubble called Berlin

I was anxious to talk with Wolfgang, and took the streetcar to the S-Bahn station Treptow Park. The S-Bahn, ran only for a distance of two stations, then I had to leave the train, and walk across to the other side of the platform. From where another train would proceed two more stations and I had to again transfer to the other side and continue. The reason for this system became clear, when I looked at the railroad tracks. The second set of tracks had been removed by the Russians for reparations, and in order to maintain any kind of traffic this clever flip flop system had been devised. From the train, which ran elevated through the center of Berlin, I could look down into Georgenstrasse to see the building I was born and grew up in. Only the street side facade was still standing, the rest of the building had been destroyed.

When I arrived at Aunt Kläre's apartment, I was amazed at what I saw. During the house to house fighting in the center of Berlin an artillery shell had exploded on the second floor of the apartment building, and the whole staircase and much of the upper floors had collapsed. The debris completely concealed their ground level apartment entrance and windows, so that no plundering Russians were able to clean out their belongings. My Aunt Kläre, Wolfgang's mother, had been in the air raid shelter underneath the house when it was hit by artillery, and she was trapped there for a few days. When she finally dug herself out, the fighting was over, and she hid in the ruins without being detected.

Since Wolfgang was about my size, he gave me some of his clothing. Wolfgang was wheeling and dealing in the Berlin black market already and not just in small quantities. Wolfgang and I limped through the old parts of Berlin around Kupfergraben and Lustgarten and down Unter den Linden where we had roamed as kids. The beautiful city I was born in had been leveled by bombs and artillery.

I visited my great-uncle Leopold whom I had never met. Leopold had been an employee of Lufthansa at the Tempelhof airport, and had just started working for the Americans there. Leopold gave me some clothing that GIs had discarded. I gradually returned to a semi-civilized looking human being again. It would be a long time before I would recover from the humiliation of having to go around and beg for clothes and food.

Seeing all the dirty, unkempt Russian soldiers pushing everybody around at will, reminded me too much of the early Nazi era's brown shirted Sturm Abteilungen (SA), when they rounded up Jewish people. It was the same goddamn brutality. Even the colors of the uniforms matched, and they also marched behind a red flag! What difference did it make if there was a swastika or a hammer and sickle in it? The same attitude and mental deficiency, "If you don't want to be my brother, I'll bash your head in" prevailed. I decided to leave all that behind me, and make a new start someplace else.

Just before my arrival in Berlin the Allied Control Commission had been established and declared itself the sole Government of Germany. People in the streets said, "This is democracy? We don't have anything to say again?" Well, I was not going to be dragged into any political discussions here, because like in Nazi days, the communists now listened in on conversations, and reported people with the "wrong" attitude to the Russians. I had learned my lesson when I was jailed by the NKVD.

My mother understood my feelings, and also thought it would be better for me to leave. She had decided to stay with her mother, where she had a habitable home, which hundreds of thousands of Berliners didn't have anymore. Mother told me that Shell Oil Company, shortly before the Russian troops closed in on Berlin, had decided to evacuate to Hamburg, where their main refinery was. In the middle of the night they had packed up their documents, crammed all the employees who wanted to leave, including my father, into a few remaining vehicles, and convoyed out of Berlin. Father was in the British occupation zone, and there wasn't a way to find out whether he was still alive. What Mother didn't tell me was that she and my father had separated. I found that out only 50 years later, but I could never find out why they separated.

On November 1, 1945, the intrazonal postal service was finally opened. A few days later we got letters from my father and from my uncle Gert Rausch in Reichenbach. Uncle Gert wrote that when I returned from Russia, I should come down to stay with them and he would help me to get reestablished. That was incredibly good news. As if I had foreseen this, I had given uncle Gert's address as a residency on my Russian release paper. Now I could legitimately claim that I lived in the US occupation zone.

Mother received a letter from a former business acquaintance of father by the name of Otto Friese. Otto had channeled many business contacts towards father. Otto and his wife Johanna were heavy drinkers, had four children and mother claimed, each child was from a different father. I was stunned when mother told me that Otto had been a Nazi-SD man and a Gestapo informer.

As a young man Otto had learned the blacksmith trade and later he started in the automobile business. He wrote that he and his whole family had reestablished themselves in a small village near the town of Brandenburg, and if mother needed any food to come out and visit them. My mother was really angry that Otto, despite his past, had already fallen back on his feet again. I guessed she was envious and who could blame her. My parents had worked hard for 25 years and had nothing to show for it, while Otto was established and probably an informer again, this time for the Russians .

Since mother had to work, she didn't have the time and maybe not the guts, to use the unreliable train connections to pick up badly needed produce at Otto Friese's place. She asked me if I would go to get potatoes for her. I was reluctant to do so, because I was sick and tired of traveling on trains, and didn't want to jeopardize my newly won freedom. But I felt guilty for having stayed at Grandma's place and using their scarce supplies and I agreed to give it a try.

I put on my old faded and dirty POW uniform and set out to Lehrter Railroad Station to catch a train that would carry me in the direction of Brandenburg. Lehrter Station used to be one of the big dead end railway stations in the center of Berlin. When I got there, not much of the station buildings was left standing. Only a bombed out, burned out shell without roof remained, but the railroad tracks were intact and occasionally a train would pull into, or out of the station.

The fight to board a train

There were hundreds of people waiting for the trains, and it required a robust physique and sharp elbows to get into the train. As a released POW I didn't have to pay for the train ticket, I only showed my sprawka. Through a simple trick I was able to get into the first train to Brandenburg that came in. When the train overloaded with people pulled into the station, I quickly jumped across the car's bumpers to the other side of the car away from the station platform, and casually went into the car while the people in the car were trying to push their way out to the station platform. It was as hard for the passengers to get out of the train, as it was to get in.

Regular battles were fought. People were climbing through the car's windows, climbing on the car's roofs and standing on the runners and even the bumpers to go where they had to go. It was impossible for the railway personnel to discourage people from these dangerous practices. People had waited for countless hours just to get into the station, and they were not going to get off that train again. Finally, with two hours of delay, the train started to roll.

When I finally reached my destination, I had to walk to Otto's farmhouse, where they welcomed me with open arms. I had my first hearty meal in ages. As a matter of fact the sausage was so fat I almost couldn't eat it. Otto had taken over the large farm of a former local Nazi who had been deported to Siberia. He wasn't the least bit ashamed about it and told me that the Russians knew about his background, and after what my mother had told me I could guess what Otto meant. The farmers in the area had needed a blacksmith to shoe the horses, so Otto fit right in. Otto was pleased to hear that all of my family was OK. The next day Otto's wife had a big breakfast on the table and we discussed what I wanted to take back to Berlin. I filled the rucksack with some potatoes and they gave me bread, bacon and eggs, and then filled another sack with about 100 pounds of the precious potatoes.

Otto found out that the next train would probably leave either late at night or early in the morning. Due to the curfew I had to arrive at the station just prior to the curfew hour and camp out in the station's waiting room all night. Otto got a horse drawn cart and took me and a total of 140 lbs. of potatoes to the station. On the way to the station I kidded Otto saying that this vehicle wasn't as fast as his Opel "Admiral," and he laughed and said, just you wait, that will come again too.

The waiting room at the station was already packed with people and at the onset of the curfew two armed Russian soldiers took position outside the doors. The train was overdue and didn't arrive until 7:00 am. Since I wasn't strong enough to schlepp the big sack with potatoes with me, I had the audacity to check it in at the freight counter to be shipped to mother's address. I carried the 40 pound rucksack with me.

The train was a freight train, with open lorries full of potatoes. We boarded it and sat on top of the potatoes. As we rolled through the countryside I enjoyed the beautiful autumn scenery. It was already the 6th of November and the weather was exceptionally nice for this time of the year. I expected that at the end of this train ride a big raid would be conducted and I wanted to avoid that.

When our train rolled into a Berlin S-Bahn station in the western suburbs and stopped right at the station platform to wait for another train in the opposite direction, I quickly got off the freight train and casually walked across the platform to wait for the next S-Bahn train. Some Russian soldiers glanced at me, but with my "woyna pleny" uniform and my cane I didn't arouse any suspicion.

Mother couldn't believe what all I had brought home. She was skeptical about the shipped potatoes and said they would never arrive. As it turned out they arrived two weeks after I had left.

The next morning mother passed the newspaper to me and I read that by getting off earlier, I had avoided the big raid that took place at the Lehrter station. The raids were conducted to prevent people from bringing stolen food items in from the surrounding farm areas. Apparently the hundreds of passengers on the potato train had also filled their luggage with the cargo of the train, which was illegal and many ended in jail.

When my ten days of "tolerated presence" in Berlin were over, I decided to get the hell out of Berlin, and go to the U.S. occupation zone. Wolfgang had told me that there was an Allied transfer camp operating in Berlin-Staaken to channel all POWs returning from Russia and residing in the western occupation zones to release camps in these zones. I went out to Staaken, a suburb on the western fringes of Berlin. When I left the S-Bahn station there, streams of ragged looking former Russian POWs were all walking in one direction. At the camp entrance, which was under British administration, I showed my "Sprawka" and even though I was in civilian clothes now, was immediately admitted.

They asked a lot of questions about name, destination, from what POW camp, from what German unit etc. Then two husky English soldiers armed with enormously large wooden syringes (they were at least 4" in diameter and about 18" long) blew clouds of powdered DDT into every hole of everybody's clothing. Into pants legs, pockets, shirt collars, sleeves, every piece of luggage, everything was dusted with DDT. The western Allies didn't want to admit Russian pests into their territories.

The camp was militaristic, with a typical British arrogance and the proverbial stiff upper lip. When POWs did not move aside fast enough to make room for British officers, they just slapped them with their swagger sticks. On the positive side, the food was good, it consisted of American K-Rations. The cigarettes and chewing gum had been removed from the boxes, but the POWs sure liked what was left.

In this enormous heap of humanity I had a chance to talk to all sorts of people. I met another civilian who turned out to be a former Luftwaffen physician, Dr. Werner Hauser, who, after the collapse of German forces east of Berlin, had walked into an abandoned medical practice and set himself up to help the local people to deal with the many serious medical problems arising out of the occupation. Rape, venereal diseases and unwanted pregnancy were on top of the list. He had been able to help many and made a lot of money, but wasn't able to continue for lack of the most basic medical supplies. We had a long talk and then boarded a freight train together.

Into the U.S. Occupation Zone

These freight trains, running between the western occupation zones and West-Berlin, ferried supplies to British, French and US troops. When going back, they carried returning POWs who needed to go to the western zones. The trips were scheduled to go west during the night, so there wouldn't be much interference by the Russians. Armed US soldiers accompanied each train. After we had passed across the zonal border, the train stopped in Marburg, Lahn, and Dr. Hauser and

I decided to bail out. We were both in civilian clothes so it was not too difficult. We saw that standard passenger trains were in service here already, so we walked across the tracks, went to the ticket booth and paid for tickets to Heidelberg, where Dr. Hauser had studied and had many friends. Our departure from the POW train may have saved us also unpleasant problems at the U.S. discharge camp the train was destined for. As it turned out the camp was notorious for transferring POWs to the French Army, who shipped them to France to work in the reparation work force.

I could not help but think that I now had finally escaped the Russian Bear as well as the Berlin Bear.

Back to civilization?

Like every place else, train traffic in the US zone was impaired by the damage and destruction of the German rail network. However it was possible to detour around the destruction. The double spur rail system, common on all railroad lines of Germany, was intact, no rails had been removed for reparation. Passenger trains were running pretty well according to schedule, but were overloaded with passengers.

We slept in Red Cross dorms and railroad stations and slowly worked our way south. Thanks to Dr. Hauser's knowledge we made it to Heidelberg in about three days. The normal prewar travel time would have been a few hours. I enjoyed the trip, because I had never been to southern Germany before. The ride in an electric suburban trolley from Weinheim to a northern suburb of Heidelberg was very picturesque. From the end of that line, we had to walk the last few kilometers. I vividly remember walking down to the Neckar River and for the first time seeing the beautiful city of Heidelberg.

A fairy tale image?

I felt like I was walking into a fairy tale town. The town looked as if World War II had never happened. The Neckar river valley overwhelmed me emotionally and tears rolled down my cheeks. Dr. Hauser gave me a questioning look, but he understood how I felt after what I had been through. When we walked over the Neckar bridge, I stopped every once in a while and looked at the old monuments and my adoration for this town knew no limits. I would have liked to settle here.

Dr. Hauser found his friends in Heidelberg, and I was anxious to talk to them to find out how best to continue to Stuttgart and Reichenbach. We all had so much to talk about that there was not much time left to sleep. The next morning I thanked Dr. Hauser and his friends for their help and made off for the rail station.

Walking through Heidelberg was dreamlike. No bombed out houses along the beautiful Neckar river valley, trees ablaze with fall colors, vineyards climbing up the steep slopes, and above it all, the old Heidelberg Schloss. It was like a dream, a fantasy of what the real world should look like, but didn't.

Later in the day I arrived in Pforzheim and was reminded that Heidelberg was an exception. I could not understand why the famous jewelry center was of such a strategic value that it had to be destroyed. I could not get a train connection and had to stay overnight at a Red Cross shelter. After seeing Heidelberg, it was a nightmare to walk through the rows and rows of destroyed buildings in Pforzheim, with almost no trace of human beings.

I got into Stuttgart around noon and found that rail connections here were better than any place else. The diligent Swabians had many things functioning again, even though there was a tremendous amount of bomb damage here too.

Finally at my destination

I finally embarked on the last stretch to Reichenbach/Fils. When the train stopped I was surprised to see my Uncle Gert and Aunt Wally waiting across the station platform. They were speechless when they saw me getting off the train and said that they were on their way to Stuttgart. There was a big hello, and we walked back to their place.

Grandma's apartment, still intact, Berlin, 1945.

Brandenburg Gate, Berlin, 1945.

It is an unhealthy attitude to think success a trivial incident in life.
Edward Young

19
To be Human Again

It was Sunday November 18, 1945, and I was finally at the location I had given on my release papers. Uncle Gert asked me if I had come alone. I didn't get what he was driving at. When he saw the questionable look on my face, he explained that he meant, "Do you have any lice or whatever else?" I laughed and told him about his mother's action in Berlin, and about the DDT attack at the transfer camp. I said that after the DDT attack all the lice had fallen out of my pockets dead, with no survivors. We broke out laughing. Uncle Gert had an identical experience with his mother when he came back from World War I.

The world is good once more

I started to tell them about my trip, but said that I would like a bath first, because I again hadn't been able to clean myself since my departure from Berlin. I sank into the large bathtub with warm water up to my neck and the world seemed to be good again. I considered my arrival here as my "magnum opus" as the old Romans would have said. Here I was at my dreamed of destination in Reichenbach, 192 days after I had started on May 9, 1945. Not only had I made it back to Berlin, but I was now already 500 miles farther west in the US occupation zone, approximately 1,250 miles from my starting point in Courland. That, I calculated to be about 6.5 miles (10 km) per day, not bad since I didn't have a car. I figured the odds for me to have succeeded in this venture must have been at least 1:10,000,000. I had made my mind up about doing it, planned it, prepared for it, and accomplished what I had planned and was really proud of it

When I finished my bath I recited some poetry by Ringelnatz, probably the first real hippy poet in Germany. Translated it would read, "The knowledge surrounds me like heavenly magic, I am able to show myself today, because I am clean." This was enthusiastically applauded by the family.

I sat down with the family and was introduced to my cousin Christa, four years old, and to Aunt Wally's mother, Frieda Voigt, who was in her late seventies. Gert and Wally Rausch were renting the upper floor above the local elementary school. Aunt Wally was a dentist and had her dental practice on the same floor. Uncle Gert, a textile chemist like his father, was employed by a large textile manufacturer in Leinfelden and commuted there by train. They had not experienced any food shortages during the entire war since most of Wally's patients were local farmers, who often paid with produce, rather than money. They had the best of everything and plenty of it. I thought, that's the way it is, in every disaster there are a few lucky ones.

When we sat down for a meal, I didn't dare to eat the quantities my stomach asked for. I had to be polite and civilized at the table in order not to wear out my welcome. After dinner I would sneak into the kitchen and snatch some of the leftover food. Aunt Wally had gallons of fresh milk from one of her patients and she let the cream rise to the top and then scooped it into a separate container in the refrigerator. When enough was accumulated she would get out a small hand-driven butter churn and I had to crank for hours to produce their butter.

They had a maid, but much of the housework was done by Wally's fragile mother, who was treated as if she were just a servant. Little Christa was quite a spoiled brat, who would cuss her grandmother and called her names. I had never heard any kid call an adult names like that. This was a type of household I had not experienced before.

The next day uncle Gert opened the doors of a huge wardrobe in the master bedroom and my eyes just about popped out. There were stacks of brand new linens, underwear, shirts, handkerchiefs, socks, you name it, and it was there and in quantity. Gert had also rounded up material for two complete suits for me. The material was not the best, simply "German Forest", as synthetic material was sarcastically called in those days, but it was a start. I was infinitely grateful about those gifts.

The biggest problem was to find a tailor who could make me the suits, because more than just the outer fabric was needed to finish them. When I was growing up, my mother had always taught me to be independent and to stand on my own feet. She told me never to rely on other people to do things for me. That philosophy was so deeply imbedded in my brain that it bothered me having to ask for something. Sometimes I simply didn't ask, because I was too ashamed to receive gifts without being able to reciprocate.

Soon I looked like a civilized person again. I had no identification papers and in Germany they were essential for getting work, for getting permission to move to a place that had work, and above all to get ration tickets. My only document was the Russian release document, and nobody here could read it. Uncle Gert took me under his wing and took me to the local mayor and vouched for me so I would get a temporary ID card.

Next thing was to look for a job. That was a hell of a lot more difficult. I was a refugee and had lost all papers pertaining to my technical education. I was an optician and optometrist, had finished an apprenticeship and passed all the final exams required, but, how could I prove that to a potential employer? I wrote to the board of examiners back in Frankfurt/Oder. They replied that all documentation had been maliciously destroyed, but they sent me questionnaires to fill out. I had to have them verified by at least two people who were familiar with my technical education. That was a sick joke. I didn't know where the teachers, master opticians, and the board examiner lived, or even if they were still alive.

The next task was to get permission to move to Stuttgart, because that would be a place were I could get a job. All living space was rigorously rationed in Germany because every city and community had to cope with the enormous destruction of buildings and the influx of millions of refugees. Most had been deported from the eastern parts of Germany now under Polish administration. There was a set number of square feet allowed per person. If a family had more space than their quota, they were forced to rent to other people. In order to be eligible for rental space in Stuttgart, I would have to have a job in Stuttgart. So it was a ridiculously complex world, but I was determined to get off and stand on my own feet.

On January 28, 1946, I was in Stuttgart. The city of Stuttgart had 55% of all buildings destroyed by bombs. Rebuilding was a job of gigantic proportions, it included everything from buildings to office equipment. So, I learned to fix typewriters in a dinky basement shop to make some money. I was able to rent a room in a house but had to sleep on a couch in the dining room. The woman's husband had not come back from a British POW camp and she needed the money.

There was considerable resentment and discrimination against refugees. In Schwaben that was not a new trend, it had been there before the war. They didn't like people who didn't speak their dialect, which had only a loose resemblance to high German. Fortunately I was a very adaptive person and had a knack for languages, so I didn't have much of a problem.

The food ration tickets were barely enough to live on. As a bachelors the food situation was particularly bad, since I had to eat in restaurants. There was no way that I could cook in my cubbyhole room. The official "calories per day" count was about 1100 calories during 1946 in the U.S. occupation zone, but at times even these few calories were not available.

I had to find additional food that wasn't rationed, and find the restaurants that gave the biggest portions for the ration tickets. This was almost a full time job. Everybody helped by telling where to get what, and the papers announced if there was an additional amount of food available and on what ration cards. There was a widespread practice of "modifying" the ration tickets to get additional food. People who had the equipment started to print ration tickets and sold them on the black market. As a single person I had little to fear if I got caught, but for the blackmarket sharks there was a definite risk of going to jail. The retail trade had many opportunities to get additional supplies by falsifying their returns of ration tickets to the occupational government office responsible for food distribution. Personnel who worked for retail stores and who had to glue these various tickets on sheets, which had to be turned in at the end of each calendar month, could also get "rich" by letting some tickets disappear into their own pockets. Everybody was hungry and honesty often fell by the wayside.

Finally in Reichenbach, 1945

Thus oft a struggle to escape, but lands us in a still worse scrape.
La Fontaine

20
To Start Life Over

I had arrived in Stuttgart with the clothes my Uncle Gert had given me, that was all. I had no friends or contacts in the city. My job was not paying much, but even with money, there was little to buy. Every article of value was available on the black market for exorbitant prices, or for American cigarettes. I could truthfully say that Chesterfields, Lucky Strikes, and Camels, preferably by the carton, opened every door, got every service, and bought any goods. It was the only currency that was universally accepted, since the "Reichsmark" was nothing but a worthless piece of paper.

I could buy American cigarettes on the black market for five to ten Reichsmarks per cigarette, but I didn't have that much money. I smoked and could occasionally afford a few cigarettes for my own use. I had to have either items of value that were in demand by the GIs, such as Leica cameras, binoculars, Mercedes cars, or be of female gender and willing to make a deal.

A horrible encounter

Going home from work one evening, I was in a streetcar when a man came on board who looked like the spitting image of Adolf Hitler. I couldn't believe what I was seeing. The streetcar was crowded, and the "Hitler type" gradually worked his way towards the center of the car. He wore a light colored trench coat, the way Hitler often did in his earlier years. There was no sign of any makeup, which would have identified him as an actor involved in a play. The people in the streetcar did not instantly recognize this "image" before them, because in those miserable postwar years everybody had a lot more important things on their minds. Then people gradually started to wake up and alerted their neighbors to the Führer image. I expected everybody to raise their arms and shout "Sieg Heil", and address him as "Mein Führer", but the reactions were dead stares, with expressions of disbelief, even fear, on some of the faces. I wished I could have filmed the faces of the people as they eyed the man standing there in an authoritarian posture. He was staring out of the window with a cold and arrogant expression on his face, projecting every bit the image of the real Adolf Hitler.

I didn't know if a Stuttgart theater was playing Zuckmayer's "The Devils General", it was possible. It was also possible that he was an intelligence agent testing peoples' reactions. Anything was possible in those post war days. When he left the streetcar a few stops later, I heard, "My God I thought he was dead and I hope he is."

The place were I was living was nice but expensive and it was quite a distance from where I worked. Finally Mr. Schmidt, who worked with me, suggested that if I wanted to stay with them, they would make room for me. He and his wife lived in Heslach, a few blocks from where we worked. The Schmidt's had a small apartment on the third floor, with a storage space, actually a room with a door, right under the roof. The room was fairly large, and the ceiling was the slope of the roof with a small swing out window, but it had no heat or water. Fortunately there was a toilet and wash basin on the same floor. I immediately saw that I could have a nice little place of my own, and was delighted to get it. There was a bed, a set of drawers with a stoneware wash basin on top, a table and a chair, and enough room for big steamer trunks, book shelves or such, and maybe even a stove. It was primitive, but adequate.

Repairing typewriters

My employer was a man from Saxonia, probably also a refugee, by the name of Möckel. The company's name was Schreier & Möckel. The shop was in a semi-basement with windows above ground, about 20 by 20 feet in size and had several work benches with simple equipment. Mr. Schmidt, who was a master tool maker, showed me how to repair various typewriters. I was a fast learner and we soon had a good working relationship. Mr. Schmidt had been a manager of the tool department of a large company, but because of his membership in the Nazi party he was not allowed to work as a manager anymore. Such was the decision of the de-Nazification court.

No existence without papers

My most serious problem was to get duplicates of my technical education papers, birth certificates and savings account books. I was also putting my feelers out for a job as an optician. I wrote numerous letters to the appropriate institutions, but they either had been destroyed during the war, or the archives had been evacuated and were still inaccessible. The whole tragedy of war, and its senseless destruction came back to haunt me again and again. It was a constant uphill battle, even in these "peace" times.

Here and there were signs of small improvements, manifestations of the indestructibility of the human spirit which warmed the heart. Despite the mountains of misery, destruction and tragic personal circumstances that surrounded me, I began to believe that there might be better days ahead.

Early in 1946 I was able to buy stationary to write Hannes Rhode's wife in East Germany about what had happened to him. Several weeks later she replied, she had just received a Red Cross card from Hannes, saying that he was OK. She was surprised to hear that he had been shot, since Hannes hadn't mentioned it on his card. I was relieved to hear that he had come through all right. I also wrote to Kurt König's (King's) mother to find out if she had heard anything from Kurt.

The Russians had confiscated all of my notes and addresses, and the chaotic situation between the occupation zones made communications difficult. The postal system, like anything else, was not back to normal, and all the interzonal mail went through a censor. I wrote to the von Collins family in Austria and to my distress got an answer from his sister telling me that Sepp had shot himself. I was distressed about that. She referred me to Siegfried Penzel, who was with the other group that had attempted the "Journey of no return". He wrote me that they also had been caught near the former German border with Lithuania, and when that happened, Sepp von Collins had committed suicide by shooting himself. I just couldn't believe that an intelligent and well educated person would do that. Siegfried had notified Sepp's family. I send a letter of condolence to them and later on got a reply, saying that she and the family just couldn't comprehend that it happened, especially since he had survived the war.

I missed having a close friend I could talk with. Most of all I missed my father, with whom I could sit down and objectively analyze the problems on hand, and find the best solution. When I had left my parents in Landsberg, I was seventeen years old. I spent the next four years in the military. At age twenty-two I had no experience dealing with civilian human problems.

Solving a mystery

One day I hit upon a magazine article about the radio station "Soldaten Sender West", which I had listened to so often in Courland. At the end of the war the station had gone off the air, without revealing anything about its identity. The general public concluded that it might have been a German underground transmitter that was shut down by Germany's surrender. Nothing was further from the truth. The station was in England and was manned by German internees, many of them Jewish, who were well informed about events in Germany during the war. The security surrounding the station was incredibly tight. At its peak, the station had over 2,000 reporters all over Germany. I was sure that hardly any of the "reporters" knew that they were not contributing to a German Armed Forces radio station, but to a British propaganda effort instead. The information these reporters gathered were usually only of minor military significance. They were reporting the daily lives of the people in towns and villages. It was sprinkled with sarcastic comments on occurrences in Germany, mixed with very detailed military information. That is why it looked like legitimate German information.

The radio announcer would for instance say, "The clock in the steeple of St. Mary's Cathedral in Munich has been ten minutes late, since the clock custodian Hubertus Huber has been drafted into the "Volkssturm". Nobody else seems to know how to correct the problem." This information was factual, of no military significance, but it made people in Munich, who could verify that information, think that they were listening to a German radio station.

The chief editor of the station turned out to be a top English newspaper man by the name of Sefton Delmer. After the war he packed a rucksack and hiked through Germany to personally interview people about the effects of his information service. I considered his efforts and his accomplishments the ultimate of intelligent Allied propaganda. The listeners had just loved it.

More facts emerged about the effects of the war. Of my birth year, 1923, only 30 percent of the males came back from the war, that is, 70 percent were killed. The years from about 1920 on to 1926 suffered equal or higher losses. It was only natural that the few men of these birth years who did return had enormous opportunities. Young women were looking for boyfriends, widows were looking for husbands, and businesses were looking for bosses. I had made a fundamental mistake by staying in Stuttgart but was trying to correct it.

I had found a job in Straubing, Bavaria. The owner of the store had been killed in the war, and his daughter was trying to keep the business in the family. She was a pleasant woman in her mid twenties, and I thought we might be compatible. The town bureaucracy told me that with only my Russian release papers I could not get permission to live in Straubing. They advised me to go through the U.S. release camp in Regensburg to get American release papers. I thought they were kidding, but they were not. I told them, thank you, I will not voluntarily go behind barbed wire again. I later read that the Regensburg US POW camp was notorious for transferring POWs to France to work there.

When I got back to Stuttgart, I had to move to another room, because the one I had occupied was given to a couple. My new room was only about half as large, there was just enough room for a bed, a night stand and a wash basin, but I was glad to have a roof over my head. In winter time it was damn cold up there. The temperature often didn't climb above 50°F. Sometimes Mrs. Schmidt brought me a hot water bottle to keep my feet warm in bed.

Shortly before Christmas 1946 I met Traudl, who was also a refugee. She was from Silesia and was teaching home economics at a high school for girls. She had a small apartment and was lonely too. She told me that she would have to confess to her priest about any extramarital sex. I couldn't believe such nonsense, and asked her what damn business of the priest's it was if we made love. She was hemming and hawing about it, and told me "that's just the way it is." I had broken with the Protestant church shortly after my confirmation. I considered all religions to be man made inventions conceived to manipulate the mass of the people for the advantage of a few, the priests. I had seen enough of mankind's senselessness with respect to religion during the war. The war prayers on both sides of the combatants, and the "God with us" blasphemy on our military belt buckles, told me not to believe in religion any more. I considered it as bad as the games the politicians played, just another way to enslave man's mind. I tried to discuss it with Traudl, but I didn't get anywhere.

Shortly after my 23rd birthday, she came up to my room to borrow two suitcases. She was going to spend Christmas with her family somewhere in Bavaria. When we were in bed, she actually had to teach me how. It was my first time, and I was embarrassed about my ignorance. We hugged and kissed and did it again, and it felt so good. She told me that she had done it before, but didn't really like it much, because of the confession requirement in her church. She got up, dressed and left with the suitcases. I was very disappointed that she was so businesslike about sex.

After she came back from Bavaria we had sex again, but like the first time, she was not enthusiastic. We did it without a condom a couple of times, and it felt even better, but I had to withdraw before I went off. That wasn't satisfactory. When I started to explore her body and caress her breasts, she didn't like that either. She wanted to get married in the worst way and have children, but she seemed to be completely indifferent to enjoyable sex, as if it was an unpleasant duty. Her attitude about sex and religion turned me off completely. Anyway, I wasn't ready to get married since I didn't have a pot to piss in. I could also see that she would not change after we were married. About a month later she told me that her period was overdue. Two weeks later her period came and we were both relieved. I had the feeling that she was trying to manipulate me, and we parted amiably.

We lived in a bombed out city, with food rations so small that we could barely survive, no available living quarters to raise a family in, and prospects for improvement years away. Birth control pills had not been invented and abortions were illegal in Germany. Doctors faced severe penalties if they were caught. I felt that it would have been irresponsible to bring children into this world.

Finally I found a job with a local optician in downtown Stuttgart. The store was in the old part of town in temporary quarters. The workshop was extremely crammed, but the owner, Mr. Milten, already had plans and permits for a store in another building nearby.

I was replacing another optician, with whom I worked just long enough to be shown how things were done in this company. I questioned him about his next employment, and to my surprise he said that he was going to move into the Russian occupation zone to work there. I just shook my head and told him about my experiences in Russia and East Berlin. The man was not to be deterred. In his opinion the only power that had any say in Europe would be Russia. I told him that would be the worst thing that could happen to all of us. He said that I was not realistic and didn't want to see the facts. He seemed to be a genuine communist and as far as I was concerned it was good that he left.

The new store construction for my employer progressed despite the fact that all the building material had to be bought on the black market. Mr. Milten had a business partner, who appeared to be a big black market racketeer. His mannerisms resembled that of an SS officer. I wasn't at ease with that guy at all. He pulled too many shady deals, but that was how people were getting ahead. In a way I was envious of people like him. They were the only ones who seemed to accomplished anything. All one had to have were connections and absolutely ruthless determination.

When we moved into the new store, I set up a nice work area. Mr. Milten hired an apprentice I would train. Next to the new store was an old established orthopedic business, that employed a podiatrist, an attractive woman, who took an instant liking to me. Hedi was a dyed-in-the-wool Schwab from Ravensburg. She knew her way around Stuttgart, had many friends, and even more connections. She was tall, blond, well-dressed, spoke French and German, was a terrific dancer, and a good figure skater, with the muscular legs that are essential for that sport. She wore glasses and hence the interest in me. She had beautiful green eyes, and was one of the first people I knew who used contact lenses. She had an unusual tolerance for these large hard glass contacts lenses and could wear them up to eight hours. I bought some for myself, but could only tolerate them for four hours, since I had tight eyelids.

The first time I went out with Hedi was to a Carnival dance, for which costumes were required. Since I didn't have much in the way of clothing and couldn't afford to rent a costume, I wore the white lab coat I usually worked in, and put a stethoscope around my neck. It was an unexpected hit, because women walked up to me to have their "hearts" checked. I was often embarrassed since many wore transparent, skimpy tops. My dancing was too rusty to dance well with Hedi who was in a dance club, and did competitive ball room dancing, but we had a good time anyway. Hedi acknowledged my popularity with the ladies at the dance and to prevent my escape, she asked me to share her bed for the rest of the night. She motioned me to walk quietly to her room. She had a single bed, and for two tall people, it was on the snug side. We bedded down in spoon position, made love and went to sleep.

The next morning, a Sunday, we had to wait until the family Hedi lived with had left for church before we could get up. We had slept in the nude, and it was fun to be with somebody who wasn't shy and inhibited. Hedi had lots of sexual experience, small firm breasts, and a good muscular body. We made love several more times during the morning. Since she had other commitments for the day, I left. I sensed that she wasn't quite sure about me, probably because I was so inexperienced and a couple of years younger than she was.

After my return from the Russian POW camp I had started to think about leaving Germany. I had contacted some ophthalmic companies in Sweden, Holland and Switzerland for job opportunities, but nothing came to fruition. There were too many obstacles in the form of time limited employment permits and too much hatred of Germans.

In late 1948 I finally got mail from my old Luftwaffen buddy King (Kurt König). He had just returned from a Russian POW camp, and he wrote that he had worked in a coal mine in the Ukrainian Donez region. He said his health wasn't the best, so I sent him a parcel with vitamin tablets and condoms, all goods that were in short supply in the Russian occupation zone. He thanked me and told me, that he had joined the "Volkspolizei". I was appalled, he was a very intelligent, well educated man, whom I really liked, and he was now working for the Russian police force. I tried to talk him into emigrating with me, but I could not convince him. I sensed that he was in a political straight jacket, particularly since he was in a police unit housed in a compound. It was obviously not an ordinary police unit he belonged to, but a paramilitary unit. Never in my wildest dreams would I have thought that we would be on opposite sides of the political spectrum, and in case of another war would have to shoot at each other.

Kurt had been drafted right after high school, and didn't have a professional skill to fall back on. His mother had lost their belongings in the war, so he had to provide for both of them. The work he had chosen was an easy way out for him. Our correspondence was interrupted by political pressure from the unit he had joined. All interzonal correspondence still went through mail censorship.

At the U.S. Immigration Department I learned that the waiting list for German emigration to the U.S. was about two years long and I dropped the idea. My relatives in New York might have been willing to do something for me, but I was too shy to ask them. They would have to post a security bond for me, and I knew that they were not well off, so I applied for an immigration visa to Canada instead. I also applied for a visa to Brazil. This odd combination came about because I had met a gentleman who was a specialist in the newest ophthalmic field, contact lenses. He worked for the only contact lens manufacturer in Germany, the Müller-Welt Company in Stuttgart. I had met him through the South German Optical Journal that I occasionally wrote articles for. He was going to Sao Paulo, Brazil, to open his own business there. He promised to help me, if I decided to come to Brazil. I took courses in Portuguese and in American English languages to prepare myself.

The Canadian Immigration Mission was in Karlsruhe. In Stuttgart, where I lived, it was impossible to get any information of preferred professions or skills wanted in Canada, or anything else that would be helpful. Everybody wanted to get out of the piles of rubble left by World War II. We all waited patiently, hoped, prepared and cursed the snail's pace of the institutions which issued the coveted immigration visas.

In the meantime Hedi had found a better place to live. It was a small, attractive place, that she decorated with unique, contemporary style furniture. I liked her taste. We were both busy, so had rarely time to spend a whole weekend together, but we made passionate love and enjoyed each other's company as often as we could. Sometimes we just talked or soaked up the sun on her balcony.

Hedi's past was shrouded in mystery. During the war she had been working in a hospital in Ravensburg which treated wounded soldiers, a hospital that also specialized in VD treatments. She told me horrible stories of soldiers dying of syphilis. Having lost a grandfather to the same disease, I knew enough about it. Penicillin had not been available in Germany during the war.

For Hedi's birthday I brought her a large bouquet of lilac, but to my dismay she told me that she hated lilac. She finally told me about her tempestuous love affair with a French POW during the war, strictly forbidden during the Nazi regime. They got engaged after the war and planned to get married. Just days before the wedding however, Pierre was killed in an automobile accident. At his funeral it had been lilac time and since flowers were hard to get in those days, there were huge bouquets of lilac in the chapel during the funeral service.

I also started to date Martha, a salesclerk in a grocery store just around the corner from where I worked. As a bachelor I had to live on skimpy ration tickets, and a little extra food would be welcome. The initial feelings in the relationship were of mutual antipathy. I didn't like her legs, they were flabby and she didn't walk gracefully, she waddled. She wasn't the athletic type that I adored. I should have followed my first impressions and left her alone. I was naïve and didn't know that it is impossible to change a person.

Even our first attempt to make love was a problem. We had gone to a quaint little inn near Stuttgart but had to keep that camouflaged, because Martha's parents were so old fashioned.

We took a lot of trips into the beautiful countryside around Stuttgart. The public transportation system gradually returned to normal, and more areas became accessible. We took busses or the railroad to an area and then went on hikes. We went along the Neckar River Valley and to the Schwabian Alps and at times made love out in the forest. At one time, even on top of a wooden observation tower with a Hornets' nest right above our heads. Another time we did it on a stone wall surrounding a cemetery. Whenever we felt like doing it, we did, and probed every possible position. Pregnancy was a constant worry.

A new start with new money

In the late spring of 1948, there were rumors about a replacement of the worthless Reichsmark. The old Reichsmark had been stabilized once before in 1923, and that had ended the most disastrous inflation in German history. Twenty-five years later the Reichsmark was totally overvalued again. It was obvious that a devaluation had to take place to get the West German economy on its feet again.

I was working with a different optician now. Next to the optician store was a small, boutique which had elegant woman's fashions. Ronney was an employee there, a super good-looking woman, with a typical model figure, tall and skinny. She was young, maybe 19 years old. Her boyfriend was an American civilian, Henry Kaminski from New York, who was in his thirties, overweight, and overbearing at times, but a hell of a nice guy. He drove a light blue 1946 Dodge coupe, and supposedly worked for the Joint Export/Import Agency (J.E.I.A.) of the American Military Government in Stuttgart. Martha, Ronney, Henry and I became good friends, and did a lot of fun things together.

I think an American customer gave me a draft copy of the scenario for the planned reevaluation of the money. What I read was shocking to me and everybody with whom I shared the information. I remember the reactions of my aunt and uncle in Reichenbach, they just couldn't believe it would happen that way.

A new currency was going to be issued. Only a small amount of cash and savings up to 3,000 Reichsmarks were going to be exchanged at a 1:1 ratio. Everything else would be exchanged later at a 10:1 ratio. That is, for ten old Reichsmarks, one would get one new Deutschemark. All debts were to be exchanged at a 1:1 ratio, with only a short extension. The biggest surprise was that every property owner who's house was not destroyed during the war would be saddled with an additional 50 % mortgage on the property. That mortgage was payable to the future German Government's reconstruction fund and would be used to finance the rebuilding of housing in Germany.

On Friday, June 18, 1948, the law about the change of the currency was published, and the old Reichsmark was declared invalid. All business involving an exchange of money came to an instant stop. On Saturday June 19, large convoys of American military trucks with armed guards on each vehicle, plus armored personnel carriers, rolled up to the banks and unloaded the new bank notes.

On Sunday, June 20, the banks opened to issue only 40 new Deutschmarks for 40 old Reichsmarks, but made no savings account exchanges yet.

Over night the store windows filled with goods that people hadn't seen in years. The furious citizens were cussing the merchants who had hidden all these goods. I saw everything I needed in the stores now, but had no money to buy it. In addition, a general price increase of up to 300 percent was permitted officially.

That action by the western Military Governments brought the whole economical situation back to a more normal condition. Now businesses would sell or render services for just plain money, and the Camel or Lucky Strike "currency" was eliminated and reduced to just a commodity. Most people's savings accounts were later reduced 10:1. The Russian Military Government didn't like these Allied actions and on June 24, started the blockade of West Berlin, as a retaliation.

My mother suddenly left Berlin, and moved to Hamburg and didn't explain why. Mother was always holding her cards close to her chest. I had often suspected that she didn't like sex, and that my father had extramarital affairs.

A short time later, my mother wrote me that father was in a hospital with a kidney infection. She said that he had gotten numerous penicillin injections, but that he wasn't doing well. When I asked if I should come to see him, she answered that my appearance in Hamburg would only tell my father that his condition was hopeless and she didn't think that was a good idea.

A week later, I got a telegram, telling me that father had passed away and to please attend the funeral. I was very angry at my mother. I would have liked to see my father once more before he died.

November is not the best time for weather in Germany, and the November of 1948 was no exception. I used a private bus service to go to Hamburg. When the bus reached the main northbound Autobahn, we ran into impenetrable fog in the area around Frankfurt. The fog was so dense that the driver asked the backup driver to sit on the front fender of the bus, and show with hand signs where to steer the vehicle. He had to slow to a crawl, and I didn't envy the poor guy out there, because it was beastly cold. The two drivers changed positions every 15 minutes, but even the inside of the bus, an old diesel burner, was not warm. The girl next to me moved closer and we spread a blanket over our legs to keep warm. After about ten hours of this misery, the bus arrived in Hannover at five o'clock in the morning. The passengers going to Hamburg had to walk through the bombed out inner city to the main railway station, which was also heavily damaged, but functional. About three hours later the train rolled into Hamburg-Dammtor Station.

Mother had rented a small room in a larger apartment. When I entered her room, the first thing I saw was my father's picture on top of a dresser, with lit candles on each side. Mother said hello to me in tears. She fixed coffee and cake, and we smoked a cigarette. Then she told me about father's sickness and his last days. He was down to 90 pounds when he died.

In those days all the doctors believed that penicillin was THE cure-all and administered it indiscriminately, not knowing that it was ineffective against inflammations of the urinary tract. Penicillin also kills the bacteria of the intestinal tract, which are essential for digestion and absorption of the food into the body. Father got so many penicillin injections that he was literally starved to death.

The next day mother introduced me to father's girlfriend who, as she put it, "Did it just for chocolate." I could not figure out how she meant that. Was this woman just a prostitute, or father's lover, who happened to like chocolate? When the woman came to visit, I could not warm up to her. She was a young woman, maybe in her late twenties, tall and fairly attractive. If I had been more diplomatic, we could have met privately and I would have found out more about my parents' relationship.

Mother never explained to me why she went to work for a widower with a large farm and five kids during the war. She claimed that she had to go to work and didn't want to work in a factory. Maybe her decision was the reason for the separation. I was sure father also had some affairs in Berlin. It also seem to explain why my mother didn't want me to come and talk to father before he died. I was really offended by all that secrecy.

The funeral was attended by many former colleagues of my father, his girlfriend, and some old friends from Landsberg. To my surprise Anni Timmerman, the oldest daughter of our Dutch neighbors in Landsberg, was there too. I had been very fond of her in Landsberg, and the feeling hadn't changed. Hildegard Piechatzeck and her son Frank were also present. I sadly said good-bye to my father. Due to his profession and constant absence from home, I never had a chance to know him well. After the very moving nonreligious service was over, we all went to a restaurant and had a farewell dinner together, and later I saw Anni, Hildegard and little Frank off at the railway station.

I finally questioned my Mother by putting pressure on her to reveal the reason for her hasty trip out of Berlin. She apparently had pulled some illegal deals with food stamps and was due to be arrested, but had been warned and fled to West Berlin. From there she flew to Hamburg. There were too many loose ends in her story. I was at the end of my patience and returned to Stuttgart. Mother had hinted that I could stay in Hamburg, since father's boss at the Shell Oil Company had offered to help me get a job at the company. I didn't like the Hamburg ambiance and atmosphere, so my answer was "no."

Back in Stuttgart, Martha and I continued to improve our relationship. I told her that I had applied for immigration to Canada and she accepted that. She had two cousins in Chicago, and if she had been on the ball, she could have asked them to sponsor our immigration to the States. These relatives were sending her CARE packages, they were well off, and all were active in the "Schwaben Verein", a big Chicago German Club.

About a month after I had applied for immigration to Canada. I got a letter from my mother, telling me to contact people in Stuttgart-Weil im Dorf by the name of Woltmann. An old friend, Dieter Bergner from Landsberg, was living with them.

Finding an old friend

The Woltmann's house had bomb damage which they had temporarily repaired. Dieter was surprised to see me. He introduced us to the Woltmann family and to his cousin Vera, who was the oldest of the four Woltmann girls. Vera and Dieter were engaged and were going to get married soon, because a baby was on the way.

We talked about what had happened since we had last seen each other in Landsberg. Dee had been sent to a so called NAPOLA (a Nazi Political school) by his half Jewish father. In those schools they were trained to be the future cadres for the Nazi upper crust. Peter Bergner might have thought that it was a good way to save Dieter from going to a concentration camp.

Two days before the Russian troops had reached Landsberg, Dieter came home from school to urge his father to crank up the old Packard car and flee with the whole family. His father told him that was nonsense. He was convinced the Russians would need his dry cleaning and laundry services and so he was going to stay. After the Russian Army entered Landsberg, Peter Bergner, a capitalist, was deported to a labor camp in the Ural Mountains, where he died. Dieter's youngest sister Inge was abducted by a Russian officer and was never heard of again. All efforts to locate her through the Red Cross failed. She was probably raped and then murdered. Dieter's oldest sister Anneliese had been murdered earlier in the war by her husband, a staff sergeant in the Luftwaffe. He had learned that she had an affair with another man while he was at the front in Russia. He took an emergency furlough, came home, confronted her while she was walking down the street and point blank shot her. Dieter's mother, and the two other sisters survived the war. I was shocked to hear the gruesome news, especially about Inge, who had been a good friend of mine.

Whenever Martha and I went out to visit Dieter we had to keep an eye on the clock, because the last streetcar departed at 10:30 PM. We each lived about 15 miles away, and in two different parts of Stuttgart. We often had to sprint to catch the last car.

On my first visit with Dieter I had mentioned that I had applied for immigration to Canada, and Dieter said that sounded interesting, and that he would also apply. I was skeptical, because he was not the type of person to do something in a hurry. On one of my following visits Dieter mentioned that he had filled out an application and sent it to the Canadian Immigration Consulate. Dieter was at odds with his uncle and father-in-law. Mr. Woltmann, who was Jewish, had been a member of the communist party, and had spent time in a concentration camp during the Nazi era. He was still convinced that communism was the solution for the world's problems.

Dee, Vera, Martha and I became close friends, and I especially liked Vera. After she had given birth to their first daughter, Judith, we often went on hikes and trips together. We exchanged a lot of ideas and enjoyed the beautiful surroundings of Stuttgart.

Traveling American style

Sometimes Henry and Ronney invited Martha and me to go on trips with them. Since Henry had a car it was a lot more fun than squeezing into crowded trains or buses. Henry smoked cigarettes and he always had some good cigars in his car. One time he offered me one, but even though I smoked, the cigar didn't sit too well and I got sick to my stomach. Henry came to a screeching halt at the next farmhouse and got some Alka-Seltzer from his glove compartment. Ronney got a glass of water from the farmer. It worked and we continued on our way to Heidelberg.

The trouble with Henry was that it took an unreasonably long time to get from A to B. He was a compulsive eater, and whenever he saw a nice restaurant, he had to stop. He had an encyclopedic knowledge of good restaurants in southern Germany. He dragged us to far-out places that we didn't even know existed. We roamed down the Neckar River valley, stopped at a place that he knew, and had a fantastic steak, at a time when the average German restaurant didn't even know what a steak was. How he managed to have all these connections was a constant puzzle to me. Henry could hardly speak German, but he always got what he asked for.

I suspected that Henry was connected with a different American organization than what he said. Ronney sometimes had to retrieve his car from someplace, supposedly because he couldn't show his face there anymore. Other times he disappeared for weeks. We never knew what he was up to. Ronney finally broke up with him, but a considerable time later he showed up at our place, this time in U.S. Army uniform, and with a new girl friend. Then we lost track of him.

Years later we discovered a picture in a Canadian magazine of the same Henry Kaminski, and just about keeled over. He was getting married to a German lady right on the border bridge between Canada and the USA. Henry was standing on the Canadian side, and his bride on the U.S. side. For some reason Henry, who was divorced, couldn't remarry in the States, but could in Canada.

Getting married

In 1949 Martha and I finally decided to get married. Her parents were pissed off, because I didn't want a church wedding, just a simple civil ceremony. My father-in-law immediately accused me of being a communist. To me that was the dumbest accusation I had ever heard. He was a member of the Social Democrat Party and his party was closer to the communists than any other party.

At breakfast on our wedding day, her mother served us only a piece of dry bread. She said that it was just a day like any other day. I had never encountered anyone that rude and obnoxious in my entire life, except in the military, and I should have walked out right there and then. But Martha wasn't on good terms with her parents either, so I didn't want to let her down.

After the civil ceremony was over we had a nice dinner at her parent's home with Martha's brother and his girl friend and a few other people. Martha wore a pretty white dress that had come from Chicago, and I wore the dark pin-striped suit that had been tailored from the material my uncle had given me. The wedding was small and simple and in tune with the tough times.

The biggest problem was to get a place of our own. We were not willing to put up with the constant complains and sarcastic remarks by Martha's parents and her brother. Martha and I tried every possible angle with the bureaucracy that rationed living space, and the agency that tried to help refugees to get reestablished. It took us several months to get a reasonable room in the western part of Stuttgart.

Our 20 x 20 foot "apartment" (compartment would have been a better definition) soon started to look quite livable. It was on the third floor, and the windows opened towards the street side. There wasn't a wash basin or toilet in the room, and we had to go over to the landlord's flat for these conveniences. We got along just fine with the landlord's family and there were never any problems.

Now that we had our own four walls, and privacy, we could have sex any time we wanted, and we took advantage of it. However Martha was beginning to have serious female problems. At first we thought it was because we had so much sex, but after a consultation with a gynecologist, he discovered that there were several problems with her ovaries and fallopian tubes. The physician couldn't determine exactly where the problem was, and suggested exploratory surgery.

At first we were both against it, but since she had a history of severe menstrual problems, and had several times been in the hospital for curettage, she finally decided to have the surgery. After that was over the doctor told me that he had to removed one ovary and fallopian tube. In his opinion she would not be able to have any children.

This information upset me, and I contemplated a divorce. Martha had a difficult time coping with the problem herself. It took her a long time to recover from the surgery, and I think that was an emotional turning point in our relationship. We made love like we had before, but something was missing. As time progressed, I, who was aware that I was the last male member of my family, felt that I was betraying my ancestors by not having any children.

I worked part time, and found another job in Ludwigsburg, but not in ophthalmic optics. The company was a nationally known manufacturer of fire extinguishers. It was an interesting job and the pay was much better, but I developed a severe reaction to a protective nitrocellulose lacquer that the company sprayed on the finished product. It was done in a spray booth that was supposed to have adequate ventilation, but the fumes were everywhere in the building.

My face and hands broke out in a rash, and I even had a rash on my penis. The doctor did not know of any medication for this particular allergy, so he decided to give me intramuscular calcium injections. His theory was that the calcium would "seal" the skin against external irritants. That theory sounded like believing the moon was made of green cheese. The physical sensation of these calcium injections was weird. The liquid was injected into the thigh muscles, it took a few seconds to get into the bloodstream. It felt like a hot liquid being slowly distributed throughout my body. After a few minutes the sensation ended. I must have had at least 10 injections and the rash didn't even lessen. Then he put me on a high dose of vitamin A and that seemed to have an effect. I had no choice but to quit the job. It took me a long time to get over it completely.

What vintage is that?

I enjoyed writing articles for the South German Optical Journal and liked the owner and chief editor, Rudy Neuss. Rudy was a real character who had started the Journal on a shoestring. It filled an urgent need for trade information in the field of ophthalmic optics. Writing for a technical journal is a highly specialized field, which requires a thorough knowledge of the technical subject and an exact writing style, without being boring. Rudy was a very strict editor, and in the beginning I had to rewrite almost every article that I submitted. Rudy taught me good technical writing.

Rudy had another skill. He was a wine connoisseur, who had been trained by his father who was a vintner. One could present Rudy with a glass of wine, and without seeing the bottle, he could tell what wine and what vintage year it was. I tested him many times at home and at restaurants and he never failed a test. Martha and I tried to trick him at times, but we couldn't lead him astray. He loved wine, had grown up with it, and at times drank too much of it. When he was in one of those "drink just to forget" moods, he did crazy things.

He came to our place with several bottles of Piesporter Goldtröpfchen, and we went into a long "sampling session". All of a sudden Rudy crushed an empty wineglass in the palm of his hand, as if it were a piece of paper. He cut his hand of course, but he then took a piece of the broken glass and chewed it. It was really crazy. We bandaged his hand before he left for home and I had to go down the staircase with him to unlock the main entrance door. Rudy slid down on the banister to the bottom of the staircase, grabbed the carved wooden ball on top of the last banister and twisted it off. He said nonchalantly good-bye and left. Martha and I were at a loss about his behavior, something must have really bothered him that day. May be it was the fact that I was married now, and he wasn't. I carefully reattached the knob, but the next day somebody else grabbed it, and it came off again. The lady who owned the building was bitching about it for days. I never said a thing, for fear of being evicted. Rudy sincerely apologized.

Another time Rudy took me to a restaurant to have me sample a wine that he had discovered there. He told the waiter what to bring.

After he had tasted the wine, Rudy said to the waiter, "That's not the wine I had yesterday." When the waiter assured him that it was, Rudy got angry and demanded to see the owner of the restaurant. When the waiter introduced the owner, Rudy asked him if that was indeed the so and so wine, and the owner assured him it was. Rudy stared at him for a few seconds, and then asked him how he stored that wine. The owner now sensed that he had a real expert on his hands, and got a little fidgety and visibly uncomfortable. Rudy waited, staring at him, and the owner then had to admit that he had put yesterday's bottle back into the refrigerator, and the wine Rudy had sampled today was from that same bottle. Rudy was really pissed, asked him for another bottle, and ordered him to "uncork at the table." This was done, and after Rudy had tasted it, he declared that it now tasted like the one he had the previous day. After that, he let me sample it too. It was so good that we emptied two bottles of it. When we left the restaurant, he told me that he had noticed the distinct change in the bouquet of the wine. He knew his wines inside out, and over the years all the restaurant owners who served wine in and around Stuttgart must have known and feared him. There was no way to cheat him.

As mentioned before, I had written a number of technical articles on ophthalmic subjects for his magazine, just to get recognition. I was a frequent visiter at the America House, the US library in Stuttgart. The ophthalmic articles published in the USA were most interesting to me. Since almost the entire German optical industry had been destroyed or dismantled during and after the war, there was an enormous product information gap. To fill that gap, I wrote an article about Bausch & Lomb's frames and lenses for the Optical Journal. It was published, and I sent a copy of the article to Bausch & Lomb in Rochester, New York. They wrote back thanking me for the article and they asked me if there was anything they could send me as a token of appreciation. I replied that one of their Ray-Ban frames with prescription sunglasses would be most welcome, since I couldn't get anything like that in Germany. I provided my prescription and frame dimensions, and was surprised when they sent me exactly what I wanted. I never got anything from a German manufacturer after writing about their products.

How did he get away that fast?

In the summer of 1951 Dieter Bergner, much to my envy, got his immigration visa for Canada. It irked me that he was going first, especially since he had applied much later than I. Dieter had a job offer in

Edmonton, Alberta. We had one hell of a going-away-party for him, and I made him promise to help me to get over there after he was established in Canada.

Dieter was in Edmonton, Alberta for a few months, where he worked in a coal mine, then he found a job in dry cleaning and moved to Grande Prairie, 400 miles northwest of Edmonton. He bought an old house for $ 2,500 and wrote to Vera to come over. He wrote that she didn't need to bring any household goods, because he had everything. Knowing Dieter I was a bit skeptical, but that was Vera's problem.

In December of that year Vera and her two little kids boarded a ship for Canada. Vera, with Judith, 2 1/2 years old, and Regina, about 1 1/2 years old, got into one hellish crossing on an old Greek passenger liner. They got into the same storm that sank the "Flying Enterprise" near the southwestern coast of England. The three Bergners were dreadfully sick when they arrived in Halifax, Nova Scotia. They still had a five day train trip to Grande Prairie ahead of them. Vera couldn't speak any English and when they arrived in Edmonton, Regina was in critical condition. The Canadian Red Cross finally helped them. When they reached Grande Prairie, the temperature was 20 below zero and the kids were just barely alive.

Vera went into the kitchen to prepare a bath for the kids, and looked around for a water tap. Dee pointed to a closet door, and when Vera opened it, there was a 55 gallon drum filled with water. So much for conveniences Canadian style. Vera was furious with Dee. She wrote to Martha and me that he only had the most rudimentary household items on hand. She also enclosed a picture of herself with a little baby and we couldn't figure out who that was. When we looked at the back of the photo it read: Stewart 4 weeks old. We couldn't believe that they already had another kid.

After I had recovered from my skin allergy, I went job hunting in Stuttgart again. I found a job with Marwitz & Hauser, a company with a modern factory in the Heusteigstrasse which manufactured high quality frames for eyeglasses. The company was owned by a Mr. Schneider, who ran a very tight ship, but offered extraordinary facilities and benefits to the employees. His company was miles ahead of any other in the field. He had made his money during the depression in the United States, returned to Stuttgart around 1930, and bought the company. The manufacturing operation was housed in a cheerfully painted building, and had the best machinery, manned by hand-picked employees. By 1950 they were already exporting their non-plus-ultra lens frames to over 50 countries. Their products were sold to well qualified opticians only, and were the envy of the frame industry throughout the world. They were at a quality level of the Mercedes Benz cars that come from the same city. The company had about 350 employees at that time.

I was trained to work in the final quality control department. Every frame went through that department where 20 men shaped and aligned the product into its final shape. There was a nice dining area, with menued meals that were subsidized by the company. There were no coffee breaks, but about 10:00 am and 3:00 pm a food and beverage cart came to each work area, and we could buy a sandwich or Danish, cookies, coffee or tea. Friday afternoon we could even buy a bottle of beer. This system eliminated time consuming runarounds by employees during ten minute breaks, and made efficient use of work hours.

One attraction was an unheard of employee weekend outing with all family members to the wine growing area along the Rhein River. The company rented an entire railway train for the outing. On a Saturday morning we left for Rüdesheim am Rhein, where we embarked on an excursion steamer. It went up one side of the Rhein and down the other, stopping at all the famous wine growing towns so we could sample their products. All that "sampling" caused a few casualties, unfortunately including my wife. She could normally hold her liquor well, but she got sick on this trip. This was an embarrassment for me, because each employee was being scrutinized by the bosses. We all had a lot to drink, but there was little tolerance for uncouth behavior and if there was, the bosses took notice. We returned late on Sunday, and I had to take a taxi to get Martha home and into bed. She was sick for several days.

I wasn't too keen on events like that because I was never comfortable in the presence of masses of people, and I didn't like to drink with that much "observation" either. Oktoberfest type of activities were not my thing. I was much more comfortable with friends, whom I could trust and drink with, without being scrutinized. Probably a hangover from the Nazi times and their mass rallies and marches.

Despite the good working conditions, I was restless and putting out feelers to other companies for a better job. At Marwitz & Hauser the atmosphere was too restrictive. Mr. Schneider was convinced that only he knew how to manufacture top quality frames. He laughed about all competitors, saying they didn't even know what good lens frames looked like, let alone how to make them.

My articles in the optical journal had attracted industry attention, and a number of frame manufacturers contacted me, to see if I wanted to work for them. Only one looked worth the effort. I had to keep all contacts with competitors secret, or I would have been fired. After I had come to an agreement in Frankfurt/Main with a Mr. Boeller, I didn't mention my reason for leaving at Marwitz & Hauser. I told the personnel office that my emigration to Canada had come through, and that I would be leaving via Frankfurt in the near future. That way they couldn't force me to sign an exclusion document.

My colleagues kidded me right away and called me "Canada Hannes." They said I would be drafted into the Royal Canadian Air Force. Since there was no conscription in Canada that was nonsense, but these guys didn't know that and they had invented that reason just to ridicule me.

Former top Nazis reappeared in the newly formed West German Government. The mistrust among the former Allies, particularly towards Russia, had developed into the cold war. That was one of the reasons why they needed the German's "expertise" about Russia, and why the old Nazis were able to resurface and offer their services. Of course the same happened in East Germany and I figured, that sooner or later they would try to outdo each other and merrily go to war again. I hoped to be away from Europe when this scenario took place. I didn't trust the Russians, but I didn't trust the western Allies either. The Canadian Government seemed to be the only one that kept out of this insane paranoia.

In 1951 after some hard bargaining I had an agreement with Mr. Boeller to come to Frankfurt and design a whole new line of eyeglass frames for his company and update his manufacturing facility to manufacture the new merchandise. We had to move to Frankfurt, but I thought my immigration to Canada would soon come through.

Looking civilized again, 1947.

Back into opthalmic optics, 1947

Farewell party given by colleagues at Marwitz and Hauser, before leaving for Canada, 1951.

My friend, Kurt König, as a political Kommissar with the VolksPolizei, 1951

The Price of this goddamn war

The first statistics about the human losses in the war became available and they boggled my mind. They said that it is the first time in a war that the Civilian losses exceeded the Military losses. I thought that was hard to believe.

Germany, Military KIA:	3,250,000
Civilians killed	3,810,000
Total losses:	7,585,000
Austria, Military KIA	380,000
Civilians killed	145,000
Total losses:	525,000
All losses on German side	8,110,000*

* **These are not exact figures, which will never be available!**

A wise man's country is the world.
Astippus

21
Last Stage Before Exit

After the hustle and bustle of packing our meager belongings and having them picked up by a trucking company, we were off on the express train to Frankfurt/Main, not Frankfurt/Oder. From the main railway station in Frankfurt, I called Mr. Boeller, and his secretary gave me the address of a family in a suburb of Frankfurt who put business travelers up in their house.

This rooming business was widespread in Frankfurt, a city which had numerous business conventions and exhibitions, called "Messen" (trade shows). These shows often brought tens of thousands of visitors to the city, far in excess of the hotel room capacity. Residents set up a room or rooms in their apartments or houses to accommodate these guests, and make extra money. Martha and I got one of these rooms, and Martha went out hunting for a permanent place, since I had to start working right away.

Even six years after the end of the war it was difficult in Frankfurt, or any other German City to find a room or apartment. Rebuilding was progressing slowly due to a shortage of capital and material. In Frankfurt about 50 percent of all buildings were still rubble. The situation was aggravated by the occupational forces, who had confiscated many of the inhabitable buildings for their own purposes.

Being a city person, Martha felt right at home in Frankfurt, and found us a large room in a ten room apartment. Mrs. Zureck, the apartment owner, had thirteen family members and relatives living in the huge flat, but still rented two rooms to outsiders. Occasionally there were problems as far as kitchen and bathroom use was concerned. Everybody was used to these high density accommodations in the postwar period and tried to make them as frictionless as possible. Mrs. Zureck's husband, an art dealer, had died during the war, and had left her with three kids and no income. She had done remarkably well by renting part of her flat, and selling off some of her valuable art objects. The place was right on Fürstenberger Strasse, a couple of blocks from the huge I. G. Farben Hochhaus, the headquarters of the U.S. military government in Germany.

Boeller & Co. was family owned, which I didn't know when I agreed to join the company. Shortages caused by the war and the destruction of many manufacturing plants, as well as the complete dismantling of the ophthalmic industry in the Russian occupation zone, created a booming market for optical goods.

Boeller & Co. produced frames for eye glasses. It was a fairly small manufacturer with about 150 employees, and was not a top quality company. Technically their manufacturing techniques were "medieval" compared to the company I had left in Stuttgart, but that was Mr. Boeller's reason for hiring me. I was to update the company's manufacturing processes. It was a job I loved to do, and was good at.

I had to win support within the company for my improvements. My salary was good, so I was able to stomach the work climate for a while. Valuable help and support came from a Hungarian woman by the name of Elizabeth, who was a skilled draftsperson. My prime job was to design new lens frames and set up the manufacturing processes for them, and she was exceedingly helpful at the documentation end of that task. She also had an uncanny way of handling some of the difficult human relations problems for me.

She knew that at times I bit off more than I could chew, and gave me advice and support. Another colleague, a fellow optician, and a mechanical engineer, also gave support and help.

It was just a matter of time for the good working relationship with Elizabeth to blossom into an extramarital love affair. Elizabeth was not married, and was more than willing to lure me away from Martha. She knew that Martha could not have children, because we had talked about her female problems. Elizabeth showed that she was exceedingly good in handling children when we surveyed a kindergarten to determine what kind and size of lens frames fit small children. This was needed information for me as a frame designer. I was surprised how gently, but firmly she handled these rambunctious children, and thought to myself, "Now, here is a woman I could have a family with." However, "Where there is much light, there is also much shadow," as an old Greek philosopher observed two thousand years ago.

Elizabeth's parents, with whom she lived, were from Hungary. Her mother, a short, immensely energetic person was a nurse at a local hospital. She was called the "Short Force" because she wasn't more than 5'-1" tall. Elizabeth's father was an "artist", a painter of church art and a typical Bohemian character. Since both his wife and daughter worked, Mr. Loewe didn't expend much effort to do likewise. He behaved like an oriental potentate. The only hobby he had was growing peppers (paprika) and he claimed he could determine how hot a particular pepper was just by looking at it. In my opinion that was not a cash producing business skill, because there wasn't that much of a demand for paprika. Elizabeth's parents liked me, but I just could not see supporting the "artist" for the rest of his life. The Loewes had already applied for emigration to Brazil, with their church organization footing the bill.

Martha had found herself a job at a food chain store near our apartment. She smoked heavily and never had any desire for any physical activities. Biking was a good and fast way of getting around in Frankfurt, a large city, in flat country and much of the city had bike lanes on the sidewalks. Automobile traffic was still minimal in the early fifties. To own a car was financially out of the question for us. After much discussion I finally convinced Martha that we should buy two bikes, and since she never had a bike in her childhood, I was going to teach her how to ride it. It was another case of underestimating the difficulty of a task. I finally succeeded in teaching her how to ride, but it was a long struggle. Painful for her, and frustrating for me.

After weeks of practice on Martha's part, we went on bike tours throughout the beautiful parks and countryside around Frankfurt, and Martha began to enjoy the bike rides. I often went on more strenuous tours on my own, especially since Martha had to work on Saturdays.

Now 1952, we enjoyed the improvements that showed up in Frankfurt, a new store that opened, or a concert, or merchandise that reappeared on the market. Martha had been able to get us two tickets for a performance by Louis Armstrong and Ella Fitzgerald, two of our favorites. The concert was a smash hit in more than one way because big Ella fell off the stage and crashed into the orchestra pit.

Swing, bebop and classical jazz were reappearing everywhere, and the presence of GIs and civilian Americans made these events possible. In those days they called Frankfurt the Chicago of Germany.

On one of our bike outings we went to see an old friend, Max Scholz, from Landsberg, whom I had found through other refugees in West Germany. Max and I had been in the rowing club together. Max had gotten married and had established a successful Ma and Pa type store in a small town east of Frankfurt. We had exchanged information about former Landsberg friends and their fates and whereabouts.

Starting for home, Martha did not pay attention to her biking, and raced down the cobblestone street from Max's house. She went way too fast to turn the corner, ran right into the curb and crashed onto the sidewalk. It happened so fast I couldn't even open my mouth to tell her to brake and slow down. She had painful bruises on her lower leg and thigh and was crying. Max's wife had observed the whole accident, and she brought Martha a big glass of brandy and applied cold compresses to her leg. Then we biked slowly to the nearest streetcar stop and I helped her to get on.

I biked home leading her bike by the handlebar, since we couldn't take it on the streetcar. Fortunately we had a doctor living in the same building and she was willing to have a look at Martha's leg. Nothing was broken, but Martha had real nasty bruises and was ordered to stay home and preferably in bed for a few days. During the next days the color of her leg went through the rainbow spectrum, but no lasting damage was done.

Hot Hungarian paprika

Elizabeth had shown me a picture of a small girl, and asked if I thought that this child was adorable. I told her that the girl was cute. She hadn't told anyone in the office who the child was, or what her name was.

Weeks later she told me that she would love to go to bed with me, but didn't know where this would be possible. She absolutely insisted that it had to be in a bed. We couldn't do it at her place, since her father was always home. I had overheard a fellow renter telling of a woman who rented rooms by the hour. The man told me that I could give his name as a reference. Of course this was strictly confidential information, he said, since the police didn't look kindly at that kind of business. He mentioned that he himself had used her place, and that it was clean and safe.

When I mentioned it to Elizabeth, she was apprehensive, but willing to try it. We met at the house, and walked up to the third floor. When I rang the doorbell, an older, prissy looking woman opened the door. When I told her who had recommended her, she let us in and mentioned a stiff hourly price. She showed us a small, clean room with a bed, a wash basin and a door to an adjacent toilet. The bed linen was spotlessly laundered.

We undressed and she snuggled up to me and we made love. When you have sex with somebody for the first time it is exciting, and as long as it feels good for both partners, size doesn't matter. I was young and horny all the time. With all that abstinence during the war years, I had a large sexual backlog. After the euphoria wore off, we got dressed and parted in a joyous mood.

Back at work on Monday she asked me how I liked it, and I said that I enjoyed it, but that I was surprised about her size. She asked if that really mattered and I said, didn't you know the old German saying "no joy without friction", and she broke down laughing. She reminded me that both men and women came in different sizes, and that was just the size she was.

Later that week she told me that she and her family had just received a formal notification that their immigration visa to Brazil had been approved. She told me I should make up my mind whether I wanted to go to Brazil too, and that it would be fun to start a new life over there.

Four weeks later she told me that she was pregnant. I was surprised, because I was still under the impression that during a woman's period conception wasn't possible. It showed that I was woefully misinformed. Thinking back it started to dawn on me that she might have deliberately misled me about her period when we made love.

Martha had gotten wind of my affair and had managed to confront Elizabeth somewhere in downtown Frankfurt. Elizabeth had coldly told her that she was carrying my child and that she was not going to give me up. When Martha talked to me about it, I began to realize that the whole thing had been a set up by Elizabeth, and I told Martha so. I told her if she wanted a divorce, she should see a lawyer.

I talked to Elizabeth and said that in my opinion it would not be a good idea to emigrate to Brazil being pregnant. We discussed the reasons and I thought she agreed with me. I asked her what I could do to help her out of that situation. She stated that she didn't know of any physician who would perform an abortion. I promised to talk to my physician and did so immediately. I mentioned to him that Elizabeth was going to Brazil and she didn't want to arrive there pregnant. He agreed to perform the procedure, if she was less than eight weeks pregnant. Elizabeth promised to see him and I checked with her to see how it went. She mentioned that the doctor had asked her whose fault it was that she was pregnant, and she had told him it was her boyfriend's fault. No names were mentioned in the discussion.

Later I wondered whether she really had been pregnant, and whether she actually had an abortion. Elizabeth and her parents left for Brazil a few weeks later, and when she came to say good-bye at Boeller & Co. she said to me, "Remember, I am going to wait for you over there."

Later I often thought about our affair, and regretted that despite it all we didn't get married. We could have stayed in Germany and had a nice family. I also wondered of course, if there might be a child of mine living in Brazil with grandchildren etc.

Two months later I got a letter from Sao Paulo, Brazil, telling me that they had arrived, and that Peter had been there to greet them. I didn't know who this Peter was. She wrote that she had gotten a job, but that the work climate for women was not the best.

Another great escape

In the meantime I was busy with my own emigration plans. We were writing the year 1953 and I still had not heard from the Canadian Immigration Department in Karlsruhe, despite several letters and a trip to their office. I was getting annoyed at these Canadians for not turning their hearing aids on and at least giving me an answer.

In the meantime I heard from the Brazilian Consulate that there was no problem letting me immigrate into their country. However in light of Elizabeth telling me about Peter, whom I suspected of being her former lover and possibly the father of the little girl in the picture, I abandoned the idea of following her.

I was increasingly uncomfortable in my job, particularly since Elizabeth was gone. She had been a great help in the design work. The new girl who took her job was a dud in her work, as well as in her character. I had secretly contacted the Rhodenstock company in München. Their product line showed that they had a more modern attitude in frame design, and I would have liked to work for them. They asked me for references, and a resume. Mr. Boeller must have smelled a rat, and made me sign a three year employment contract.

Then, on February 28, I got a letter and questionnaire from the Canadian Immigration Department, the first positive sign in two years! Yippee, that just came at the right moment. I filled it out and returned it immediately. I also started to think that this might be the only way out of my contract. I immediately send off a note to Dieter in Grande Prairie, Alberta, Canada, asking him to send me a letter of "intend to employ" no matter how fictitious.

In March of 1953 the International Automobile Exhibition took place in Frankfurt. This was a big event, and Martha and I had to go and see it. Since there weren't many German cars available, we were particularly interested in the U.S. display. One of the most popular cars to me was a Buick "Skylark" convertible, which was of impressive size and luxury.

Coming home from work on Monday the 13th (!), while crossing in front of an approaching streetcar, I had a head on collision with another biker, who had tried to do the same in the opposite direction. Even though I instinctively turned my right shoulder forward to cushion the crash, the impact was considerable. I had terrible pains in my right shoulder, and could hardly move my right arm. The other guy had a good sized lump on his forehead, but was otherwise OK. The bikes had survived with minimal damage.

Martha got hold of the female physician on the first floor, who examined my shoulder and thought it was dislocated. She said that she wasn't strong enough to reset it herself, but gave me a painkiller and a transfer to an emergency hospital, at the other end of town.

We rode the streetcar to the emergency station located in an old underground bomb shelter. The waiting room was filled with at least 20 people, all waiting to get first aid. After two hours it was my turn. An X-ray showed that my shoulder was not dislocated, but that I had torn the ligaments that connect the outer end of the clavicle with the shoulder blade. The doctor said there was nothing that could be done and that it would eventually heal. He put a huge wire brace under my right arm and bandaged everything up. It looked like the wing of a "Stuka," the notorious German dive bomber, and was actually called that. He gave me a referral to an orthopedic specialist.

The injury was the least welcome thing at this time, and could possibly spoil my chances of getting out of Germany. We went home, and I had a couple of good shots of cognac, to numb both the physical and psychological pain. At midnight I finally went to bed, only to find that sleeping was not easy with this "Stuka". I was depressed.

A few days later the "Stuka" brace was taken off, and an orthopedic surgeon put a stiff bandage around the shoulder and put my right arm in a sling. He told me that there were several ways to surgically reattach the clavicle to the shoulder blade, but in his experience that was not satisfactory and would cause additional problems later on. "Why me, Lord?", I thought to myself. First the childhood injury to my right leg which was an ever present impediment and now another permanent problem with my right shoulder. I was a physical wreck at an early age. But as Nietsche said, and as I was told many times in the Hitler Youth and the military, "What doesn't kill you, makes you stronger." Fine piece of bullshit that was. Only a masochistic German philosopher could have come up with that.

On Saturday, April 18, I received another letter from the Immigration Authority, requesting that I get the enclosed long list of documents together and have them in my possession when I came to Karlsruhe on June 12, for my medical screening. Bang! That was me "fainting." I had been waiting for over two years to be called for this screening, and when did it happen? Right after an accident. I didn't know about Murphy's Laws then, but old Murphy was looking over my shoulder already.

I had to bring my passport, a chest x-ray, proof of immunization, a document from the police department that I had never been convicted of a crime, nor that I was a parolee, a bum, a Nazi, a prostitute, or any other undesirable element of society. I had to get a release from the German equivalent of the IRS, saying that I had paid all my taxes and didn't owe anybody any money. Furthermore, I had to have at least five sworn statements by prominent citizens, such as lawyers, bankers, professors or physicians, that I was a law-abiding human being, of solid moral foundation, and that I polished my halo daily, was wearing it above the right forehead, and similar demands. They apparently wanted saints, not hard workers, in Canada. For a refugee who hadn't lived longer then five years anywhere in Germany, getting all these papers together within six weeks, while working for a living, going to physical therapy, and getting the money together to book a passage to Canada, was a superhuman task. But I really wanted to go, so it had to be done. They made it tough to leave ye olde Fatherland, and the next six weeks were like episodes of the Keystone Cops chasing after all these documents.

Good-bye Fatherland

I first checked my passport, and discovered that it expired within the next 60 days. That meant I had to get it extended immediately. Then I wrote letters to five prominent citizens, in order to get my character whitewashed, and I made appointments with my dentist to get all my teeth in top condition so I could bite the immigration officials in Karlsruhe, in case they wouldn't let me go to the "promised land". I made an appointment with a physical therapist to get my shoulder into shape.

Next my boss called and got all upset that I hadn't come back to work. I had designed a new lens frame based on the Bausch & Lomb "Bal-Grip" principle, on which production was starting, and I was urgently needed to smooth things over. I had written the instructions for the dispensing opticians already, but the literature needed to be proofread. In other words, "Hans, get your ass back to work, we need you." I told him, "The doctor has not released me yet." Of course I couldn't tell my boss that I had all these other "super important" things to do, and no time to come back to work.

I went to various travel bureaus to find out what ship passages were available, and that was when the shit hit the fan. It was the year of Queen Elizabeth II's coronation, and a peak postwar tourist year. Half of America's population was traveling to Europe and all ships and flights were booked solid. I ran from one travel bureau to the next until I finally latched onto a ticket for a dorm type accommodation on a converted Liberty ship by the name of "M. S. Fairsea." It was leaving Bremerhaven on July 17, 1953, going to Quebec City, but I didn't have the money to buy the ticket.

The following week I was at the Department of Public Health getting my immunization, and persuading the X-ray technician to move the film an inch to the left when taking my lung X-ray, so that the right hand shoulder blade would not show up on the film. My injury would have been too obvious, and I couldn't take that chance. Finally on May seventh I went back to work even though the doctor had not released me.

On Saturday the 9th he got my X-ray film and it was "good," I picked up my extended passport at the police station, and received a letter from Dieter in Grande Prairie with an attached "letter of intent" to employ me there. Wow, some obstacles out of the way.

During the next weeks I went to physical therapy every other evening after work. The female therapist was a very pleasant and good looking lady and obviously interested in me, but Lord, where could I find the time for another love affair? Damn!

The following week, we found a Mercedes parked in front of our apartment building. Nobody who lived there owned a car. Well surprise, surprise, Martha's cousins from Chicago were on a trip through Europe, and had looked us up. We were delighted, even though it was the wrong time with all the other hectic things going on. The Chicagoans gave us moral support, took us out for dinner, and invited us to come celebrate with them down in Steinenbronn, their home town. One of cousin Gene's trademarks was that he paid everything from a big roll of 50 dollar bills that he carried in his pocket.

The next weekend was Whitsuntide and that was an official long weekend in Germany. We hopped on the train and went to the big reunion in Steinenbronn, a little village near Stuttgart, where Gene and Gertrud had been born. Gene, playing the bigshot from America, rented one of the restaurants for the night and invited everybody in the village for dinner and drinks. It was one hell of a bash and the singing and drinking lasted until the wee hours of the morning.

When Swabian people celebrate there is a lot of singing of old sentimental folk songs and the softer hearts, women as well as men, start to cry. I was brought up in a Prussian world were crying in public was socially not acceptable, particularly for a man.

At this celebration Martha started to bawl too, because she realized that she would soon leave for America and would not be able to see all these relatives any more. Gertrud, her Chicago cousin, was puzzled and said, "Martha you aren't even gone yet, and you are crying as if you were homesick, what is the matter with you?"

Another cousin we were staying with was a young and very sexy redhead who was going to get married the next weekend.

When we finally turned in at her house, the acidic Swabian wine and the emotional display of my wife made me sick. Since there were too many people for the available beds available, we slept wherever there was space.

After the holidays I went back to Frankfurt right away, because my immunization had to be checked and the recommendations had to be rounded up. I went to the police station to pick up my "conduct certificate", to the dentist to have more work done and to therapy to admire the therapist. My shoulder was getting slowly better and the pain had started to subside. I had all my papers together and was double-checking everything, so nothing could go wrong, could go wrong, could go wrong. On Friday June 12, 1953, I took the train to Karlsruhe, about 125 km south of Frankfurt, and appeared at the Canadian Immigration office right on time. After an initial check of all my documents, the secretary commented on how wonderfully complete all my papers were. I then apprehensively went for the physical. The doctor was polite, made a run-of-the-mill type examination, and then looked at my chest X-ray. He didn't notice the shoulder anomaly but questioned me about the evidence of scar tissues in my lungs. I told him that I had come down with pleurisy while in a Russian POW camp. He seemed to be satisfied with my answer, but questioned me at length about conditions in that POW camp. We had a fairly long chat about that, and that concluded the physical. Now I had to face the Immigration Officer but felt confident. I had the letter of intent to hire, and I was sure that would flatten the last hurdle.

The officer was a French Canadian and after looking at all of my paperwork, he asked me where I wanted to go to in Canada, and what kind of work I wanted to do. I told him I was set to go to Grande Prairie, Alberta, and had already a job there. The officer had a puzzled look on his face, and with that I handed him the letter of intent. He looked at it, smiled, and then told me that they get hundreds of these letters a week and that they didn't mean anything. He said he didn't believe I wanted to go to Grande Prairie. I assured him that my best friend was already living there, and I felt he would be a great help in getting me started. The Officer was not convinced, but after I offered to write him a postcard from Grande Prairie as soon as I arrived there, he changed his mind.

He then outlined the conditions for my entrance visa. I had to go without my wife, and I had to enter Canada no later than July 31, 1953. If I couldn't get there in time, he would not give me the visa. He continued, that after I was established over there, I would have to contact the local immigration office to obtain a permit for Martha to come and join me. Since Dieter had gone through the same formalities regarding the spouse, we knew about that. What floored me was the July 31st entry requirement. I told the officer that in light of what I knew about ship's passages, I would have a hard time meeting that deadline. The officer replied, "That's your problem. The Canadian immigration rules do not allow any deviation from that date." I was told to send my passport for the visa stamp, only if I could prove that I had a valid ticket that would get me to Canada before July 31. That was only six weeks away.

I was happy about the outcome, but worried about my ship ticket. The Keystone Cop chase was now replaced by a good size panic. Martha had to find another apartment, because she could not afford to keep the one we had, I had to sell my bike, get suitable overseas luggage and pack my belongings. I also gave some thought as to what additional skills I could acquire to help me make a living in Canada.

I didn't have much hope that I would be able to continue in the ophthalmic field. The Canadians never told anybody what they were looking for. They wanted manual labor people, plus a few highly specialized professionals such as tool and die makers and welders. I was lucky enough to latch onto welding. I took a night class at the adult education system that taught arc-welding. The class met three times a week and ran four weeks. It was a good class with theoretical and extensive hands-on training.

After my return from the Immigration Office, I had to get confirmation of a berth on a ship and the rail ticket from Quebec City to Grande Prairie. Finally on June 16, 1953, I had the money and got confirmation on all my tickets.

On this very same day a most frightening political event took place in the DDR (East Germany). There was an uprising of the workers against the Communist Government's action of trying to form the SED party and prohibiting all other political parties. Hitler had done exactly the same thing after he came to power. It verified my belief that a red flag was a red flag, no matter whether hammer and sickle or a swastika was on it.

The initial protests in Berlin and a few other localities developed into mass riots, and the Russian army stepped in with tanks to suppress it. Many people were killed. For a while it looked like the overture to World War III. I was scared shitless that I wouldn't be able to get out of Europe before things blew up.

On June 17, I sent my passport and copies of my tickets to Karlsruhe, and eight days later on June 25, I had my validated passport with the desired immigration visa stamp in it. In three weeks I would go to Bremerhaven to board the MS Fairsea and sail into a new and different life. On June 30, after getting my paycheck, I finally had all the money to pay for my trip from Frankfurt to Grande Prairie.

There was only one more thing to do, and that was to sneak out of my employment. Since I had accrued vacation time, that wouldn't be too difficult. I applied for my two weeks vacation, starting Monday July 13, and it was granted. Saturday was my last day of work. I casually went around the company and told certain key people that I would be back in two weeks, and to leave difficult problems until then. They had made life difficult for me there, so I had no qualms about giving them a snow job.

Following my "departure" from work, I went to the railway station, and checked the larger pieces of luggage through to Bremerhaven. On the way home I bought several bottles of good champagne, and hopped on the streetcar in the best of moods. We had one hell of a party with the Zureck family, and they assured me that they would keep their mouth shut about the whole affair.

We gave up the apartment on the 15th of the month. Martha had already found a smaller and cheaper place to live, and we had moved her belongings to the new place. We celebrated good-bye with a bottle of champagne and we made love for the last time in Germany. Then we left for the main railway station, had a nice dinner at the station restaurant, we kissed good bye and at 20:15 hour sharp, the train to Bremen moved out of the Frankfurt main station. The "express train" trip took ten hours, and there were no sleeper cars. I had at least two weeks of travel ahead of me. I started with the minimum amount of money for the trip, plus $ 20.- for landing money. At 6:00 am the next morning I arrived in Bremen. I carried only a large brief case with all my papers, a toiletry kit, a set of fresh underwear and pajamas. The connecting train to Bremerhaven rolled into the station in the afternoon. I called my mother to say good bye, but the conversation was rather frosty. Mother did not approve of my emigration, but I didn't let her put any guilt into my mind.

I met a lot of people who were leaving on the Fairsea, and the first friendships developed. We talked about the emigration and the situation in Canada. Naturally everybody had a different idea as to what it would be like. A few women, most with kids, had definite information from their husbands already in Canada. Since we could not board until the next day, we had to find a restaurant and bar that was open all night. We had something to eat, and drank lots of beer, talked and dozed off at times. Next morning we went on a train to the Columbus pier and were told that we could only board in the afternoon. First I had to go through the German customs check, and my passport and immigration visa were scrutinized by officials from the Canadian Immigration Department.

The MS Fairsea was an 18,000 tons Liberty ship built as a troop transport. It was now owned by the Greek Sitmar shipping line, ran under the Panamanian flag, was registered in Liberia, and had a German-Italian crew. How was that for internationalism?

The ship still had the dorm type accommodations of a typical troop transport, with some triple-deck bunk beds. There were separate dorms for men and women and also a few staterooms. The Greek owners hadn't wasted any time or money on conversions of the ship. They had stepped right into the lucrative business of transporting millions of immigrants who were leaving Europe after World War II. The "Fairsea" was booked out with 2600 immigrants for this crossing.

My dorm was on the third deck down, close to midship. The bunks were on a first come, first choice system. Since my dorm was close to the gravitational center of the ship, I figured roll and pitch in heavy seas would not be too bad, and selected an upper bunk in a corner of the dorm close to the exit. I reasoned that an upper bed was safer, because nobody could puke or pee on me. Nothing beats experience when it comes to making important decisions. What I didn't know was that the ship's water tanks were behind the wall next to my bed. The sloshing sounds that they made in heavy seas was something I had to get used to.

During the afternoon the ship slowly filled with passengers and luggage. Most of the people had never been on board a large ship and were extremely uncomfortable, especially sleeping in the same quarters with dozens of strangers. There were many young children along who were desperately clinging to their mothers, while others had no inhibitions and stuck their nose into everything. The women seemed to be especially apprehensive. In the late afternoon the last stragglers were finally on board, and the public address system called out directions to the dining areas and the eating shifts for the different decks .

The dinner arrangement was at long tables with 16 passengers per table. Stewards put large plates and bowls with the chow of the day on the table, and everybody had to help themselves. The food was reasonably good and plentiful, the cooks and stewards were Italian, so the menus were oriented in that direction.

At 20:00 hour the ship's diesel engines came to life and two tugboats moved up on the port side. We were wondering who would be the last one aboard. As the gangway was just to be lifted off the pier a totally panicked family came running and screaming towards it and just got on 10 seconds before departure.

We all went up to the top deck to say good-bye to Germany, some tearful, some glad, including me. The lines were cast off and we slowly moved away from the Columbus Pier with the PA system playing "Arrivederci Roma" and "I wonder who is kissing her now". The dumb DJ found the German "Nun ade du mein lieb Heimatland". Fifteen minutes later when we slowly moved away from our Fatherland. There was a beautiful sunset as we saw the German coastline fade away.

With my mother in Bad Homburg 1952

My place of employment in Frankfurt 1951 to 1953

Designing new eyeglass frames, Frankfurt, 1952

Elizabeth, 1952

M.S. FAIRSEA   Letzter Gruß vor der Abfahrt aus Br

Departure for Canada on the MS Fairsea, July 17, 1953

Medio tutissimus ibis.
You will go most safely in the middle.
Ovid 43 B.C.- A.D.18

22
Go West, "Old Man"

An old sailor's song came to mind, about a sea voyage which had many passengers hanging over the railing, feeding the fish. As the Fairsea slowly moved away from the pier and out into the Weser River estuary the first passengers were seasick already and hung over the railing to feed the fish. There wasn't the slightest wave action or any motion of pitch or roll in the ship. Maybe some of the "feeders" had celebrated their departure too heavily last night, or were emotionally upset about leaving the land of their birth.

As we moved into the open North Sea, the wave action on the ship was hardly perceptible, but it caused quite an increase in the amount of fish food available. I had been seasick only once, when I was in summer camp at the Baltic Sea and went on a rough small boat trip to another coastal village. About 20 of us teenagers were so sick that we refused to take the boat for the return trip and hiked back. I remembered that embarrassment, and was determined not to let it happen again. I had plenty of anti-seasick pills along. After the month long tension of my departure I was exhausted, and was soon asleep on my upper bunk.

The next morning I got up at 5:30 to beat the masses of passengers to the washroom, and hurried to the top deck to get fresh air and check on the wave action. On deck I met Walter, whom I had talked to the previous day, and we took a long walk around the deck. He had been in the German navy during the war and had sea legs. He shared his experience to help me avoid seasickness.

We had the same chow time slot, and at breakfast we noticed that already two passengers were absent from our table. Walter told me that I should not drink too much liquid, since it would slosh in my stomach. The morning was spent watching the crew fill the swimming pool on the rear deck, and we took part in shuffleboard games. Around noon the ship entered the east end of the English Channel where a boat heaved by to put a pilot on board the Fairsea.

The wave action was getting more vigorous, but it wasn't unpleasant. I took a swim because I thought it might be my only opportunity to swim above the English Channel. I saw high cirrus clouds coming up from the northwest. Which meant a storm was approximately 24-48 hours away. We passed Dover, and the sea turned considerably rougher. When the pilot left, I watched and admired his acrobatics to get into the pilot boat. It looked like the sea was preparing some "fun" for the Fairsea and it's green passengers. We saw the crew drain the swimming pool and tying everything down.

At lunchtime 12 of the 16 passengers showed up at the table and I took my first seasick pill. On the upper deck I had to be careful not to be downwind from the many passengers hanging over the railing and generously feeding Neptune and the fish. Walter and I couldn't help but poke fun at some of them. Some guys were telling one of the sea sickies that he had better watch out when that black hole came up and not spit it out, because it was his asshole, which he would need later on. That kind of rude kidding was dangerous if one was in a downwind position.

Walter and I walked the deck extensively. The sick people were a pitiful lot and I felt sorry for them. The ship pitched heavily and rolled quite a bit, making walking on deck and under deck difficult. Walter showed me how to negotiate flights of stairs in rough seas. If the timing was synchronous with the ship's motions, jumping from the top to the bottom of the stairs was quite easy.

To pee or not to pee

The worst problems were in the bathroom. The seas were so unfriendly that peeing into a urinal caused a back-splash right over one's pants. The solution was to sit on the John, but even then I had to hold on to something tightly.

About two thirds of the passengers and a good percentage of the crew were seasick. Nobody cleaned the lower decks and stairs and walking there became unsafe. Negotiating the steel stairs was downright dangerous. The ship was in constant roll, pitch and other assorted motions. Walter and I spent a minimal amount of time below deck, because the smell alone made me sick. Walking on the open deck was difficult and we had to be constantly alert for showers of sea water coming over the bow section. Waves were 30 feet high, and occasionally much higher, and tons of water came over the deck at the roped-off bow section. Getting drenched was inconvenient, because there wasn't any way to get clothes cleaned or dried.

Down below, I had an unpleasant surprise when I opened one of my suitcases. A bottle of wine earmarked for my friends in Grande Prairie had cracked and leaked its content into my clothes. I could only spread the clothes around my bunk and let them dry, making the whole dorm smell like a wine cellar and probably making more people sick.

At the dining table four out of the original 16 people were still present, and we had one hell of a good time. Since few people were eating, the stewards gave us outstanding service. We had to watch for sliding or falling dishes with or without contents. July 21 was the worst day with a wind-force of 9 on the Beaufort scale (strong gale, 47-54 miles per hour wind), after that it got better, or maybe we got used to it. Despite the rough seas, I watched the wave action and schools of dolphins jumping through the wave troughs. All sorts of seabirds could be seen, and I marveled at their ability to exist so far from land.

It was on the sixth day of our journey that we sighted icebergs of impressive size. I thought about the "Titanic" in connection with their appearance. Around noon the first land came in sight through the fog and haze, it was Belle Isle, at the mouth of the St. Lawrence River. The next day, the Fairsea entered the St. Lawrence River. Initially we couldn't see any land, because of the enormity of the river estuary.

The ship's motions finally calmed down, and the crew cleaned up the mess. Passengers crawled out of their beds and dared to come on upper deck to recuperate. I had never seen so many pale people in my life. We passed Anticosti Island and finally entered into the land of our hope, Canada.

As the St. Lawrence River narrowed, we could see houses and roads with cars. We were surprised about the variety of the roof colors, red, green, blue and yellow. In Germany the roofs were red when covered with clay tiles, gray when covered with slate, or black when covered with asphalt. It is strange what first impressions one has in a different country.

The size of the St. Lawrence River also impressed me. We had been on it for two days and were still not close to the end of the journey. Finally, after the third day on the river, and the eighth day of our crossing, the Fairsea tied up at the pier in Quebec City, Canada. It was Sunday, June 26, 1953, at about 18:00 hour. The landing pier for immigrant ships was right under the famous Chateau Frontenac, an impressive structure.

Since the immigration people didn't work on Sunday, there wouldn't be any disembarkation until Monday morning. That was fine with most of the passengers. But the husbands down on the pier, who were waiting for their wives and kids, were not happy. A customs' guard at the gangplank prevented all traffic on or off the ship.

It was a typical warm and sunny summer evening. The passengers decided to make the best of it and celebrated their safe arrival in the "promised land." We all gathered on deck and passengers who had brought musical instruments showed up with them and a regular jam session soon developed. I was impressed by a trumpet player, who already had a job offer from a band in Canada. His solos must have been audible for at least a mile around the ship.

We all talked, danced, drank, and enjoyed each other's company. Since everybody had different destinations, people knew they would never see each other again. I regretted that I had deliberately missed out on several love affairs that were offered during the crossing.

I had to get to my destination in the fastest, cheapest way possible. I had 20 Canadian dollars in landing money, and had to cross almost the entire continent. I could not afford any extra expenses.

Just in time

The next morning, Monday July 27, (please remember July 31 was the deadline for my arrival) we disembarked. We were herded into a large, two story warehouse building, where our luggage had been piled in big, disorderly mountains. We had to find our suitcases and line up in front of the customs and immigration officers who sat behind tables with the letters of the alphabet attached to the tables. We had to step up to the letters that our family name started with.

While searching for my luggage, I met three gentlemen who were bound for Vancouver. I decided to stick with them, because Frank, the leader, had been an exchange student in the United States. He was familiar with the customs and spoke excellent English.

An Italian immigrant, with a large salami sausage in his luggage, probably a gift for relatives, was told that he was not permitted to bring it into Canada. The customs officer took it away from him, and tossed it into the nearest garbage can. The Italian was absolutely infuriated and tried to talk with hand and feet to sway the customs officers mind, but had no success. After the Italian had gone through the immigration formalities, he sneaked back behind the customs guy and tried to retrieve the salami. He was caught, and was led away by another customs officer. Apparently they got an interpreter and read him the riot act, but let him get back in line.

In front of some letter desks there were long lines, while at others, such as under XYZ, there was no line at all. Frank went over to the customs officer behind that table and asked him if he would process the four of us, even though any of us didn't fall into his XYZ alphabetic name category. He didn't mind, and within 15 minutes we were through the formalities. The luggage was then checked through to the final destination by railway employees.

Since most immigrants were not fluent in English, the Canadian Immigration Department, in cooperation with the Canadian National Railroad (CNR) Company, had put together a special train. They seated passengers in the cars according to destination, and then would uncouple the cars on arrival there. We had a look at the interior of these cars. They must have come out of a railway museum. That kind of rolling stock was seen only in old cowboy movies.

We went to the CPR agent and Frank asked him if it was possible to use regular trains with the railroad tickets in our possession. The agent looked at our tickets and said there was no problem at all. He told us there was a bus line running right by the immigration hall to the downtown train station of Quebec City.

It was past noon, and we were hungry and anxious to get going. In true German tradition each of us had a briefcase, and walked to the street below to wait for a bus. However, there was no bus stop sign in the vicinity.

As a bus approached, Frank stood by the sidewalk and made a thumbs up gesture as if hitchhiking. To my surprise the bus driver stopped. We boarded the bus, but had a problem with the Canadian money to pay for the ticket. The driver gave us time and we finally got the fare together. That was the third positive impression we had of our new country, counting the courtesy and willingness of the immigration and railroad employees as the first two.

One man of the group was Paul, extraordinarily tall (probably 6'-5"), and he spoke French fluently. He had lived in Paris for several years, and was anxious to help us with his command of the language here in French speaking Quebec. He was surprised and puzzled when he found that the French-Canadians could not understand him, and he didn't understand them either. The Quebecois speak a French used in France 200 years ago. After they emigrated from France, their language got locked into that time period, because they were so far removed and isolated from France.

The four of us walked to the railroad station to find out where we would catch the Transcontinental to the west coast. Departure wasn't until 06:10 am the next morning. That was bad news because of our tight money situation. We went to the nearest eating place, and ordered a cup of coffee and a whatever low-priced item we were able to identify on the menu. I ordered a roast beef sandwich. To my surprise the "sandwich" was buried under the roast beef and mashed potatoes with a thick sauce which made the bread all soggy. I didn't like that and wondered why they bothered with the bread at all.

Frank asked the waitress' helped to find a low priced hotel, not too far from the station. We went there and the room price was $ 10.- and two guys checked into each room to save money. Frank figured how to get our food cost down to rock bottom. We went to the supermarket to purchase what we needed to feed ourselves during the next four days on the train. With the exception of Frank, none of us coming from war ravaged Germany, had ever been to a real supermarket. We roamed the isles to see what was on display. Many times we couldn't identify what certain items were, and were overwhelmed by the variety of merchandise. Frank could help out most of the time, but sometimes even he was not familiar with the merchandise.

We could only buy food that would last without refrigeration. Frank had figured out that it would cost each of us $5 to feed ourselves on this trip. We would eat mostly sandwiches with cold cuts and cheese, or with jam and peanut butter. We also bought canned fruit and soup, and I couldn't figure out what we would do with the cans of soup. Frank told us about the small kitchenettes on these long-distance trains, an unknown convenience in German trains. Frank lectured, "How do you think mothers with babies could travel for several days if they couldn't heat the bottles for the kids?" After we filled the shopping cart and checked out, we were surprised that the total was only $ 16.- dollars. Frank asked the clerk for four cardboard boxes, we packed everything neatly and went back to the hotel.

We went out to do a little sight-seeing in the downtown area of Quebec, and were not impressed at all by the city. The architecture was uninspiring, with the exception of the Chateau Frontenac, built by the Canadian Pacific Railway in 1892 and named for Louis de Frontenac, who served as the governor of "New France" in the late 17th century. The overhead power lines that crisscrossed everywhere were ugly and spoiled the views.

Our little group, after roaming the city for several hours, observing, discovering and criticizing, finally went to a small coffee shop. I had a doughnut and a cup of coffee. I really took a liking to doughnuts, but the coffee was awful. Food in Germany, even though still scarce, was always good even in restaurants. Apparently Canadians were indifferent to the quality of their meals. The emphasis was on quantity, not quality.

At the hotel, Frank made sure that the desk clerk would wake us up so we would catch the train. The $5 per person for the room really dented my budget. I had spent half of my landing money already, and I wasn't even out of Quebec City.

The next morning we walked to the railroad station with our big brief cases and cardboard boxes with groceries. In those days people in Quebec city were accustomed to strange looking characters walking around this major immigration port of entry. When we got to the station we found the station's entrance gates locked. We were told the gates would open 20 minutes before departure only. This strange custom was observed throughout Canada. We went to the coffee shop, and I had my doughnut and a cup of coffee, for a total cost of 25 cents. I was getting accustomed to my new role in life, being a POGI (Poor Old German Immigrant), so get out the violins already.

Monday is laundry day all over North America?

Just before 6:00 am we boarded the train. The railroad coaches were enormous compared to the ones in Germany, it reminded us that Canada is a BIG country. We settled into comfortable seats by the windows, so that we could have a good look at the countryside. The first thing that caught my attention was laundry flapping in the breeze to dry. Every house was "decorated" by laundry on lines. We asked Frank if all women in Canada were washing on the same day, "Yes Monday is the national laundry day on the entire North American continent." This was hard to believe, but the evidence was there for us to see. Mind you it was already Tuesday, but outdoor drying takes a while.

The scenery along the route, which more or less follows the St. Lawrence River valley, was nothing spectacular. Just low rolling hills, endless fields and forests.

Around noontime we gave our fellow Canadian travelers a luncheon show when the food boxes came out and we prepared our first rolling lunch. The Canadian coaches had a feature we had never seen before. The seats could be turned 180° so that they faced the row of seats behind. Then a fold up table between the facing seats could be brought up. We took advantage of this clever feature, and noisily prepared our sandwiches. We spiced our meal with numerous jokes and lots of laughter. I thought we annoyed the hell out of the fellow passengers, but they were all good-natured. Some tried to strike up a conversation with us, to find out where we were going. It was obvious that Canadians had a more humanistic attitude than Germans.

At 02:15 pm we rolled into Montreal. The city looked like a European city, and we felt as if we had just stepped into France. Lots of show windows, tastefully decorated, specialty stores, sidewalk cafés and even electric tramways with interesting open sight-seeing cars. These open cars had seats arranged in bleacher fashion, so that all passengers had good visibility. I was intrigued by this arrangement.

While taking in all the sights I saw a large ice cream parlor, and couldn't resist. I walked in, followed by the other three guys. Ordering from the long list of available flavors was difficult, because I was not familiar with the ice cream lingo. One of the things I could make out was, "Banana split" 55 cents. It was an enormous oval bowl with heaps of various ice creams, melted chocolate with nuts, topped by maraschino cherries, and peaking out from each end was a large banana. Wow, was that a winner with my taste buds. I had difficulty finishing the whole thing and was full for the rest of the day. This "meal" fully made up for the soggy sandwich the previous day.

On the Transcontinental

At 8:00 pm the Canadian Pacific Railways (CPR) Transcontinental train left Montreal. The train arrived from Halifax, Nova Scotia and ran across Canada, via Montreal, Ottawa, Sudbury, Winnipeg, and Calgary over to Vancouver, British Columbia. A trip of over 3,000 miles, taking five days and nights. An equivalent European distance would be from Gibraltar to Murmansk.

The train was much more comfortable and luxurious than the one from Quebec City. It had reclining individual seats in the coaches. The seats could also be turned to face a central table. It was air conditioned by large blocks of ice in compartments under the coaches, and it had a kitchenette at one end of the coach. The outside scenery was visible through huge windows that could not be opened. The train had sleeping cars which we couldn't afford and a diner, which was also too expensive for us. We all sat together, reclined our seats, and soon fell asleep. I always had problems sleeping in railroad cars, but here my tiredness from all the sight-seeing overwhelmed me. Around midnight the train stopped in Ottawa and the crew changed. They awakened everybody to check their tickets. This was strange, and was repeated at the border of each province where crew and conductors changed.

The next morning we got a glimpse of Lake Huron, later Lake Superior, and hundreds of smaller lakes north of the tracks. After the train pulled out of Thunder Bay the picture changed abruptly. We entered the Canadian prairies, the immense flat and almost treeless plain with nothing but enormous farms as far as the eye could see. It was spooky, I saw this seemingly endless, featureless expanse all day long, went to sleep and woke up the following day seeing the same featureless expanse, almost as if the train had not moved at all. We passed through the Provinces of Ontario, Manitoba and Saskatchewan with the same indistinct features being repeated.

We four guys got along just fine and I am sure we entertained all the passengers who were traveling with us. Every once in a while a German speaking person would try to practice their language on us, but there were few people who were fluent. We learned a lot of Canadian expressions, and a lot of Canadian customs as we rolled westward. The kitchenettes were really cute, if one stayed out of them when the mothers were trying to heat the food for their babies. The hungry and screaming youngsters were unnerving.

Every once in a while the train stopped at a smaller town. Passengers would file out to get fresh air, and I would get my doughnut and fresh coffee. When the train pulled into Medicine Hat, scenery became more hilly. A few more hours and we would reach Calgary where I had to get off. We had our last breakfast together. The other three guys were going to Vancouver. I thanked Frank for all the help he had given me. Frank urged me to fix myself sandwiches from what was left, because I was going to go off into the wilderness, as he put it, and I did just that.

When the Transcontinental pulled into Calgary at 09:30 am, the train was over 40 minutes late. Since I had to change trains in Calgary to go north to Edmonton, I was worried. The train conductor on the "Transcontinental" assured me that the other train would wait, but that I better hurry to catch it. He said that my luggage would follow on the next train and catch up with me in Grande Prairie.

I didn't want to bother people with questions in my school English for fear they wouldn't understand me. I could read much better than speak, and there were signs everywhere, so I had no problems. It just took a little more time. The train to Edmonton was not a deluxe one, and the engineers must have tried to get back on time after that delay of the Transcontinental. I was sure they ran the locomotive at wide open throttle. Rail beds on secondary lines were obviously not top quality either, and we were tossed around fiercely. It was almost as if I were back on the "Fairsea".

When I arrived in Edmonton I learned that the connecting train to Grande Prairie wouldn't leave until four hours later. As always: Hurry up and wait. My fanny was sore from all that sitting. I was looking forward to seeing Dieter and Vera again.

I bought a paper in Edmonton, to see if I could understand what was printed, and it wasn't easy to understand the press jargon. I understood most of the paper and that made me feel much better. Just about an hour before the train to Grande Prairie departed, Gottfried walked up to me. He was the guy who had been so sick during the ocean crossing. He had opted for the immigrant train which was run by the Canadian National Railways (CNR) and which followed a more northerly route to Edmonton. Gottfried was an excellent harmonica, piano and organ player, and was looking for a job with a church and/or small radio station. He decided to join me, and go to Grande Prairie (GP), I though however that my connections there wouldn't help him much.

When we boarded the train, I found to my consternation, that this last leg of my journey, 400 miles long, would take more than 12 hours. It stopped at every little village and loaded and unloaded milk cans and other assorted goods. The fellow passengers were also of a different kind. Most of them were farmers, housewives and blue collar workers. Some of the older women tried to talk to us. They wanted to know what church we belonged to and whether we were married. This was odd. I could not figure out why they wanted to know all these personal things and I often declined to answer. Maybe they had daughters they wanted to marry off. What I didn't realize was that I had encountered the oral community network. They wanted to know everybody, and especially new faces that were moving into the area, to see if they would "fit in."

The scenery outside was flat, with lots of trees and an occasional farm, and the godforsaken ramshackle houses, with old cars and tractors around them. I felt as if I were back in Russia again. Finally after 18 hours, on Saturday, August 1, 1953, the damn train rolled into Grande Prairie at noon. Later on when the movie "High Noon" came out, they often kidded me about my arrival time in Grande Prairie.

Dieter or Dee as they called him here and his boss Fred Reeves were at the station to pick me up in Fred's car. Fred was, I later found out, the biggest bullshitter in town, and came to the station just to know who arrived. We went to Dee's house and Vera and the kids, came out to welcome me. Then Fred Reeves took Gottfried Sprecher under his wing and left.

Arrival in Quebec City, Canada, July 26, 1953

Getting on the Transcontinental to western Canada, 1953

From Quebec to Grande Prairie, Alberta, 1953

How much a dunce that has been send to roam excels a dunce that has been kept at home!
Cowper

23
This is the Promised Land?

The way from the rail station to Dee's house reminded me of my experiences in Russia. The streets were dirt, the sidewalks were wooden boards and the wooden houses, some with false fronts, looked like "Potemkin's villages."

In the Peace River Country

It felt good to be with familiar faces and to be able to talk things over with old friends. My trip had taken 17 days from Frankfurt to Grande Prairie, Alberta. I had an urgent need to walk on solid ground, so Dee and I walked right into downtown, and he showed me where all the important stores and cafes were. Dee had a story on hand about everyone. We walked to the York Hotel and into the beer parlor, where Dee treated me to a glass of Canadian beer. The Canadian beer was good, that meant the country was good too. The beer parlor had an entrance for the ordinary lush, and an extra one for ladies and escorts. I thought that was hilarious. In the "For Ladies and Escorts" area, I saw Indian women drink a red liquid. Dee said they were mixing their beer with tomato juice. What a way to ruin perfectly good beer.

Since it was Saturday, the whole hinterland was in town, and there were quite a few "huge" cars. Dee introduced me to at least a dozen people as we walked through the shopping district. It seemed as if all of Grande Prairie knew that I had arrived. I didn't know how to respond to people when I was introduced to them. My school English wasn't good enough for chitchatting in Prairie English, but I was very impressed by the friendly attitude of people.

At Dee's house he told me he had bought it for $2,500. The inside of the house, although sparsely furnished, was reasonably comfy. There wasn't any indoor plumbing or toilet, only an outhouse in the backyard. Water was stored in a 55 gallon drum inside a kitchen closet. The drum was filled twice a week from a water truck, at 25 cents for ten gallons. I couldn't help but think, here I come from a civilized country and I have to put up with these "medieval" conveniences . That was certainly not a move in the right direction. The address for the house was: Main Street, Fifth house east of Windsor Motors. I had never seen an address like that before.

Vera had prepared hamburger with all the trimmings for supper. The weekend evening meal would become a tradition in Bergner's kitchen. Dee would always act out the Bumstead bit (as in the Blondie comic strip), by piling layers and layers of salad leaves, tomatoes, onions, pickles, mustard, relish and what have you on his hamburger bun. He would open the fridge and looked to see what else was in there that he could pile on. Eating his super-burger was another thing. We had a lot of fun, just horsing around at the kitchen table during those meals.

Then I heard steps outside, and Dee and Vera sighed, rolled their eyes, and said, "Oh no, not the Stuttgart gang again!" Several scruffy looking characters stormed in shouting in German-English, "Welcome in Grande Prairie, de Arsch of de World." Hanke, Godel, and George came in, the other two of the Stuttgart gang were in Vancouver on vacation. They schlepped several gallons of Whisky in. Well, it was one hell of a party, but I pooped out around midnight. I had to sleep in the living room on a sofa bed, because the two upstairs rooms which I was supposed to get were still rented to Kurt Elsner, a chap from Hamburg.

I negotiated the price of $25.- for room and board per week. I didn't have a job yet, but Dee said to pay him back when I had my first paycheck. Then we discussed the rental of the two bedrooms upstairs. Kurt would stay until my wife arrived because Dee needed the money.

On Monday, Dee told me that Fred Reeves had talked to Ray Menard at Steel Industries Ltd., a machine shop, and I should apply for a job. I was scared as hell, because I didn't know what to say or what kind of a job it was. I talked with Ray and he told me to start the next day, at 95 cents an hour. That was supposedly five cents more than the going rate for greenhorns, since I could speak some English. I was going to work as a machinist. I had not worked on an engine lathe before, but had work experience on pantograph milling machines and knew arc welding. What the hell, I was going to give it a try.

I had to change the language, the profession, and above all, the measuring system, and was expected to perform instantly. I was supposed to know how to set up the lathe, how to grind the tools that were used to remove metal from the work-piece, what spindle speeds and feeds to use for a specific task, and how to measure various dimensions during the machining process.

Other strange customs in Canada where the "strike anywhere" matches. These types were long prohibited in Germany because of the problems with kids. Another strange habit of smokers was using the cuffs of pants for an ashtray.

Who Me Fixing Bulldozers?

The shop foreman, Art Fenton, an old Scotsman, wasn't pleased with me, because he had to explain everything. At times I didn't understand what he said and that scared the hell out of me, because I had to earn a living.

My first assignment was to remove the hinge pins off a dozer blade on a D-6 Caterpillar bulldozer. I didn't know if this was a joke, or a test of my determination. I tried to drift the 2.50" diameter pins out using a fairly big hammer, but they just wouldn't budge. Finally Orville Nellis, one of the other workers, took pity for me and gave me a hand. He started up the engine of the D-6, and manipulated the hydraulic system to take the weight of the dozer blade off the hinge pins. Then I drove the pins out with a sledge hammer. That I couldn't have known how to do that job, didn't concern anybody. Just do it! What a great philosophy, if you succeed that is.

On my second day one of the other workers, who could speak a bit of German, told me to wait until Kurt Hofmeister, a German from Stuttgart, returned from his vacation. Kurt was a top-notch machinist, and so they assumed everybody from Germany was like him.

On Monday Kurt took me under his wing. We got along just fine and I learned quickly. Every once in a while I goofed, but it wasn't long before the shop foreman could give me any type of work. When the shop manager found out that I had drafting experience, he put me on a job designing a portable sawmill for a customer. By that time I had seen a lot of the woodworking machinery used by the local mills, but not a portable sawmill. Ray told me what he had in mind and I had some ideas that I thought would work.

The principle customers of Steel Industries Ltd. were the sawmills, the plywood factory and many oil companies. The oil guys had moved into the Peace River area in the early 1950s. Their seismic work crews were looking for oil all over the Peace River country.

Many of their jobs were beyond the equipment we had at the machine shop, but we just did them as best as we could. Even in those days the hourly expenses of an oil drilling derrick were in the thousand Dollar region. Any German shop supervisor would have had an instant heart attack, had he seen how we executed some of these jobs.

Sometimes daring, and sometimes foolhardy would be an appropriate description of the work principles involved.

On the first of September I got my first paycheck of $195.18, of which $100 went to the Bergners for room and board, and with the rest I bought a few tools needed for work.

It was time to see Mr. Ledger, the local immigration officer, and apply for a permit to bring Martha over. Vera was looking forward to her arrival, but I had mixed feelings because of our prior marital problems in Germany. I should have told her, Grande Prairie is the most miserable area I ever lived in, so it would be better if you didn't come over there. But I also had a look at the girls available here and then decided to change my mind.

By the end of September I had permission to bring her over. I rented the two small upstairs bedrooms, and with my next paycheck I bought a bed, and converted a 4x4 ft. closet, with an outside window, into a tiny kitchen. An oil heater was the next thing I installed, and there was some money left for a couple of chairs and a table. The place was livable and I was broke.

A Halloween Arrival

On October 17, Martha boarded the ship in Bremerhaven, arrived in Quebec City on the 26th, and rolled into Grande Prairie on Halloween Day. As we walked from the station she saw all the kids in costumes running around to collect their treats. This was a custom not practised in Germany. When Martha asked why all the kids were running around in funny costumes, I told her, "That is because you arrived in town," and Dee asked, "Where is your broom" but she didn't get our jokes.

There was a big hello at the Bergners, particularly from the kids, and combined with the Halloween gangs coming and going, it was a riotous reception. To top it all, the Stuttgart gang showed up to greet the newly arrived Stuttgarter. They discreetly stayed down stairs while we tried out the bed. Vera told us later that Rolf had jokingly supported the ceiling below our bedroom while we were making love.

When Rolf came up the stairs later on, he hollered in the broadest Schwabian dialect the equivalent of, "I can smell a pussy," and burst into the room. I was angry, and Martha was surprised, but that's the way these guys were. They were helpful in so many ways that one had to ignore their vulgarities.

Martha's arrival was an excuse for a party. Ray Menard and his boss Mel Rodacker came by from the shop, and Gottfried came with his accordion. Since Schwabian people always have to sing when they have a party, it was a noisy party 'til early in the morning. It was so noisy that the next door neighbors had called the Royal Canadian Mounted Police (RCMP), complaining about a bunch of DPs (Displaced Persons) making one hell of a racket. When the RCMP drove up to the house and saw Mel Rodacker's Lincoln Continental parked in front, they concluded that it was an "acceptable party" and didn't even bother knocking at the door.

After we had slept off our hangovers, Martha and I went to the supermarket to replace the food Vera had put out for the party. The variety of goods in the supermarket overwhelmed Martha and I had to translate a lot. We were very selective, since there wasn't room for a refrigerator upstairs, and we couldn't park too many things in Vera's fridge. Finally the shopping cart was filled to the top. Martha was flustered and asked if I had enough money to pay for that much food. I said sure, no problem. The total checkout came to $ 15.- she couldn't believe how cheap food was. Since Martha had worked in the food business in Germany she had a good way of comparing the prices. Of course the expression "cheap" always has to be brought into relationship with wages, and the wages were rock bottom in Grande Prairie.

In the following weeks Martha was frustrated because she couldn't read and understand the newspapers. That was not surprising, since journalistic slang baffled even the Canadians. I told her the best way to learn English would be to get a job, because it would force her to speak the language and interact with other people. She put out her feelers through "the immigrant network", and found a job at the local "Dairy Pool" (DP).

The DP was a dairy cooperative and the collection point for milk. The farmers shipped their milk in big metal cans. Some farmers were so far away that they had to ship by railroad, others shipped by routing trucks, and some delivered directly. One can imagine what the delivery mode did to the quality of the milk. At the DP the milk was graded for taste and butterfat, which determined how much the farmers got paid. Depending on quality, the DP processed the milk into various grades of drinking milk, butter, ice cream, sweet and sour cream, and then shipped the rest to a cheese or glue factory.

Martha, much to her satisfaction, started in the ice cream processing department. We all loved good ice cream. As an employee she got ten percent off the price of dairy products. Every Friday (payday) she carried home gallons of ice cream and pounds of unsalted butter for the seven people in the house. Martha's pay at the DP was 60 cents an hour, and combined with my 95 cents an hour, we just made decent wages for one person. Later on, Martha got a special license to be able to work in the laboratory, where she determined the butterfat of the milk. This job entailed a raise of two (2) cents an hour, for the grand total of 62 cents. She couldn't complain about that, or could she?

The Tank that Blew the Walls

On December 23. 1953 it was bitterly cold, around 25°F below zero, with two feet of snow on the ground. A customer had brought a five-ton truck with an oval shaped tank on its bed into the shop. The truck had hauled crude oil from an experimental oil well to the next railway stop, where the crude was pumped into a tank car. The tank was leaking because of a crack, and the shop was supposed to weld the crack. Before the truck came into the shop, the tank had been "steamed" for 24 hours, to get rid of any oil residue. It was parked in the back shop for several hours, so that the metal of the tank was at room temperature before any work was begun. On the shop wall behind the truck was a big storage rack for the company's metal bar stock. I had to machine a new wheel spindle, and needed some bar stock. I asked our old Irish shop helper to give me a hand to carry an appropriate steel bar over to the cutoff saw. I was just setting up the saw, when Orville the welder crawled halfway under the truck to start welding the crack in the tank. All the hatches of the tank were open and soon I saw thick white fumes coming out of them. As I pointed to the tank and opened my mouth to shout a warning, a tremendous explosion rocked the shop. Orville, who had been under the truck, ran out the door. A split second later we heard a terrifying roar and now everyone ran out of the building. The storage rack had been torn from the wall and dumped tons of metal bar stock to the shop floor where my helper and I had been just a minute before.

After everything had calmed down we went back into the building and our eyes could not believe the damage in both shop buildings. The explosion had pushed the wooden walls in the back shop a foot off the foundation, and had blown out all windows and doors. In the front shop, where all the machinery was, a 40 lb. four jaw lathe chuck was blown off the shelves and had crashed to the floor. It was a miracle that nobody was killed or injured.

Within minutes the siren of the Voluntary Fire Department was wailing and their engine was pulling up at the door. The firemen were stunned, and Ray Menard was really pissed off. As manager, he was going to be held responsible for this accident. With all the windows and doors blown, the temperature in the shop dropped like a rock.

We hastily grabbed a few plywood sheets and boarded up all openings, and then searched for the bottle that the Irishman always had handy. It circled until it was empty and we gave Jack money to get another one. Orville was the luckiest of the bunch, some of his clothes had caught fire and he beat the world record in 50 m sprint when he ran outside to roll in the snow to get his burning clothes extinguished. He wasn't even injured. The next ones were my helper and I. Had we been two minutes slower we would have been crushed by the collapsing storage rack of steel bars.

The truck and its tank looked like a big beer can that had been hit by a giant sledge hammer halfway between the two ends and was a total loss. Not only had it popped the tie-down straps to the truck bed, but the explosion had bent the ten-inch wide steel beams of the truck bed. Very expensive damage. Mel Rodacker, the owner of the company, came over to see what the hell had happened. He was speechless, probably calculating the cost of the damage. Both Mel and Ray were relieved that nobody was hurt and told us to go home, have a Merry Christmas, and report back after the holidays.

A Thankful Christmas

When I came home slightly drunk, I had to give them all the details of the explosion and we celebrated my survival some more. Wow, my guardian angel sure had protected me. We now had one more day to prepare for Christmas and it would be one of the best in my life. We were treated to good organ music from the local radio station. Gottfried had found a home as an organist there.

Boxing day, a Canadian tradition, is the day after Christmas, when all the gift boxes of Christmas are discarded. People go from house to house to visit their friends and neighbors, and usually have a drink. It is an excuse for one hell of a party all over town. That year we had so many friends and neighbors come to the house to hear what had happen at the shop, that we drank considerably more than usual.

After the holidays we went back to repair the damage to the shop and the truck. The entire back shop would have to be torn down and rebuilt if we couldn't get the walls back on the foundation. Ray Menard and Art Fenton came up with an idea that had me in stitches. The back shop was about 40 feet wide by 80 feet long, and about 30 feet high. Not a small building. Ray had us drill several 1.5 inch diameter holes equally spaced through the wooden outside walls. Then we threaded a number of long 1.5 inch diameter steel rods. Next we drilled a 1.5 inch diameter holes through 1/2 inch thick steel plates. These would function as large washers. The steel rods were pushed from the outside of the building through the holes in the wayward walls, with the plates and a heavy duty nut on the threaded end of the rods outside the walls. This was done also to the opposite wall of the building. Inside, in the middle of the shop, these long rods over lapped and were welded together. We now had a huge vice that had the building walls between the "jaws".

After this clever preparation, an awful lot of screwing took place in the bitterly cold winter weather and it wasn't sexy at all. As we turned the various nuts at the end of the rods in sequence, the walls started returning back in the direction they had come from, and surprise, surprise, were soon back on the foundation. A bit of fine adjustment with a 20 pound sledgehammer here and there, and the building was as good as new. A triumph of latter-day-engineering-architecture.

We had everything back to normal in the shop, everything but the truck and the tank. The repair and the fabrication of that tank turned out to be another epic of "flatbilly engineering " (there were no hills around Grande Prairie).

To begin with, the Steel Industries shop was not equipped to do large sheet metal work, because there was no demand for it. After the building restoration, I was prepared for anything. Coming from Germany's rigidly structured industrial society, I had never been trained in improvisations. I respected Canadian ingenuity in solving unusual technical problems, with unsuitable tools and with the material that was on hand. When the tank was finished it looked every bit as good as the original tank.

Looking at the new tank my "calibrated eyeballs" told me that the tank was much too long. I asked Ray if he had calculated the volume of the oval tank. To my surprise Ray told me with the straightest of face, that there wasn't any formula to figure the surface area of an oval, and hence it was impossible to calculate the volume of an oval cylinder. I didn't know if he was trying to pull my leg and stared at him in disbelief. As a greenhorn immigrant, I didn't have the vocabulary to start a mathematical debate with him. I walked away muttering to myself in German, "Das darf doch nicht wahr sein (this cannot be true)." Mind you, I hadn't figured the volume of an oval cylindrical body since my school days but I knew there was a formula for it.

How many gallons in that "bucket"?

At home I looked into my technical books. I knew that the surface area of an oval was calculated by adding the large diameter of the oval to the small diameter, dividing the sum by two, and then treating it like the diameter of a regular circle. Its radius squared, times pi, times the length of the tank, yields the volume. I found that there is another formula which calculates the area by large diameter times short diameter times 0.785, times the length. It was a simple calculation if you knew how. The problem for me was that I had to do all that in the medieval British-American measuring system. It drove me nuts, I was accustomed to the much simpler metric system.

Since all dimensions were in feet I now had the tank volume in cubic feet, that was the easy part. I now had to convert cubic feet into cubic decimeters (the equivalent of 1 liter), because all specific weights of water or oil etc. are given per these metric units. After I had calculated that, I had to reconvert that into Imperial gallons, to give Ray an idea of what the volume and the weight of the filled tank would be. This was the more difficult problem, since I didn't know the specific weight of the crude oil carried by the truck. Electronic calculators didn't exist then, so I was figuring it with a slide rule and paper. Since I had an itzy-bitzy doubt about my own memory on the subject, I was going to have my results verified by a local high school math teacher, who happened to also teach the English language class for immigrants that Martha and I attended.

A high school teacher with an "F" in math?

The teacher didn't know what the "oval formula" was. I couldn't believe that a high school math teacher didn't know something that basic off the top of his head.

I was convinced I had done it correctly and went to work to present my case. Ray was not inclined to be lectured by a newcomer, and didn't believe my numbers, but I bet him a case of beer and he accepted. My results showed that the weight of the full tank was close to eleven tons, and I didn't think that would be a safe load for a five ton truck, especially with the road conditions around Grande Prairie.

Then came the tense moment, as the saying goes, "When the elephant lets the water," and the tank was hoisted atop the truck bed. It was way too long, and the tank had to be taken off and shortened by about three feet. After that, the full tank still weighed about seven tons plus, but that was "acceptable, since they had reinforced the truck bed." I never saw my case of beer, but from there on I had considerably more clout in the shop. Ray never accepted another "steamed" oil tank for repairs, either.

The Grande Prairie experience was a very valuable apprenticeship. Even though life was hard and often uncomfortable, especially in winter, we lived a contented life with many friends and not many worries.

In God's Deep-Freeze

One of the hazards in Grande Prairie was the extremely cold winters. In the three winters I spent there, the lowest temperature was 55 degrees below zero. That is goddamn cold! The folks there determined whether it was cold, damn cold, or goddamn cold in the following way: If they spit on the ground and the saliva stayed liquid for a few moments it was cold; if it froze quickly after it hit the ground it was damn cold (20 degrees below zero); and if it froze before it hit the ground, it was goddamn cold (40 degrees below zero). Cars wouldn't start, or if they started the wheels had ceased because the bearing grease was frozen solid. In the early fifties multigrade oils were just being introduced, but people didn't believe the claims of the oil companies. Engine block and dipstick heaters helped to keep the motors alive, but batteries and bearing lubricants were the biggest problem.

Everything slowed down in such low temperatures except the people. They hurried into the warmth of their home or a store, or a coffee shop or to work, to escape freezing to death. Every house and store was overheated, and therein lay the other danger. When I came to Grande Prairie we didn't have natural gas to heat our houses, even though it was in the ground right under our feet. Everybody heated with oil, wood or coal. The wood stoves were dangerous, since most of them were improperly installed and overheated adjacent walls and ceilings. Most of the houses were built without a building code. In wintertime an average of one house per week burned down, because even with the best fire department, there wasn't anything that could be done to stop the fires once the temperature was 20 degrees below zero. Hydrants and hoses froze, and firemen could only try to keep the fire from spreading to adjacent structures.

One of the worst fires in Grande Prairie was in a general store on main street, across the back lane from Steel Industry's shop. It was late in the afternoon when the fire started, and the fire engines were on the spot within minutes. There wasn't much that they could do to save the store, but the firemen battled for hours to save the adjacent buildings because if those had started to burn, the whole downtown could have gone up in flames. Enormous amounts of water were used to keep the fire localized.

When I returned to work the next day the runoff water from the fire hoses had formed a foot-thick sheet of ice in the back lane. I went outside to get a steel plate out of the racks, and the lower tiers were covered with ice that had to be melted with a blowtorch before I could get the plate out. While I was working at it, I heard what sounded like a cat howling somewhere in the material yard. The cat was in one corner, with its tail frozen solidly to the ground. The poor beast had been sitting too long in one place with a wet tail. Orville put his welding gloves on and held the cat, while I carefully tried to melt the ice with a blowtorch. The cat was scared as the dickens by the noise of the torch, and fought like hell to get away. It took three guys to do the job without burning the cat's tail off. It ran off like a streak of greased lightning.

Far more serious troubles developed during the spring thaw-out period. That time is messy in any cold climate, because the water from the melting snow cannot be absorbed by the frozen soil underneath. In the back lane the additional amount of ice caused by the fire fighting effort inundated the entire shop with water. We had to put on our Wellingtons (rubber boots) and were standing in at least eight inches of water while operating the lathe and milling machines. Quite dangerous in light of the quality of the electrical wiring in the area. I put on thick gloves to work on the machinery because one faulty ground in the electrical wiring of a machine could kill me instantly. We had to rig up pumps to get the shop reasonably dry, but it took weeks to get everything cleaned up. Since the shop also had an outhouse along the back lane, it didn't smell too good either. I was reminded of conditions in Russia during the war.

The Stuttgart gang was a perpetual source of hilarity. At least one of them was always in trouble, either with the law, or with the girls, which sometimes also led to brushes with the law. All of them liked to drink, as did everybody else there, and the RCMP wasn't always looking the other way when it came to driving under the influence.

Rolf was employed by a local body shop and on Christmas eve he was driving the company's big new tow truck to pick up a car in trouble. At the downtown intersection the RCMP stopped him, and found that he had been drinking. They ordered him out of the truck right in the intersection, and an officer was going to drive the truck back to Lou's Autobody. It was one of those fancy rigs, with umpteen gears and hydraulic actuators, and the officer couldn't figure out how to get the big rig out of the intersection, where it was blocking the heavy Christmas traffic. It was snowing, and cars were soon lined up in all directions, with angry drivers honking, and rear ending each other due to the slippery street. Finally the poor RCMP officer had to admit defeat and let Rolf back into the truck. He ordered him to drive right back to Lou's and he stayed behind Rolf, to make sure he got there safely. Then he went into the office and read Rolf's boss the riot act. What happened behind closed doors was never disclosed, but Rolf stayed out of jail.

Opa Stamp

I was intrigued by the odd characters I met in the Peace River area. People were loners, some of them real "originals", others absolute loonies. I attributed much of it to the remoteness of the area which seemed to attract unusual people. Even in the small German colony there were unconventional characters. It was fun to observe and talk to them to find out what made them tick.

One of the old time Germans was Opa (German short form of grandpa) Stamp, a wheat farmer who had come to Canada after World War I. He owned a quarter section of land quite a distance from Grande Prairie, and came into town every Saturday to sell cream, eggs and homemade butter. He was from the northwestern corner of Germany, and spoke in a strong dialect, called Plattdeutsch. In summertime he often got thirsty from all that dust on the gravel roads and to have company he would invite some of us guys to the beer parlor. Between several of us a lot of beer was required, especially during hot summer days. We didn't mind keeping Opa Stamp company, as long as he was paying. The Stuttgart gang would sometimes make pigs out of themselves and guzzle down a dozen glasses each without batting an eyelid. Opa Stamp would then go home without making any profit and his wife would rake him over the coals, but he was well preserved by then, and it didn't bother him at all.

One time a whole bunch of us went out to his farm and he drove us around in his little Austin car which we named his "English Cadillac." It had a four-on-the-floor gearshift, which Stamp still hadn't quite figured out. He stomped on the clutch and then bent over to look at the shift pattern, which was marked on the floor. He didn't pay attention to where he was going and drove into a ditch. We all helped to push his car out, and then we shifted gears in tandem. He pushed the clutch and told whoever was sitting next to him which gear he needed and they would operate the shift lever and tell him to put the clutch in again.

At another time four of us went out to his place and found nobody home. Kurt Elsner, his nephew, was looking around the kitchen and discovered a freshly baked cake. So, we all sat around the table and ate the whole cake, leaving a note telling Grandma Stamp how good it was. The gang sure had a lot of nerve.

In 1954, Dee noticed that many of his kids' marbles had disappeared under one end of the living room couch. After much observation he concluded that this corner of the house was either lower than the rest, or some strange gravitational anomaly was present. Dee and I discussed that problem endlessly in "well oiled conditions" and figured that more research was necessary to determine what the problem was, and that a nonpartisan verification was necessary.

A Speed Queen vacuum cleaner salesman, would routinely demonstrated the extreme power of his machines by sucking 1" diameter steel balls clear across living room floors. We called him over to Dee's house for a demonstration. His machine was unable to overcome the gravitational disadvantages of Dee's living room floor. Having saved money by not buying a vacuum cleaner, Dee decided to spend it on leveling the living room floor and/or the house.

Greenhorn's House Raising

We started early in March. We dug away the soil bank along the sagging corner of the house to determine the corrective action necessary. Opa Stamp stopped by and said, "Na Jungs is man nen bischen früh" (Hey boys, its a little too early). We ignored him, and of course two days later it started to snow. Dee hastily covered the exposed side of the house with burlap sacks, we relaxed and waited for spring.

Spring came early in May and we now had the only house in the neighborhood situated above a lake. The melting snow and rain had filled the area under the house with water, because we had removed the soil bank. So we again relaxed and waited for summer to dry out the lake.

It was a very slow dry-out and frogs, attracted by the lake, started to disrupt everybody's sleep with their nightly concerts. Their concert couldn't compete with "Eine Kleine Nachtmusik" by Mozart. It became obvious that action was required. Fortunately an earthen cellar was under the middle of the house, so Dee emptied out the cellar and let the water drain into it. Then we pumped it out. The crawl space under the floor joists was about 15 inches and the ground was still muddy, so we greenhorn house movers removed all the earthen banks around the house. Then we relaxed one more time hoping the ground would dry.

We were into the middle of July and finally ready to start the job. The plan was to push long 6 x 6 beams under the house and then lift and level it. We discovered that there was not enough clearance to push four 6 x 6 x 30 foot long beams under the length of the house. We discovered that the house, originally just a two room shack, had been randomly expanded in all directions by using scrap lumber material. We couldn't raise the house without a support structure underneath, and the house had none.

We had to rethink the project. We would have to assemble the beams in pieces under the house, in miserably confined quarters between the floor joists and the muddy ground. Eventually we accomplished that with much sweating and even more cursing.

Now the "fun" of lifting and leveling could start. For this task we needed a minimum of nine hydraulic jacks and also cement blocks to put under the beams when they were raised. First Dee talked all of his friends out of their hydraulic car jacks and told them to call him if they had a flat tire. I borrowed several big jacks from my workplace. After we had used these jacks for two weeks, Ray Menard finally missed them. He hollered, "Where in the hell are the jacks?" I told him where they were, and to please give me a couple more days to finish the job. That kindled Ray's curiosity. He showed up at the house to see what the crazy Krauts were doing. When he saw our project, he cracked up laughing, and said, "Keep the jacks long enough to finish the job."

The biggest problem was to synchronize the jacking and lifting of the house without breaking it into pieces. Very slowly, very sequentially, very carefully, we jacked up the beams, and with much creaking, the poor old house followed the upward pressure.

The house had two brick chimneys which we had completely ignored. During a casual glance upward Dee noticed that one of them resembled the leaning tower of Pisa. Dee hollered at his family to get out of the house immediately. When the kids saw what the chimney looked like, they bet on whether it would topple or not. After inspecting the bases of these chimneys, Dee found that they rested on two 4x4s inside the framework and should have moved with the house. We managed to prop them up with long 2x4s to keep them from collapsing. After 12 hours of hard work we were able to get everything on an even keel and the family was allowed back into the house again.

The next task was to put "something solid" under the beams on which the whole house would rest. Dee found chunks of a foundation on his boss's property, and brought home several large pieces in an old one-ton pickup. After much digging and shoving these were placed under the beams. We lowered the jacks slowly, and with much audible protest, the house followed and settled down again. I checked whether the house was level. We let loose a bunch of steel balls on the living room floor, and they rolled randomly.

The house was not absolutely level, but within one inch end-to-end. We considered that ultimate precision, knowing how it was accomplished. A lot of cracks in the house and the chimneys had to be patched, but we figured by the time the next snow fell we could accomplish that. First we had to have one hell of a party to celebrate our accomplishment. I bought a bottle of Johnny Walker Red Label and the four of us drank the bottle all by ourselves.

The Sheriff from Chicago

On a Sunday afternoon during the summer of 1954 Dee opened the door to our stairway and hollered, "Hans, the sheriff is here and wants to talk to you." I thought, what sheriff and "What does he want? I haven't done anything wrong." When I went downstairs it wasn't the sheriff, but Martha's cousin Gene and his wife Mildred from Chicago.

They had driven all the way from Chicago in their new 1954 Chevrolet Bel Air coupe. Their car was covered with a thick layer of dust inside and out, since Gene liked to drive with his windows open. It gave them the right impression of summer driving in the Prairies. They had checked in at the York Hotel, and Gene had already washed down all his inside dust with Canadian beer, which he said he liked a lot better than the beer in Chicago. They had brought a huge salami sausage, because Martha had complained that something like that wasn't available in Grande Prairie. Gene and Mildred even let us use their shower at the hotel, because there still wasn't any indoor plumbing at Dee's house. After looking at the "Grande Prairie milieu" they shook their heads and said you guys ought to come down to Chicago. We promised we would, as soon as we had the money and a car.

I decided that having been in Grande Prairie for 18 months, it was time to get my own four wheels. The first step was to get a driver's license. According to all the information I got from the guys at work, that was the easiest thing in the world. All you had to do was go to the Department of Motor Vehicles, tell them that you want a driver's license, answer a few questions, tell them you had driven before, and after paying one dollar you were a licensed driver. I had a German class IV license for motorcycles. My father had shown me how to drive a car, on deserted roads out in the farm country. In the military I had driven vehicles for short distances, but I never had a formal driver's education. Here in the Canadian boonies all that was required

260 / From Bär to Bear

was knowing the traffic signs and having one dollar. Truly the land of opportunity.

Many of our friends lived a considerable distance from Grande Prairie, so I started to think about buying a car of my own. My boss had the Lincoln/Mercury agency, and I looked there first, but he didn't have any dependable used car in my price bracket. Besides that, because of the harsh climate and horrible roads, a car was only reliable for three years. The road to Edmonton, the nearest big city, was 450 miles long, 400 miles of which was gravel.

I had wondered why General Motors spent millions of dollars to build test tracks for their cars. All they had to do was send the cars to Grande Prairie, drive them over the local roads and they would certainly know what lasted and what didn't. Car maintenance was an uphill fight because of weather and the mud and gravel on the roads. Broken windshields, axles and wheel spindles provided a constant business for all the automotive shops in town. It was worse in the spring when cars got stuck in the foot deep mud, and better in winter time, after the snow had been compacted on the roads. The problem then was icy ruts in the snow.

On long trips we had to have a jack, shovel, ax, cable or chains, a come-along, and critical car parts, such as fan belts, extra spare tires, preferably snow and mud tires. Also water, food and matches for a fire, in case we got stuck out in the wilderness.

Greenhorn's car caper

In early spring of 1955 Dee and I decided to go down to Edmonton to look for a used car. The weather had turned warm prematurely but the roads were still frozen and in good shape. Dee hitched a ride with a truck driver and I took the bus. Dee knew businessmen down there who directed me to a finance company and several used car dealers. I didn't want to spend more then $1,500 for the vehicle. I finally decided on a 1953 Buick Custom sedan, black in color, with a straight-8 engine, automatic transmission, radio and heater. It had an Ontario license plate, which meant it had been driven on relatively good roads. It was 18 months old, looked in good shape, and had 15,000 miles on the odometer. The car dealer looked like a Mafia guy, wore black clothing and had two more guys around him who looked the same. They acted like his personal guards. When I mentioned the car that I wanted, the guy strangely enough went into a defensive mode. He said that car was his car, etc. He wanted $1,800, but we finally, after much haggling got it down to $1,700, big deal.

As we drove the car off the lot it began to snow. In the middle of the next intersection we ran out of gas. Luckily there was a service station at one corner, so we pushed the car to the pump and filled it with 16 Imperial gallons. That sucker had a big tank.

We wanted to stay one more night and take off early the next morning. The hotel must have had nylon carpets because the static electricity was so bad, we got zapped every time we touched a doorknob or some other metal object. We listened to the weather report, and when we heard another cold wave was coming down from Alaska, we decided to leave immediately. We cancelled the hotel, bought some food and went on the road. We drove the car alternately to get used to it, and detect any flaws. We soon discovered that the temperature gauge was not coming off the peg, and that the heater wasn't warming up. Other than that, there seemed to be no trouble. We pulled into the last service station at Westlock, north of Edmonton along Highway 2 and filled her up, checked the oil and I asked the mechanic for advice about the heater and the gauge. He suggested putting a piece of card board in front of the radiator, to allow better warm-up. We followed that advice, but it didn't make any difference.

After Westlock the pavement ended, and we had about 400 miles of gravel road ahead of us. The temperature outside was dropping rapidly. The route to Grande Prairie along the old No. 2 highway ran through very sparsely populated areas. Since the roads were smooth due to compacted snow, we drove at 70 M.P.H. Around 1:00 am we finally saw an open coffee shop at Faust, got a cup of coffee, and asked for the next open service station. The gas gauge showed over 1/4 full and we were told that the nearest station open 24 hours was in Valley View, 65 miles ahead. Holy Moses, it finally dawned on us what fools we were. The thermometer at Faust showed 28 degrees below zero.

Dee and I looked at each other and then at the fuel gauge and decided to try and make it to the station. Dee was driving and he said, "Well, we'll just have to drive a little faster to get there quicker, that's all." By now we were shivering badly because the heater wasn't working. Even our European overcoats couldn't keep us warm. The bananas we had bought were frozen and black, but we had cookies. There was no traffic to catch a ride and we didn't have any matches to light a fire either. At 30 below zero we would last about 30 minutes in the clothing we wore.

When we were 20 miles from Valley View the gas gauge showed empty. I told Dee to slow down to save on gas, but he said, "Hell, then it will take us longer to get there."

We reached Valley View, and the service station was open. The kid who filled the tank looked at his pump gauge, and said, "You guys have a hole in the tank?" I said, "No, but why do you ask?" He replied, "I filled in 15 gallons, and it isn't full yet." All three of us now stared with fascination at the pump's gauge as it slowly went to 15.75 gallons, and stopped. When we told the kid that the tank capacity was 16 gallons, he just shook his head and said, "Are you two lucky. "

Relieved, and refreshed after a cup of hot coffee, I drove the last 70 miles to Grande Prairie. We tuned to the Grande Prairie radio station whose slogan was, "The voice of the mighty Peace" (Peace River Country), but more often referred to as "The Boys with the mighty piece." We both had one hell of a time to stay awake. The low temperature and the fatigue were taking their toll. We sang and told old jokes just to keep awake. When I drove into Grande Prairie at about 6:00 am we were close to collapse. I almost rammed a lamp pole when I turned the last corner too quickly and skidded on the snow. We had brought her home. I parked in front of the house, and we literally dragged ourselves in.

Martha asked what car I had bought, and I told her. She didn't believe it. I told her to look out the window, but it was too dark to see. Vera greeted us with the news that the newly installed indoor plumbing had frozen, despite her leaving a faucet dripping. Fortunately she had some water in a water kettle. Since we couldn't do anything about the frozen pipes at the moment, we had a cup of hot tea with lots of rum, and crawled into bed. It took me two hours to get warm enough to be able to sleep. We had been at the brink of hypothermia. Another greenhorn chapter closed.

The next morning Dee couldn't thaw out the plumbing, so I said I'd drive to the shop and try to get somebody to come with the welding truck to warm up the pipes. When I tried to start my car, it wouldn't, no matter what I tried. I thought that the coolant might have frozen and called Kurt to see if he could help. Kurt towed my car into the shop, to let it warm up.

Kurt and I drove the shop's welder truck back to the house. We fired up the big arc welder/generator and clamped one pole to one end of the copper pipe, and the other pole to the farthest end of it, and then turned the juice on (about 80 Amps.) for a few seconds. That did it, and the water started running again.

Returning to the shop, Kurt and I couldn't find anything wrong with my car. I thought that the coolant in the radiator was frozen and proceeded to heat it carefully with a blowtorch, not realizing that I was melting some solder joints of the radiator. Now it leaked, so I had to plug the radiator with what we called "bearshit", a brown syrupy gunk that was added to the coolant to seal small leaks. The news that I had bought a car had spread and Ray Menard showed up to look it over. He was impressed but peeved that I hadn't bought from Mel Rodacker, even though he knew Mel didn't have anything I could afford. Finally Ray located the problem, badly burned distributor points. The automotive store was closed on Sundays, but Ray called the manager at home to come and sell me new points and plugs.

After we replaced points and plugs the engine ran just fine. Ray said that the engine must have been running on five cylinders. I thought that was a bit farfetched, Ray was always trying to pull my leg, but it may have been the reason we reached that Valleyview filling station. I found the heater trouble and fixed it. Now everybody wanted a test ride, so I drove them around, and we stopped at the beer parlor to treat these guys for helping me. Then the whole Bergner family went for a ride in it and the kids were especially excited.

I had to learn the technical end of car ownership, and how to drive properly. I bought a service manual for the car, and did all the maintenance and minor repair work myself. I had the advantage of having experts around, but always got umpteen different answers to my questions. Soon we went on longer trips around the Peace River country. I had grown up in densely populated Europe, and it was a wonderful experience to drive through this vast, sparsely populated country, where I could sometimes drive for 50 miles without seeing another town or car. It required careful planning to stay out of trouble on longer trips. There were few service stations along the roads.

Gone fishing?

Dee always wanted to go fishing and he had heard that Stony Lake was tops. Stony Lake was in the middle of nowhere, about 65 miles from the nearest highway, in an area of muskeg. The area was traversed by one or two "roads", bulldozed out of the wilderness by oil exploration crews. Muskeg is an unusual type of terrain and safe only in winter, when the ground is frozen. During the winter the oil and sawmill crews operated in that area. When the spring thaw-out came these crews had to hustle to get their equipment out to prevent it from sinking into the muck. Countless pieces of equipment had been lost there. We had heard all these stories, and wanted to see for ourselves what it was like "in the bush". The road to Stony Lake was supposed to be usable during the summer, so we were going to give it a try. Dee had his own car now, a Nash Rambler, and we planned on taking both vehicles in case of trouble.

Initially we were driving through a densely forested area on a good narrow gravel road. Then the road narrowed more and turned yellow in color. The color was unusual, so we stopped, after fording several creeks, to have a closer look. Despite going just 15 M.P.H. we had kicked up an enormous cloud of dust. The road seemed smooth but the material on top was fine textured, almost like flour. While walking on the road, the ground seemed to move under our weight. It was like walking on a plush carpet. Dee, Vera, Martha and I were puzzled, and concluded that the roadbed must be floating on permafrost several feet underneath it. We dared to continue ahead.

We were just getting some picnic stuff out when a thunderstorm formed over the Rocky Mountains and we decided that this was not the place to wait it out. We had also noticed numerous piles of bear shit along the road and that gave us one more reason to get out. We managed to turn the cars around, and started to drive back with Dee's car in the lead. Suddenly my rear wheels broke right through the road bed, or more precisely road crust, and sank into the muck right up to the rear axle. The differential was sitting on the road surface. Dee had stopped to see what my problem was and how he could help.

First I tried the bumper jack to lift the wheels back up to the road surface. That didn't work, because the jack sank into the ground, rather then lifting up the rear end of the car. Next came the shovel, to dig a small ramp ahead of each rear wheel, to try and ease moving ahead. That did nothing for forward locomotion. The rear wheels were stuck so solidly that gunning the engine didn't even spin the wheels. The engine output was all absorbed in the torque converter.

Next my axe came out of the trunk. I chopped down several thin trees, and put them across the road behind the rear wheels. Now the jack had a solid base and the rear wheels finally came up level with the road surface. Next I strung a long steel cable with tow hooks from the front end of my car to Dee's car. We left some slack in the cable to give Dee a chance to gain forward momentum to literally jerk my car forward on to a more solid road surface. When Dee's car moved it did indeed jerked my car forward, with the bumper jack flying off the rear end. We went back and looked at the holes where my wheels had sunk into. The cross section of the road looked like a pie, with a thin crust on top and the gooey filling underneath. The crust was no thicker than two inches. That put the fear of god into us and we very gingerly drove our cars out of that area. So much for another adventure in the Peace River country.

In vacation wonderland

In the summer of 1955 we went on our first vacation, to Jasper-Banff National Park. We left early on Saturday morning, and took the recently opened shortcut Highway 43 down to Whitecourt, which was a wonderful experience compared to my trip from Edmonton after the car purchase. It was a paved and straight highway. On our way to the Park entrance I approached an unguarded railroad crossing, then I heard a train coming at full speed. I slammed on the brakes, because I am not the type who tries to outrun trains at crossings. Martha wasn't paying attention, and since we lived in pre-seatbelt times, she banged her head against the windshield. She cussed me for braking that abruptly and I asked her if she would have felt better being banged around by the cow catcher of the locomotive. Naturally that didn't sit too well with her and she complained for the rest of the day about her headache.

We followed what is now called the Yellowhead Highway, and drove through Edson and Hinton to the park entrance near Pocahontas. After a look at Miette Hot Springs we continued to Jasper, where we stayed overnight.

Jasper was neat and clean, but we were surprised by the lack of facilities. It was unlike European resort towns in similar settings. To my great disappointment the 150 mile main road through the park was only a gravel road.

The scenery along the road was breathtaking. We marveled at the 12,000 foot mountains on both sides. I had never been in mountainous country before, and I thoroughly enjoyed it.

We stopped near the Sunwapta Pass to see the Columbia ice field, the largest glacier in the Rocky Mountains. It's surface area including the side glaciers is 150 sq. miles and 650 to 950 feet thick. It straddles the continental divide and its waters feed into the Pacific and Arctic oceans. We rode in a half-track vehicle up on the 15 mile long glacier, and were not prepared for the low temperature on the ice.

Continuing south to Lake Louise we admired the view over the lake, and the majestic mountains behind it. To stay here, or even have lunch here, was beyond our meager budget, but we sat in the park of the world-famous hotel, enjoyed the view, and took pictures. The Chateau was comparable to the best of European alpine hotels.

Down the Parkway a road branched off to Moraine Lake in the "Valley of the Ten Peaks" which gave us a spectacular view of this brilliant gem in the park. The color of the lake was emerald-green, and reflected the majestic mountain peaks surrounding the lake. I took numerous pictures of this beautiful scene from above the lake.

Banff was a sleepy little place in 1955, not much traffic but interesting shops and a few good restaurants. We visited the museum and were impressed by the huge stuffed grizzly bear standing inside the museum's entrance.

Then it was on to Radium Hot Springs, where we took a swim in the hot spring waters. Next came a boat trip on Lake Minnewanka and our first chair lift ride, up to Mount Norquay. The view of Banff and the Bow River valley was magnificent from the upper terminal.

Much too soon we had to leave, but vowed to come back again with more time and more money. We drove out west to Calgary and stayed there over night. In the city we saw a sign saying "PED-XING" and couldn't figure out what that meant. I asked the motel clerk and had a good laugh when we were told what it meant. That earmarked us as real country hicks.

Finally I and Martha were back in Grande Prairie, and very pleased with our first major excursion through our new homeland.

The Peace River area has probably the most fertile soil in the world, ideally suited for wheat, rye and barley farming. The only detriment is the harsh winter climate. The farmers said that if they couldn't get the seed into the ground by May 15, because of heavy snow or late frost, they could forget about that year's harvest. At best there was a four and a half month growing season, however with an average of 19 hours daylight. That was sufficient to let grain grow and ripen.

Everything depended on the climate, including the lumber industry. As mentioned before, the heavily forested area south of the farm belt was only accessible to heavy trucks and equipment when the ground was frozen solid. That forced the lumber industry to split their work cycle into felling and rough cutting on location in the winter and the finishing and processing in summertime in town. The other source of income was the emerging petroleum industry. Seismic work, exploding a string of charges and recording the reflections from various underlying ground formations was done to determine the probability of oil bearing cavities. The existence of large oil reservoirs under the area had already been established and the first test wells were sunk. The roads to the drilling sites were cut when the ground was frozen, and the big bulldozers and heavy mud pumps could only be moved when the ground was solid.

During the winter season the bitter cold made it difficult to keep the mud slurries for the drilling operation flowing properly. Spilled drilling mud froze instantly on the derricks, creating a safety hazard.

Injuries and mechanical breakdowns were common. Metal would often fail under the extreme temperatures. That's were Steel Industries came in, to repair or replace whatever broke down, and it always had to be done in a hurry.

The "toolpush", the man responsible for the equipment at a drilling site, was always from Texas, and communicating with these guys was difficult because of their accent. They were always pushy, so their job title was appropriate. The jobs always had to be done yesterday, if not sooner. Any malfunction at the rigs cost the companies big bucks, up to $2,000 an hour. The other guys and I often had to work around the clock to get them going again.

One evening they brought in a casing expander, which was used to straighten out caved-in or buckled well casings. The expander was too large in diameter for the casing it had to be lowered into. It was an 1,100 pound piece of steel, that barely fit into the shop's largest engine lathe, which had a 20 foot long bed. The expander had to be machined down from 16 inches to 12 inches in diameter, which was one hell of a lot of steel to be removed. The lathe didn't have enough longitudinal tool-travel to machine the full length of the expander in one setup, so the heavy piece had to be turned 180° in the lathe to finish the job. The overhead hoist above the lathe couldn't handle that much weight.

Art Fenton had started the job, which was estimated to take about 12 hours of continuous machining, and I was going to work a graveyard shift to relieve Art and finish the job. At the take-over point we were going to turn the expander 180° right over the lathe bed and Art had come up with an ingenious way to do it. He placed a small hydraulic jack dead center under the expander, and used a sturdy vee-block that fit over the ram of the jack to support the expander's weight during the turn around.

After carefully loosening the chuck on one end, and the tailstock center at the other end, the expander was supported in the center only by the hydraulic jack and nothing else. The turning was the tense moment. Imagine a 1,000 pound piece of steel, about 16 feet long, supported only by a little hydraulic jack, while four hands very carefully kept it balanced and turned it. Had it rolled off the supporting center point, it could have caused extreme injury. The scheme worked and the expander was re-chucked and tail-stocked for the remainder of the machining operation. The continuous band of steel that was removed by the carbide tool was endlessly long and razor sharp and entangled everything in the vicinity of the lathe if not remove constantly during the machining operation. Another triumph of reckless engineering.

The road to nowhere

The Alaskan or Alcan Highway started at Dawson Creek, 80 miles west of Grande Prairie. Numerous horror stories by people who worked there about its construction could be heard and those stories had peaked our curiosity. Many local people had also been involved at the periphery of that project. When a construction camp was abandoned because the highway had advanced, the entire camp was auctioned off, rather then moved. That meant everything sold at rock bottom prices. Workers bought what they thought could be resold, or could be used for personal purposes. My boss had made his fortune by selling surplus tires from the Alcan Highway project and the Canadian Internal Revenue was still after him to collect their tax. A lot of used equipment "disappeared" before being auctioned off. Heavy road building machinery did indeed vanish in some swampy areas. The terrain problems were horrible along hundreds of miles, and combined with the harsh climate in winter, and billions of mosquitoes in summer, made this one of the largest and most challenging construction projects that man had undertaken.

To see what the area looked like some of us immigrants decided to drive up and have a look. We drove the initial 150 miles north from Dawson Creek to get a feel for the scenery. That was enough. North of Fort St. John civilization ended, and we didn't bother to find out where and when it would reappear.

Along the route I examined a technically interesting curved wooden bridge, actually more of a trestle, which spanned a deep gorge. The structure had been designed by an engineering student, as his first project. It supported the highway on a curved, and properly banked trestle, 200 feet above a creek bed. It looked fragile, since it was a wooden structure, but it had stood up for almost 15 years, and didn't show any signs of deterioration.

Then we also crossed the Peace River on the bridge nicknamed "The Galloping Gerti". The bridge had initially been built to span the Tacoma Narrows near Seattle. Four months after it had been opened in 1940 it collapsed in a moderate 42 miles per hour wind. The span towers, the deck and other material was salvaged and later shipped to the Alcan project for a bridge across the Peace River. It was re-erected and served the traffic needs for many years. Years later it collapsed again, because a prolonged period of torrential rain had inundated the soil around the suspension cable anchors. The huge anchors started to slide, slowly enough to get TV camera crews on location. They recorded the final hours of the "Galloping Gerti" before the collapse took place. Several years later I was fortunate enough to catch those shots on the television news. It was quite a show.

In need of a better climate

After three years of exploring and observing the Peace River Country, Martha and I decided that life was too short to put up with the climatic severity in Grande Prairie. In summer of 1956 I began to look into relocating somewhere along the Pacific coast. As so often in life, one little incident, one small bit of information, one seemingly isolated event triggers an avalanche of changes. I don't remember where I got the newspaper, or what kind of paper it was, but I saw a Help Wanted Ad for a person with pantograph milling machine experience in Vancouver. These machines were not common in machine shops, but I had used them in Frankfurt, where I milled prototype plastic lens frames on them.

After much soul searching, I called to inquire about the job. I told them about my work experience, and the owner of the company asked me to come down. The job paid $2 an hour, which was much better than the $1.25 I was making at Steel Industries Ltd. in Grande Prairie. I hoped a job in Vancouver would open other doors. I felt that my knowledge and experience was unused in Grande Prairie, and I needed to make more money, I was getting older.

When I quit my job, Ray Menard asked me where I was going, and I told him. Ray entered into the universal song and dance routine of all bosses, " If you want more money, we can negotiate". These outbursts of "generosity" always annoyed the hell out of me.

Ray told me that when he was in Vancouver he didn't see any smiling faces in the streets, as if one could see them in Grande Prairie. Friday, July 3, was my last day of work, and I loaded the car with everything I needed down in Vancouver. Martha would fly down after I had found a place to live.

For the Fourth of July, we had been invited for the celebrations of the United States Independence Day at the American D.E.W. (Distant Early Warning) line radar station near Beaverlodge. We went up to the base with the Stuttgart gang, and together with the Yanks we had a going-away-party for me. In the afternoon I said good-bye to everybody, and drove into the sunset.

Main street, Grande Prairie, July 31, 1953

Arriving at the Bergners in Grande Prairie 1953

Changing profession, language, and measuring system, all at once, 1953.

The joy of spring in Grande Prairie, 1954.

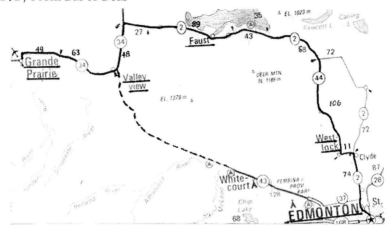

Greenhorn's car caper, 1955.

My first "compact" car, 1955.

Bartender at a housewarming

The Stuttgart Gang partying

Houselifting by the Greenhorns

Cities have always been the fireplaces of civilization, whence light and heat radiated out into the dark.
Theodor Parker

24
Back to Civilization

It was a beautiful summer day as I drove northwest out of Beaverlodge on Highway Two. The car had no air-conditioning, but on the dusty gravel roads I would choke if I opened the windows. After 50 miles I entered British Columbia (BC), and soon reached Dawson Creek (Mile Zero of the Alaska Highway) then continued west on the Hart Highway towards Chetwyn. The scenery changed to the densely forested slopes of the Rocky Mountains.

There were stretches of pavement on the road which ended abruptly and without warning, and often dropped more than six inches to the underlying gravel. The car was packed up to the driver's bench-seat, and the suspension bottomed out. The department of Highways in BC must have notoriously underestimated the amount of pavement mix needed to finish a section of the roadway. I couldn't afford any damage to my car, because I didn't have any extra money for repairs. The Buick had to get me to Vancouver, 900 miles (1400 km) ahead.

Cautiously I wound my way over the mountain passes, and shortly before midnight I turned off the road in the middle of nowhere, south of Pine Pass. I slept fitfully until about four o'clock in the morning. A scrub jay in a tree right above the car woke me up with his screeching. I stopped at a small coffee shop at McLeod Lake, filled the thermos with coffee, checked the car and continued south. At Prince George I was in for a pleasant surprise, the highway was paved from there on, with only short interruptions. The area around Prince George is well known for numerous mining operations in copper, lead, zinc, silver and gold.

South of Prince George I encountered villages with strange names, such as Woodpecker, Hixon, Strathnever, Cinema, and Quesnel. I entered the northwestern end of the central plateau around Lake Williams, where cattle ranching is practised. The area was more populated, so facilities were numerous.

I ate a the 100 Mile House, and when I was south of Cache Creek I stopped along the road, which runs right above the Thompson River, to look down into the river gorge. The air was balmy and moist and it was my first encounter with Pacific air. The difference was so distinct that it surprised me. I didn't expect that so far away from the ocean.

I continued along the Caribou Highway in steep and mountainous country and into the upper Frazer Canyon. Here the road got narrow and winding with many bad sections of roadbed and bends so sharp I couldn't see oncoming traffic. I met huge lumber trucks and was sometimes forced to pull over to let them pass. The road was certainly a far cry from the elegant, safe, and well engineered Frazer Canyon Highway that I drove again 35 years later.

Daylight disappears early in steep canyons, so I stayed overnight at a small motel right above the Frazer river near Boston Bar. I was intrigued by the way the road hugged the canyon wall on one side, while the railroad clung to the opposite side. There was only room for either the road or the rail. When the road crossed from one side of the canyon to the other, the railroad was forced to cross to the opposite side. I could imagine the engineering problems that were encountered during construction. So many fascinating new vistas, so many new experiences. I began to understand the enormous challenges that the pioneers had faced coming into this country.

Camels in British Columbia?

The Frazer River Canyon has a fascinating historical connection to the gold rush history of the upper regions around Spences Bridges. To supply the miners, goods were transported by boat from Vancouver up the Frazer River and into the canyon at Spuzzum. Upstream "Hell's Gate", a narrow gap through solid rock, made further advances by boat impossible. The goods had to be unloaded, transported over land to above the "hellish" gate, reloaded on boats and shipped to locations farther north. The many attempts to get around Hell's Gate in the olden days are legend. At one time a clever operator tried a camel caravan, because camels can carry heavier loads and don't need water constantly. His experiment ended in a disaster, because the horse or mule trains went berserk and dumped their loads and riders down the canyon when they encountered the camels. A law suit led to prohibition of camels for pack animals. Fascinating books have been written about this area and before going to sleep I read about the Frazer Canyon's history.

I stopped for breakfast at the south end of the Frazer canyon, drove through the town of Hope and entered the final stretch of road to Vancouver. All the traffic into and out of Vancouver was channeled over this two lane East-West Highway Number Three. It was the first time on my long trip that I had to concentrate on heavy traffic.

What, you have blooming fruit trees

I marveled at the fruit trees, the vegetable truck farms, and the flowers in people's gardens. After three years of living north of the 55th parallel I had forgotten what they looked like. After much bumper-to-bumper traffic, I finally wormed my way into Burnaby. On Kingsway I found a motel, had something to eat, and then went back to my room and plopped onto the bed, to have a snooze. I couldn't sleep, I was still all wound up. I finally realized that I was back in civilization and I had to get used to it again. My room even had a bath. Wow, I submersed myself in a tub of hot water. It felt almost as good as when I had returned from the POW camp in 1945.

After a cup of coffee I went out and purchased a city map and the Vancouver Sun. Back in my room, I looked at what jobs were available, in case the one I had lined up didn't pan out. Then I scanned the "For Rent" ads. The car was full of household items which would be an easy target for thieves. I called my potential employer and he advised me to find a place to live first, and then come by his place. He suggested looking over the West Point Grey area, where the University of British Columbia was. Single family home owners in that area rented to students, and now the University was in the summer break.

I was unable to sleep because of the incessant traffic noise on Kingsway. I got what had never happened before, I got homesick! I was literally homesick for Grande Prairie. That was incredible for a man who had been through as much in life as I had been. Then I remembered Wilhelm Busch's (a German humorist) sayings, "Es ist ein Brauch von alters her, wer Sorgen hat auch Likör," meaning, it is an old custom, he who has worries also has liqueur. Another saying of my military days came back which said, "Thirst is worse than homesickness." So I went to a nearby liquor store and bought a bottle of Scotch. After a couple of stiff drinks I felt a hell of a lot better.

The next morning I outlined a route on the city map, to get a gut feel for Vancouver. The more I drove around, the more I liked it. What impressed me the most was the city's location, surrounded by the ocean, the Frazer River delta and the impressive mountains of the Cascades, it overwhelmed me. I wasn't impressed with the city's architecture, and the traffic situation was terrible.

I found a small apartment in a fourplex home, in the residential area bordering the university endowment land. The building at West

13th Street had the owner living on the main floor, with two small apartments upstairs, plus a basement apartment. It was in a well kept older neighborhood, with nice gardens. Compared to Grande Prairie it looked like paradise. From a north facing window I could see the mountains across from Burrard Inlet. The apartment had one bedroom facing the street, a small kitchen and dining area and a small living room. It would have been ideal for a bachelor, but was sufficient for a couple without children. The bathroom had to be shared with the other small apartment across the hallway.

A new home

I unloaded the car and after that I went to the nearest supermarket. I stocked up the refrigerator, and prepared my first meal in the new home, which was a cup of coffee and some pastry which I was delighted to find in a nearby bakery shop. The food situation here was going to be much more to my liking. Every once in a while I peeked out the window, looked at the gardens of the neighborhood and the mountains in the background. The next door neighbor was working on his car, a Jaguar XKE coupe, and the way he went about it told me that he was British. Well, after all, I was in British Columbia now.

I decided to go for a spin in the vicinity of my new home. Following University Boulevard, I looked at the university complex. The first thing that came in sight after entering the gate, was a golf course. Oh dear, I truly was in Britain now, but I told myself, "Steady chaps, this requires a behavioral adjustment and then we shall fit right in."

I continued through the campus and turned into NW Marine Drive down to Spanish Banks Beach. "Heavens my good man, they even have beaches here," I said to myself. "One can actually swim here and watch girls in bikinis and it isn't far from home. Extraordinarily well done old chap, you choose your location with impeccable care." I continued on to Locarno and Jerico Beach, past the Royal Vancouver Yacht Club and Kitsilano Beach and then returned home. I knew that Martha would like this much better than Grande Prairie. She was a city person too. I called her and she was eager to come and join me.

My potential employer had a small machine shop on the main floor, and one pantograph milling machine and two pantograph engraving machines upstairs. One of them was operated by a young woman. She appeared to be in charge of that department. Nothing looked organized, so I wasn't impressed. I didn't have any experience in engraving brass plaques and trophies, but what the heck, I decided to give it a try. I was going to start the next day, so I was introduced to some of the other machinists. Two of them were German guys, one of them a tool and die-maker from Berlin. That gave me a little more confidence, since I would be able to get technical advice from them.

The next day Sally, the woman who was doing the engraving work, showed me what I needed to know, and gave me work to perform. Since I thought I knew how to grind the special engraving cutters, I didn't ask any questions about that, and just went ahead and did it. She wanted to look everything over I did, and she didn't like any of it. In the beginning I was accommodating, since she obviously had more experience then I did. But as time went on, she became more and more bossy. That didn't sit well with me and I let her know it. I found no way of getting into a harmonious work relationship with her. After a few weeks I talked to the guys downstairs about it, and they told me that she had even tried to tell them how to do their jobs. Those guys, who had many more years of experience than she did, told her off in no uncertain terms, and were poking fun at her at every conceivable opportunity. Maybe that was the problem, but I couldn't see myself working comfortably under "gender combat" conditions. The guys downstairs told me about another company that was hiring.

A new job

The other company was Boyles Brothers Drilling Company, and I filled out a job application there. In the meantime Martha had quit her job, packed her things and had come down to join me. She was overwhelmed by the many gardens, fruit trees and flowers, and happy to be in a big city again.

She liked the apartment, and specifically the kitchen, which was several times the size of the cubbyhole in Grande Prairie, and the view of the mountains. We didn't like flat country. It didn't have to be mountainous, but had to have hills and valleys to make it interesting. We enjoyed a cup of coffee, and pastry that I had bought at a German store in downtown Vancouver. That surprised her even more, because up in GP we never saw European style food. After seeing that she was pleased with what I had accomplished, I suggested that we better check to see if the bed was satisfactory too. Well, we proved that in a lengthy tryout and increased the satisfaction on both sides.

Martha said that she would look for at least a part-time job as soon as she knew her way around Vancouver. Since we had only one car, and she did not know how to drive, her job would have to be located close to public transportation. Vancouver had electric busses that got their power through overhead lines, like the old track type streetcars, but they were more maneuverable due to the absence of tracks. Downtown parking was always at a premium, so we used the buses whenever we had to go downtown.

There was an enormous number of attractions for the "Prairie gophers", who had been deprived of a city life for three years. We took advantage of many attractions. We lived relatively close to the Spanish Banks Beach and I had a chance to swim. Martha couldn't swim, but she enjoyed watching the tides. The tides at that northern latitude are 10 to 12 feet, and we took extensive walks over normally flooded areas, during low tide.

I quit my job at Advance Industries because of the obnoxious woman. Martha was all shook up, but two days later I started at Boyles Brothers Ltd. It was genuine machine shop work.

The machine shop was an enormous glass roofed hall, filled with dozens of engine lathes, about ten vertical milling machines, six automatic screw machines, and several gear hobbing machines. The company was in a mass production mode, and the shop was manned 24 hours a day, in three shifts. It was tough to fit in here. I frequently had to take over the shift with a machine already setup that wasn't to my liking. I had to get used to the work habits of another operator. He was an older fellow from Estonia with a poor command of the English language, which made talking to him difficult. The job paid the princely sum of $2.50 per hour and so I had a reason to grin and bear it.

What, diamonds in a machine shop?

Boyles Brothers Ltd. manufactured and sold hard rock mining equipment. They had contracted to destroy the "Ripple Rock", a large, underwater rock pinnacle in the middle of the busiest shipping lane of the Inland Waterway to Alaska. This had been tried many times before without success. Over 50 ships had been ripped open by the rock finger, which was in a narrow shipping channel with exceedingly strong currents. Boyles Brothers Ltd., with decades of hard rock mining experience, was probably the only B. C. company that could handle a job of that magnitude and difficulty.

They had to sink a vertical shaft on the adjacent mainland from where they drilled a horizontal shaft under the ocean floor to the center of the Ripple Rock finger. Then a vertical riser shaft was to be drilled and blasted through the center of the massive rock finger. From this central shaft, numerous smaller horizontal shafts would be drilled throughout the interior of the rock finger. This was extremely dangerous, since the outer mantle of the rock finger had many cracks that let water flood into the tunneling operations. Huge pumps kept the inside of the tunneling effort dry. All these shafts and tunnels were later filled with TNT, to blow up the entire Ripple Rock. This effort was in its third year, and rapidly advancing towards completion.

In the Vancouver shop they manufactured the hard rock drilling equipment to keep them going at Ripple Rock. The most interesting and most expensive parts were the diamond studded drill bits that made drilling into hard rock possible. The biggest ones were about 10" in diameter and worth thousands of dollars. All parts for the machinery that turned the diamond bits were also manufactured here. For this job the tools had to be designed and built quickly, and the men were always under pressure to get them done.

I had two weeks on day shift, then two weeks on afternoon shift, followed by two weeks on graveyard shift. My body could never adjust to it, because my sleep was constantly interrupted by noise during the daytime. I can survive if I get at least four hours of sound sleep in every twenty-four hour period, but I wasn't even getting that much.

Martha got a job as a sales clerk at the Army & Navy store in downtown Vancouver. The owner of the store was Mr. Cohen, who had his office on a mezzanine overlooking the main floor, and who constantly had a big cigar in his mouth. Most of the salesmen were older Jewish men, giving the store an atmosphere of lower East Manhattan. Martha got along just fine, since many of them were immigrants from Europe. The customers of the store were not upper social class people, except before the Christmas holy days, when a lot of Jewish women came to buy gifts for their non-Jewish friends. Martha told me of stories about the various types that frequented the store. The ones she disliked the most were the Hindus, who rampaged through the displayed merchandise in her department, discussing loudly each item, but never buying anything.

The old downtown area of Vancouver, now known as Gastown, was indeed a gas, as far as the characters that roamed around there were concerned. Since I picked Martha up after work whenever my shift work allowed, I got to know some of these local characters. One of the most unusual ones was an old Chinese man, bent over at a 90° angle, who was pushing a wheelbarrow through the back lanes. He was collecting junk in his wheelbarrow, and everybody felt sorry for him, but he served a very necessary function. A couple of years later, I read in the Vancouver Sun that he had died, and although he lived under deplorable conditions, the mattress he slept on contained over 100,000 dollars in cash.

British weather in British Columbia

The climate in Vancouver was British, too. One could always talk about it, and hence it was a marvelous opener for any kind of conversation with a stranger. Fog of London density, 12" of snow on the ground, 65" of rain annually, and anything in between was experienced in the city. The few genuinely British people never left home without their rolled umbrellas. We could, like the British, ignore the weather, but it gave us an opportunity to open a conversation about its extremes.

One night, coming out of my shift around 12:15 am, I found more than six inches of snow on the ground. Nobody in Vancouver had prepared for it, and nobody knew how to drive on snow. I was fortunate in that I still had my snow and mud tires on the car. Driving home I had to negotiate around the stranded and abandoned vehicles from buses to police cruisers. Electric buses had skidded at right angles to traffic flow, and were stuck in that position on hills. My flair for slalom driving enabled me to circumvent the obstacles, but sometimes I had to drive on the wrong side of the street which was possible because there was no traffic. I made it home without a problem.

The City of Vancouver woke up the next morning to tons of bent and dented sheet metal and it took hundreds of tow trucks to clear the debris off the streets. The unusual cold wave lasted for almost two weeks and kept the plumbers working overtime. The most hilarious sight was the university golf course. We drove through there just to look at the winter wonderland. Hardy, undoubtedly British souls, were trying to ignore the snow and played golf. Since colored golf balls were not invented yet, they spent more time trying to find the ball than hitting it, which happen to golfers even when the grass is green.

The Pre-Colombian professor

The bigger the city the more difficult it is to make contact with other people. Vancouver was an exception for us. In the apartment below us lived Dick Fredeman and his wife Pat, who had moved to Vancouver from Oklahoma, to teach at the University of British Columbia. We got together over a cup of coffee one day, and hit it off right away. Dick had an outgoing personality and Pat's was the opposite. She had been one of his student at a southern university, and apparently didn't feel too comfortable in their marriage yet. Dick had a Ph.D. specializing in Pre-Colombian history. Martha and I often had problems following his southern puns. We were allowed to attend

Pat's English literature classes. She gave an overview of the classical English literature.

Later the Fredemans moved out to university housing, and I often went out to have high level intellectual discussions with various professors. Some of the professors were European Jews and it was especially interesting to listen to their political views. There was a lot of political tension in the cold war world and also differences of opinion over the future of western democracies versus world communism. The typically left leaning academic world was much in favor of a Marxist world federation. The irony was that they had never lived, nor could they in my opinion bear to live, under such a regime. I had lived under Stalin, hence I considered their "liberal communism" a bunch of hogwash, and told them so in no uncertain terms. "Very interesting but stupid," was my frequently used expression after listening to their utopian socialistic-communistic fantasies.

Dick had an assortment of pornographic art pictures that he had gotten at the world's largest collection of ancient pornographic artifacts, the Vatican. This Vatican collection was only accessible to researchers, and only by special permission. Whether one also had to be Catholic to gain access, Dick didn't say. Dick was Catholic, but he never went to church. After I looked at the depiction of Greek and Roman penises, I changed Dick's title to "Professor of pre-Colombian pornography", and introduced him as such.

A frightfully British scientist

Dick and Pat had rented one room of their apartment to a British student, Jim Farmer, who was working on a graduate degree in biology. He was doing extensive research in UV radiation. Jim was the typical British scientist, conservative to the bone, impeccable English, and unwilling to drive a car on the "wrong side of the road". He was exceedingly knowledgeable about a very narrow segment of science. He had the British dry sense of humor, and listening to his interactions with the "Pre-Colombian Professor" from the southern U.S. was so comical at times, that I wished I could have recorded it for posterity. What wasn't so amusing was Dick's chauffeuring Jim to church on Sundays. Dick then showed up at our place to have breakfast with us while waiting for the service to end, so he could pick Jim up again. It got to be quite a nuisance and I was especially upset when I had worked graveyard shift, and wanted to sleep as long as I could. I still maintain to this day that all Ph.D.s have to take a compulsory course in "leechography" before they get their degree, and Dick certainly practiced it.

Since Martha and I liked the life in Vancouver, we tried to persuade Dee and Vera Bergner up in Grande Prairie to consider moving down too. Dee finally sold out his share of the business and they came down and rented an apartment. Dee got a job with a large dry cleaning company, but wasn't happy there. He found another job over on Vancouver Island, and after a short stay they moved to Victoria. It was a good move for them, because the economical situation in Vancouver was going downhill in 1957.

One day two more guests, Geesche Glimm and her mother, acquaintances from good old Grande Prairie, came to visit. Geesche was an attractive, tall and slim brunette, barely 20 years old, and she looked like the twin sister of the actress Jane Wyman, only younger. Geesche had changed her first name to Kay, because nobody could pronounce the old Plattdeutsch name of Geesche. She had been born in Westmark, a small farm village north of the Peace River, and had never lived anywhere but in the Peace River Country. She had never seen blooming fruit trees before her visit in Vancouver. Kay's mother was a pleasant and intelligent woman, who had divorced Kay's father, and was now living in a common law marriage. She liked the good Canadian beer, and lots of it, without ever showing any signs of drunkenness. Unfortunately Kay stepped into her mother's footsteps, but both of them stayed well mannered, even when filled up to their eyeballs. I had a crush on Kay when we still lived in Grande Prairie. She was a telephone switch board operator, and later worked in Dee's dry cleaning business.

Kay and her mother were good story tellers, and shared many anecdotes about inhabitants of the far North. Kay's father had a degree in agriculture from Hohenheim, a well known German agricultural college, but never had any hands-on experience in crop farming as it is commonly practiced in northern Canada. He took out a homestead, and somehow managed to survive a number of years on it. When Kay's brothers grew up, they had to take over the manual chores on the farm. He worked them like a Prussian drill sergeant, giving his orders from a rocking chair on the front porch. Small wonder the women left the great "dictator" as soon as they could.

My departure from GP must have stirred many of the people up there into considering a similar move, because we were getting all sorts of inquiries. The next couple who showed up were Hank and Erna Appel, on a vacation trip. They took the usual grand tour of the city, and were impressed. Hank asked me to look for a job opening at a local Ford dealer. I could have opened an employment brokerage for all these visitors from up north.

A ship from Hamburg

My mother's friend, Hans Haak, was a merchant marine officer at the Hapag Lloyd shipping company. From time to time he had the shipping route from Hamburg or Bremen to the Caribbean, through the Panama Canal and up the west coast to Vancouver. My mother would notify me whenever he was coming to Vancouver. When his ship was in the harbor, we went on board.

Many of the German guys at Boyles Brothers looked up the arrival lists at the harbor, and then ganged up on these ships. One idiot got into trouble for trying to smuggle hard liquor off the ship, and was caught in the act by customs officers. That didn't sit well with the captain of the ship, because he got called on the carpet for selling liquor illegally. Consequently some of the captains prohibited visitors, and on several occasion they had signs at the gangway saying, "Gott schütze uns von Sturm und Wind, und den Deutschen die im Ausland sind," which in English means, "God, protect us from storm and wind, and the Germans who live in foreign countries." A fine slap in the face, but well deserved.

I pointed some of the offenders out to Hans Haak, to keep "my captain" out of trouble. We always got good food and drinks on board, and were sharing the expenses with Hans Haak. We had interesting conversations often lasting into the wee hours of the morning. The ships of Hapag Lloyd were a combination freighter and passenger ship, which accommodated up to 12 passengers in first class staterooms. It was a reasonably priced way to travel, if one had the time, since the ships were not the fastest on the oceans.

One day I got a phone call from Kay Glimm in Grande Prairie, telling me that she had broken up with her boyfriend, and was coming to live in Vancouver. We were delighted, especially since the other small apartment on our floor was vacant. We wouldn't mind sharing the bathroom with her. A few days later she started to work at the local phone company. We introduced Kay to the exciting city life. When her shifts and mine coincided, I took her to the beach, and when Martha's work time ran parallel to Kay's, they would go shopping. Kay didn't have a car and didn't have much practice in driving either, so the two used the bus to go places.

Vancouver's climate was generally moderate, with plenty of rain coming out of low pressure systems rolling in from the Gulf of Alaska.

286 / From Bär to Bear

Geographically it is at the same latitude as Le Harvre, France, and Mannheim, Germany. When unusual weather patterns occurred, like the winter scenes described before, they provided wonderful conversational material. When I read books about London's notorious high density fog, I often asked myself how much of the fog stories were writer's imagination and/or exaggeration? I could not imagine people climbing up a street sign post to read the name on it, until fog came to Vancouver.

When I was on graveyard shift it took me 25 minutes to get to work. One night fog rolled in and it took me an hour to get to Boyles Brothers Ltd. Fortunately I picked up a fellow employee not far from my home. I had to roll the window of the car down, and steer by the barely visible white center line, while my copilot watched out for parked cars along the curb and helped me count the traffic lights we had to go through. We would drive up to an intersection and couldn't see the traffic lights suspended above the center of the intersection until we were almost under them. Thank God the Buick's old fashioned straight-8 engine was a quiet performer, so I could hear other vehicles. We had a few close calls, but never had an accident. After a few days the fog took on a distinctly amber hue from all the oil-fired heating systems in the city. Vancouver now had a regular London killer fog on hand, and people were coughing, and wheezing. The air literally stank. People became so disoriented that they couldn't find their homes, and tried to flag down taxis or police cars to get them to their destination. It lasted for a whole week and then cleared completely. I was convinced now that the London fogs were not writer's imagination.

Dee and Vera had settled in Victoria, and had bought a new house in the northern Saanich area. They had four kids now, so they were always short of money. We decided one day to visit unannounced. On our way to the ferry we stopped at Freybe's German delicatessen on Robson Street, and bought a supply of bread, cold cuts, pretzels and cakes, etc. to take with us.

We left at 8:30 pm on one of the ferries to Victoria harbor. We were hell bent on surprising them before breakfast. Since we were too stingy to pay for a stateroom, we had to spend the night in uncomfortable chairs. The ferry was in Victoria earlier than we had anticipated, and at 4:45 am we didn't dare to knock at their front door. We slept a few winks in the car, and rang the door bell at 6:00 am. When Vera opened the door she just about fainted as I said, "Is coffee ready, and here are the rolls, we're hungry." That woke the Bergner's household up in a hurry.

First we had to look at the new house, which was nice, but without much furniture. We talked over coffee and breakfast, just like in the "bad old days" in Grande Prairie. Dee had bought a new Volkswagen Beetle, and we wondered how two adults and now four kids could fit into that car. Yes, there was another addition to the family by the name of Jeffrey, and Dee and Vera had to take a lot of good natured joking about their sex life again. I offered to teach Vera how to do it without getting pregnant, but she refused my generous offer. They really didn't want another child, but the other three kids were old enough now to help with the new baby.

Waiting for the big bang

The Bergners had a television, and so we could see live on TV what I had been working for during the last 18 months, the Ripple Rock blast. It was going to be the biggest non-atomic blast in history. The television cameras were set up on the side of the shipping channel, about one mile from the blast center. The crews who manned the cameras all wore steel helmets for safety. Since most of the blast surface was going to be under water, it was impossible to know what effect the explosion would have on the surrounding area. There were doubts whether Ripple Rock could really be pulverized. At Boyles Brothers Ltd. we had been shown diagrams of the tunneling and the amount of TNT that had been packed into the shafts. It was a staggering amount, and unless something went wrong with the ignition sequence, the rock could not survive.

The TV announcers were afraid that something could go wrong. The tension climbed as ignition time minus one (minute) approached, and the TV crews braced for the big bang. It came right on time, and with tons of water mixed with big chunks of rocks climbing about 150 feet in the air, and then falling into the channel waters. The first living things back over the blast area were sea gulls, who feasted on the fish killed or stunned by the explosion. Nobody could tell immediately if the rock had been destroyed, the current was so strong that even hard hat divers could not go down to check. It later turned out that the blast was successful, and the narrow channel was now safe for maritime traffic.

The miserable aftermath

What was no longer safe was my job at Boyles. I and many other employees were laid off in November of 1957. In the following months I desperately tried to find another job.

At the beginning of my unemployment, Martha had asked at Army & Navy if she could work full time to help us over the lean times. That was OK'd and Martha's income kept us going. Fortunately a cheaper basement apartment was available right across the street. It was a dinky place, but the landlord was OK, and so we moved in.

A few weeks before my layoff, I had run into my old buddy Walter Golz again, with whom I had shared the "Fairsea" trip. We had lost track of each other because Walter had stayed in the province of Quebec to work in a coal mine on the Gaspè peninsula. He had brought his wife over, and later on they moved to Vancouver. Walter was an electrician, and was also interested in electronics. He urged me to enroll in a night school and update my wartime electronics background. I selected television repair courses. After graduation, I found that the job prospects were not any better than in the machine shop field. Everybody wanted a 20 year old kid with 15 years of hands-on experience. I was dismayed. My unemployment insurance had long run out, and I had spent all my savings to get through the school.

Kay Glimm decided to return to Grande Prairie. She couldn't find any friends beside us and she was not cut out for city life. I had always wanted her as my lover, but I didn't have the guts to tell her. When she came to say good-bye, she looked pathetic. She wore a flowery dress and a little old fashioned hat, like one would see in a Norman Rockwell cartoon. I had tears in my eyes when I hugged and kissed her. She was such a lovable, but such a lonesome person, that I felt guilty for not taking better care of her. I saw her off at the bus depot. I also had to take care of the things she had left behind. My garage was full of her empty beer bottles.

Shortly after that Hank Appel called, telling me that he had been fired upon his return from vacation, and was looking for a job around Vancouver. I promised to keep an eye open. What I found, looking through the job ads, was a radio and television business for sale out in Mission City. Mission City was on the Frazer River about 40 miles east of Vancouver. I called the number, and was encouraged by the owner to come out and talk to him. We hit it off right away. Ed Master wanted to retire to Santa Barbara, California, even though he was only in his late thirties. He was going to help me learn to run the business.

I didn't have a penny in my pocket to purchase the business. So I called Hank and reported to him what I had seen in Mission City. I asked him if he would be willing to go into business with me. Two days later Hank called back and said that he would come down and look the books over to see if it was worth the price that Ed wanted.

If you can't get a job, start a business.

Hank came down in a brand new 1958 Ford Edsel, which had been the reason for his dismissal. Hank had paid the stripped price for the car, yet it was fully equipped. He had buried the difference in the books.

Hank found things in order in Ed Master's books, and we sat down and negotiated the terms. Hank had put his house up for sale, but it would take time to get his money out. In order to purchase Master Television, Hank had to sell the Edsel, and buy a Ford Fairlane. He lent me half the business purchase price, to be paid back in monthly installments to him. It was a risky, iffy kind of a deal.

The long way back into civilization, 1956.

Making tools for the Ripple Rock blast, Vancouver, British Columbia, 1957

The greatest of evils and the worst of crimes is poverty.
George Bernhard Shaw

25
Poor Old German Immigrant
(P.O.G.I.)

I didn't have a penny in my pocket, but nerve enough to buy an established business with a partner in the sleepy little town of Mission City, population 5,000, with a large hinterland. Well, if you can't get a job, start a business. The success of the endeavor would hinge on my ability to satisfy the customers, people hopelessly addicted to the boob tube. I was introverted and shy when dealing with people, and in this business I would have to deal with many people, most of them crabby because their TV was on the fritz.

Martha and I didn't even own a television. I thought that 90 percent of the programming was trash, and now I was trying to make a living with something I didn't believe in.

Hank, my business partner, had no inhibitions, he was a wheeler-dealer. Hank was a street smart fighter, and Hank also had a way of winning at negotiations, which I lacked.

Hank was also born in Berlin, Germany, and at age 18 he had joined the 100,000 men German Army of the Weimar Republic. He started out with the cavalry. After Hitler came to power and Goering started a new Luftwaffe, Hank trained as a bomber pilot. At the beginning of World War II he flew a He-111 bomber. In 1940 he was shot down during a raid on Brighton, England, but managed to make a wheels up landing on the beach, and became an early POW. In 1941 all German POWs held in Great Britain were transferred by sea to Canada, because of the fear of a German invasion.

Hank, who had many stories about his trip to Canada, ended up in a big POW camp near Lethbridge, Alberta. The POWs of the camp could work outside in canneries if they wanted to and many did, just to fight the boredom. They got paid a nominal amount. Many of them were POWs for years, and consequently had money to spend.

Hank, already the wheeler-dealer in those days, operated the canteen in camp, selling merchandise to the POWs. At the end of the war Hank was doing one million dollars worth of business per year. When the camp was closed, he volunteered to stay on in Canada for another 18 months, and worked for a lumber company in Grande Prairie as a book keeper. When he had to leave, his boss told him, "Hank, if you want to come back and settle here, just write us and we'll help you."

It was 1947 when Hank returned to Schwerin, Germany and found his wife and daughter. He was dismayed about the living conditions in the Russian occupation zone. As a well dressed, well fed POW just returning from Canada, Hank stuck out. Since he also couldn't keep his mouth shut on how shitty the conditions in Germany were, he clashed with the communist officials in Schwerin almost instantly. When he was tipped off that he was on the arrest list, Hank and his family fled to East Berlin, and then crossed into West Berlin. He went straight to the Canadian Consulate there and demanded that they send him "home" again. When the consul wanted to know what he meant by that, Hank told him his story. The consul laughed and said that he would notify him as soon as immigration to Canada opened. Hank was back in Grande Prairie with his family by 1950.

When Hank and I bought the business in Mission City in 1958, we had to cut expenses to the bone so we shared a rented house. It was a nice two bedroom, two bath house with a beautiful view, overlooking the Frazer River valley and the Cascade mountains across the border in the state of Washington. Mission City was only ten miles north of the US border. Togetherness with another couple in one house is difficult, unless you have a common background. Martha was from southern Germany and Erna from the northern part. They differed in opinion on just about everything, and so did their cooking. The only thing they agreed on was soap opera time on TV.

Hank and I worked on a strict schedule. In the morning I would be in the store's workshop repairing televisions and radios that required pulling the chassis and replacing internal parts. Hank would take care of mail and banking during that time. In the afternoon I would go on service calls to customers and repair TV sets that could be fixed at the customer's home by replacing vacuum tubes.

The installation of new TV antennas was also my job. Since it was raining a lot in B. C., that was often a nasty and dangerous job. Fortunately almost all buildings were single story dwellings, but cedar shingle roofs are not safe to walk on when wet.

Hank specialized in sales of new and used TVs, radios, and hi-fi systems. He often bragged that he made more money for the company in a sale than I did in a day of service work. Hank couldn't have sold TVs in that town, if I hadn't provided reliable service. Tactless remarks like that pissed me off, because here was Hank with his ass in the warm and dry store, while I was on the road in nasty, rainy weather, jousting with bitchy customers over a few bucks for a service call.

To add to our income, Martha went to part time work at the local bus depot café. I thought it was mostly to escape Erna, but we surely needed that extra money. Many of the local business people went to the bus depot for lunch every day, including the manager of the Bank of Nova Scotia. He noticed that Martha treated the customers well and handled the money efficiently. He asked her one day if she would be interested in working at his bank. That started her career in banking, which continued for 28 years until her retirement.

Indeed a British subject now

In December of 1958 Martha and I had to go back to Vancouver just two days before Christmas, where we, together with many other immigrants, were sworn in as citizens of Canada. Canadian citizenship automatically made us British subjects too. We were proud of our newly adopted countries and considered it our best Christmas gift. The irony of ironies was that in 1945 the Russian intelligence officer interrogating me had accused me of being a British spy. I couldn't have anticipated at that time that only 13 years later I would be a British subject.

In 1959 Hank sold his house in Grande Prairie, and moved into a nice older home in Mission City on a wooded one acre lot, for the unbelievable price of $9,350. With two incomes Martha and I could buy a few pieces of modern furniture, and we even persuaded the landlord to install a natural gas furnace, which made life much more comfortable in the cool, wet climate of British Columbia.

My service work was a real eye opener, there were rich ranch and dairy farmers, and absolutely poor Canadians and Indians on the Chehalis Indian Reserve. Many of my customers didn't have a decent bed to sleep in, but they had a fancy TV set. It was often the only good piece of furniture in the whole house. To me, creature comfort was more important than the stupid boob tube, which bombarded the audience with nothing but make believe, hype and bullshit. As far as I was concerned, television had no "redeeming social value." When I talked to a social worker about it, she told me that TV is for these people the only means of keeping up their hopes and dreams. It is often their only contact to the outside world, into which they could not venture by other means. I understood, but I couldn't comprehend that people would sink so deeply into resignation.

Some of my customers lived way out in the "boonies" in appalling squalor. They were happy to get service from somebody, but I had to insist on cash payment right away, or I would have never seen my money. Many had been out of work for years because they had no saleable skills. Others were on welfare, or had suffered debilitating work injuries.

One lady in Harrison Hot Springs wanted a new television but she didn't have enough money. When I explained that she could finance the set she wasn't enthusiastic about that. She said that she had always made a "deal" with Ed Master, the previous owner of our business. I didn't dare to ask her what kind of a deal, but knowing about Ed's very active sex life, I could well imagine what kind of a deal she had in mind.

Another time a customer out near Agassiz told me that sometimes he could see, but not hear a Channel 3 TV station. In this mountainous country odd reception conditions existed at times. People sometimes had to move their antenna around, depending on weather or time of the year. When I arrived there to check it out, I saw a fairly good picture and a strange parade in some unknown city, but could not get any sound. Doing much research I found that the city was Santa Barbara, California broadcasting the annual Fiesta Parade. That city was approximately 1,500 miles away and the signal went through multiple skips in the ionosphere to reach the customer. A rare phenomenon for a TV signal, probably caused by sun spot activities.

My service district comprised a roughly 35 mile radius around Mission City. It went all the way out to Harrison Hot Springs, to Abbotsford and to Haney. Our service vehicle was a 1956 Chevrolet Sedan Delivery, in my opinion one of the best vehicles Chevrolet ever built. It took me a while to get used to the manual column gear shift. I also had to go for a test drive with a motor vehicle inspector, since my B.C. license was restricted to automatic transmissions only. This was an interesting custom in British Columbia. A driver taking the test in a car with an automatic transmission, was restricted to a car with that type of transmission. However, the test in a manual transmission car meant one could also drive cars with automatic transmission. Every 18 months there was a mandatory vehicle inspection by the motor vehicle department, not a privately owned repair shop. If the vehicle was acceptable, a sticker was attached to the windshield, giving the date for the next inspection. The system was a copy of the British and German vehicle laws.

One day Hank accepted a service call outside of our regular district as a favor to our television wholesale distributor in Vancouver. There was no money in it for us and the call was on a Saturday afternoon. On the way to the customer my car was broadsided by a driver of another '56 Chevy, who had failed to stop at a stop sign. I was going about 65 m.p.h. on the Lougheed Highway and the impact was so powerful that it pushed the tubeless tires off the wheel rims. My car careened across the oncoming lane. I hung onto the steering wheel, but couldn't control the car as it bounced into the steep ditch on the left hand side. The car finally plowed to a stop in front of a mail box and driveway to a house. Fortunately there hadn't been any traffic in the oncoming lane. The occupants of the house came running out, they had seen the disaster from their living room window.

My chest hurt from impact with the steering wheel. Our banker, who was driving behind me on the highway had seen the accident, and stopped immediately. The other driver was uninjured and came over to my vehicle and we exchanged driver's license numbers, without discussing the accident. Then the RCMP showed up and took all the particulars. The impact had opened the tailgate of my vehicle and the service tools and the tube caddy had been ejected, and vacuum tubes exploded all over the highway behind me. Our Chevy was a total loss, with the impact dead center at the right hand door. When I left Mission City I had asked Martha if she wanted to come along with me, and thank goodness she said no.

The people in the house invited me to come in to wait for the tow truck and were nice enough to offer me a cup of tea. Pretty soon Hank showed up, was surprised about the damage, and mad that he had agreed to do this call. When we drove home, he said that he had called the doctor in Mission City already, and had told him that I was inbound from an accident and needed a complete physical. Dr. McKinley gave me a good going over, but other then the chest bruises and backaches there seemed to be no damage.

The insurance paid us what the vehicle was worth, and Hank bought a cheap English Vauxhall (GM) delivery van. It was a pitiful substitute for the Chevy, and soon developed the nasty habit of refusing to start when the temperature fell below 40°F. The dealer never found the reason for this problem. I detested that van and referred to it as the British lemon.

Hank wasn't the kind of businessman who would put up with customers who didn't pay. He relentlessly went after them to collect what they owed, and the company had less than five percent of non-collectable debt, which was outstanding for a service business. When we sold a new TV set, and the customer couldn't pay cash, we financed it through a locally owned finance company. Every once in a while a customer would default on his payments, and the TV set had to be repossessed. If the finance company had to do it, it set us back $10 for the repossession. Hank didn't like to lose that money, and he often went out to get the TV back himself.

Luftwaffe Pilot raids Indian reservation

Hank had sold an expensive new TV set to an Indian who lived on the Reservation near Harrison Mills. Hank had been warned by the finance company that the Indian was a bad risk, and would probably not pay. If a customer made at least three payments, Hank said he wouldn't mind taking the TV set back, because he could turn around and resell it as a new TV at a sizeable discount.

Sure enough the customer made a couple of payments and then defaulted. Hank decided that we would go out and repossess that set ourselves. We drove onto the Indian Reservation, which was in a thickly forested area, and Hank knocked at the customer's door. There was no answer, and nobody seemed to be at home. The house owner had probably been notified by smoke signals about our coming. Hank looked through the living room window, and saw the TV set sitting there. It was a big set and would need two to carry it out. I stayed in the car with motor running in case it became necessary to withdraw quickly. Hank went to the back door, and found it open. He asked loudly if anybody was home but got no answer. He then marched right into the house and opened the locked front door, and we carried the TV set out and loaded it into the truck. Hank locked the house door again and we were on our way, watching out for a possible "ambush."

The next morning Hank got a call from the RCMP and an officer came into the store and told Hank that an Indian had filed a complaint against him for raiding his house. The officer who came to the store was my next door neighbor, and we often saw each other socially over a cup of coffee or a beer. This was an official visit, and he let Hank know in no uncertain terms that he had broken the law by going into a house on the Indian Reservation and removing the TV. He told him that not even the RCMP could do that without a special search warrant, since the Indian Reservation was an ex-territorial area, where the general Canadian law didn't apply. Hank apologized and told the officer that he didn't know that, but that the TV was our property, and we certainly had rights too. There was a hearing before a judge, who dismissed the case, because the Indian had a long list of arrests . We didn't sell any more TVs on that Reservation.

To keep up to date, I read technical and scientific publications, particularly in my professional field of optics. Late in 1960 I came upon an article in a magazine that reported on the invention of the ruby laser by Dr. Theodore Maiman at Hughes Research Laboratories, in California. After absorbing the details of the invention and understanding the significance of the coherent light output it generated, I wanted to get back into optics. One application that I could envision for the laser was the alignment of a number of optical elements with respect to their optical axis.

The answer is 9 W

The general public did not understand, or care about an invention like the laser. This was best demonstrated by the questions that Maiman was most frequently asked, " What is the laser good for?" Obviously Maiman himself couldn't envision the future applications of the laser, but having a good sense of humor, he usually replied, "Think of the laser as an answer to a question that hasn't been asked yet." Once, when he was being interviewed by reporters he was asked again, "What is it good for?" and he gave his usual answer.

The looks on the reporters' faces must have prompted the follow-on explanation. He said, "I shall give you another example. He wrote "9 W" on the blackboard and said, "That is the answer. What was the question?" Silence! Since nobody present could come up with an answer, he continued, "The question was, do you spell your name with a V(ee) Herr Wagner?" Since none of the reporters spoke German, they didn't get that one either. In the German language the English pronunciation of the number 9 means "nein" (no). I was in stitches when I read it, and for many years "nineW" was my answer to silly technical questions in any field.

The spring of 1961 was a bad time for our TV business. A prolonged strike in the lumber industry in British Columbia had its effect on all businesses. I had stayed in contact with Ed Master, the previous owner of our TV business, who had moved to Santa Barbara, California. After hearing my business complaints, Ed suggested that I take a vacation and come down to see him.

Repairing televisions, Mission City, British Columbia, 1959

The lemon, Mission City, British Columbia, 1960

Fifty cents an hour , where is the beef?

I was reluctant to leave the technical end of the business for two weeks, but Hank assured me that he would be able to handle it alone. When we had argued over business principles in the past, Hank had threatened to buy me out. I thought that my absence would be a good opportunity for both of us to sort out our feelings. I had figured out that my hourly pay rate was 50 cents an hour. I had divided my take home pay by the number of hours I spent in the business. Here I was,

38 years old, with many years of experience in optics and electronics and 50 cents per hour was my reward. The economical conditions in Canada were abominable.

Since Ed Master had mentioned that my combined experiences in optics and electronics would be a great asset in California, I decided to at least look at the job situation down there. What could I lose? Martha and I looked over our meager financial assets, and I said that I still felt like a P.O.G.I. (Poor Old German Immigrant).

Vacation in Lotus Land

In June of 1961 I got the old Buick ready, Martha gave the house keys to our next door neighbor and we crossed the border at Huntingdon and continued south to Bellingham. We followed what was then Highway 99, (now I-5) towards California, to look over another "promised land". We stayed overnight in small towns, where the motel prices were cheap.

In Olympia I tried my first glass of eastern American beer. Compared to Canadian beer, it was so bad, that I didn't drink most of it. Now I could understand why we had one hell of a time to get Martha's Chicago cousin out of the beer parlor, when he was up in Grande Prairie. Any brew master in Germany who would try to hoist that stuff on beer drinkers would be hung by his balls. From that time on we referred to it only as "pissolene."

After traversing the states of Washington and Oregon we stayed in Grants Pass overnight. Then drove over to Crescent City, and continue south along highway 101 through the Redwoods National Park. We couldn't get over the abundance of flowers, especially azaleas and rhododendrons, which grew wild in the shade under the huge redwood trees in Humboldt county. We also got our first taste of American huckersterism and kitsch right there in the beautiful redwood country. Farther south we had a first glimpse of the California wine industry, and were surprised to see grapes growing on huge, almost level pieces of land. In Germany the vineyards are always on hillsides, many of them on steep south facing ones to maximize sun exposure.

We rolled over Golden Gate Bridge into San Francisco. Martha, being a typical big city person and a shopper, went wild in the stores, interesting boutiques, restaurants, etc. We did what all tourists do in San Francisco, rode the cable cars, had a drink at the top of the Mark Hopkins, went up to Coit Tower and down to Ghiradelli Square and into China town. In 1961 San Francisco did not have beggars or drug addicts hanging around in the streets. People were well dressed, the city was clean, with a distinctly European/cosmopolitan atmosphere and above all, it had civility.

We continued south to Carmel and were charmed by its Spanish architecture, the cozy residences and beautiful gardens. After a trip over the 17 Mile Drive we continued south on Highway Number 1 to Hearst Castle, which we thought was badly overdone.

We arrived in Santa Barbara where I took the "wrong" exit at upper State Street, which in those days was full of potholes and lined by buildings in bad condition. There was a wooden water tower which was on the brink of collapse, and an old fashioned "auto-court" in a run down condition, which turned out to be the local red light business. We drove on until we hit the "real" State Street. There were many fine old homes in Spanish architecture with well kept gardens around them. Feeling better, I called the Masters.

Ed directed me to a small shack, between Brinkerhoff and Anacapa Street, which was occupied by his girlfriend Andrea. The shack was a rental behind an older Victorian house, which faced Brinkerhoff street. We felt a little out of place there, but Ed assured us that the whole thing had been prearranged, and to make ourselves comfortable. He gave me directions to his house, and invited us to a chicken barbecue in their backyard. His letters had always referred to their house as "our little shack on the hill."

Why didn't we come here right away

The weather was beautiful and we took a walk around the neighborhood, with older, well kept homes sitting in lush gardens with flowers we had only seen in flower shops. Martha and I were eager to explore the rest of this "paradise", and see if we could find jobs here.

The "little shack on the hill" up on the Mesa was a neat and comfortable three bedroom, two bath house with an attached two car garage. The barbecue was in their small backyard on a steep hillside. Ed was as always outgoing, while his wife Joyce kept her distance. Ed's two kids, Ken and Dianne, for whom I had a crush since I first met her in Mission City, and Dianne's boyfriend Ray, and girlfriend Andrea were there. Dianne looked gorgeous, and we had an amiable and interesting evening, but I sensed that something was not quite right between the family members.

The next day Ed drove us around Santa Barbara and we felt as if we had been magically transported to wonderland. I picked up a city map and we cruised around on our own, and the more we saw the better we liked it. Martha got employment application forms from several banks.

A new bank, just two years old, had a nice location on Carrillo Street. She talked to the manager and told me that this was going to be her future employer.

Ed had promised that he would be able to get me into Notron Corporation, the company where he was the sales manager. He had to drive down to Los Angeles on a business trip, and asked us to come along. He picked us up in Notron's big station wagon, which was the rage then. Ed called it the "slush pot" and we tooled down to Tinsel City. As Ed was driving through Carpinteria, just south of Santa Barbara, he pointed out a new building along Highway 101 and said, "There is another employment possibility for you, Hans." The company's name was Infrared Industries, and I liked the way it was situated right above the beach, overlooking the ocean. By now it was quite clear that we would be making Santa Barbara our home.

Ed had to tend to business in Encino and when he was finished he drove us around Hollywood and also showed us the downtown area. We got into the five o'clock rush hour and the way Ed was weaving in and out of lanes was scary. Driving north on the Hollywood freeway the traffic once came to a complete standstill. We were not impressed by Smogville.

What does it take to move here?

After a week in "Lotus Land" Martha and I returned north via Highway 101. As we came out of the Gaviota tunnel the heat hit us. My black Buick didn't have air-conditioning and was soon unpleasantly hot. We planned to visit old Vancouver friends who lived in San Leandro. The further north we drove, the hotter it got. We arrived at the Gunther's apartment at about 5:30 pm and by then the temperature was over one hundred degrees, one of those rare heat waves in the San Francisco Bay area. The Gunthers advised us to stay and take an early nap at their place to escape the worst heat. We left their place around 9:30 pm.

The temperature was still in the nineties. Going northeast on Highway 80 around Fairfield and Vacaville was like driving into a furnace. We understood why people in California had air-conditioning in their cars. I turned north onto highway 99, and drove through the area north of Woodland where we were surrounded by the pungent smell of onions. At about three am I stopped in Redding at the north end of the Sacramento Valley and the temperature was still 93°F. The filling station attendant told us that we would soon get into the cooler air around Lake Shasta. At about 4 am I was too tired to drive on, and pulled the car over to take a nap. Since the terrain was uphill, I heard trucks shifting gears all night long, and I couldn't get to sleep.

At 5:30 am I stretched my legs and had a cup of coffee out of the thermos. Despite the noise from the highway, birds were singing. A scrub jay was particularly annoyed about our presence, and made that known in no uncertain screeches. I drove while Martha slept on the rear seat. Highway 99 was a steep and curvy two lane road with few passing lanes. We were forced to hang behind strings of slow moving, smoke belching trucks for long uphill stretches. I was finally able to pull out of the traffic and into a coffee shop for breakfast.

The heat was back, and around one o'clock, somewhere in the middle of Oregon. We stopped at an air-conditioned motel, took a shower and slept a few hours. At 10:00 pm we continued on our trip north. I drove continuously throughout the night and part of the next day, only stopping for gas and food. We finally got into Vancouver around noon. Even up here it was hot.

We had decided to visit the US consulate, where we were told that we would have to go under the German immigration quota, even though we were Canadian citizens. That was surprising news, because we remembered the long lines of emigrants trying to leave for the USA after World War II. Now, since the post war boom in West Germany, hardly anybody was emigrating to the U.S.

The next day Hank and Erna invited us for dinner, and were anxious to hear about our trip. We always had a drink before eating, and I thought that was the right time to tell Hank that I had good news for him. I told him that he now could make good on his threat to buy me out, because I wanted to get out of the business. Hank was shocked. I told him he would have plenty of time to dissolve the partnership, hire a new technician and train him. It would take time for us to get all the necessary papers together.

We settled back into the usual business routine and Hank talked to the bank manager to determine how my payout could be accomplished.

A recent birth certificate?

About a week later we took our papers to the US Consulate in Vancouver. We met all of their requirements, and all our papers were in order, except for my birth certificate. I would have to get a "newer version" of it. I was stunned. Who ever heard of getting a newer birth certificate? Was I born too long ago? Then the secretary told me to look at it again. My birth certificate was a temporary one that had been issued to me at the end of World War II. Shit, getting a new certificate would not be easy, because I was born in Berlin- Central, which was now in the Russian occupation sector of the city.

I wrote to the Registrar's Office Berlin-Central, hoping that somebody at the postal office in Berlin would know where the registrars office was located. I included plenty of money for the customary fee, plus money for a return by "Airmail". I never got an answer.

I also wrote to my Great-uncle Leopold who lived in the Russian sector of Berlin, to find out where the registrar's office was located now and to get me an application form.

Several weeks later Leopold replied that he had found out that all the personal files for East Berlin and East Germany were kept at the Stasi headquarters at Berlin Alexanderplatz. He had gone there and they had told him, "If your relative (me) wants a birth certificate, he better come and get it right here (at the Stasi)." Since I knew the Soviet system from my own experience, I had fully expected that. The fact that Great-uncle Leopold had found where the papers were located, and that he had received an application form, was the most important thing. Now I could address my request directly. I filled out the form and made two copies of it. I then send the request to the Stasi and the two copies to the relatives. One copy went to Leopold and one to my uncle Gerd in Reichenbach with the request to send these copies also to the Stasi.

Three months later I finally received a new birth certificate, which they had sent by regular mail which had taken six weeks to get to Mission City. Two weeks later I got two more from the other relatives. I was now the proud owner of three new birth certificates, which would take care of any additional immigration desires that I might have in the future. The US government was also satisfied, but my job in Santa Barbara was gone, because it had taken me so long to get that damn piece of paper. The US consulate notified us in November of 1961, that our request for immigration had been granted.

To another new beginning

It was not a good time of the year to move, the rain season was in full swing, but we went full speed ahead anyway. We wanted to be in Santa Barbara for the Christmas holidays.

We decided what to sell, put an ad in the paper, and told all our friends and customers that we were leaving. Hank and I settled the business finances and Martha got our account set up for easy transfer to California. Part of my settlement with Master Television Ltd. had to be in merchandise, to leave Hank some financial elbow room. I got a German Telefunken Home entertainment center in a beautiful cherry wood cabinet and a good used TV set.

We packed the personal things needed for the trip, and let the moving company do the rest. At several "going away" parties we said goodbye to our friends. On Tuesday, December 12, 1961, the moving company came, and we took off in the old Buick.

In pouring rain we crossed the border at Sumas, Washington, and drippingly ushered in another new era of our life. After eight years in Canada I would have liked to stay there, but we never felt financially secure. I was getting older and we had to make some preparations for our retirement. We both came to the conclusion that we had done the right thing and wondered if it would be possible to convert our status from P.O.G.I. (Poor Old German Immigrant) to W.O.G.I. (Well Off German Immigrant). As we reached Seattle we started to sing "California Here I Come."

We planned the trip to Santa Barbara by the most direct, and fastest route. In Tacoma the snow came down mixed with rain. The car was acting up, it sounded like dry hydraulic valve lifters, and I wasn't going to get stuck in this slush somewhere out on the highway. We decided to wait the storm out in the motel, postpone all problems until tomorrow and get a decent dinner.

The next morning everything outside was white. I checked the car, but there was sufficient oil in the sump. I still didn't know about Murphy's laws in those days. On the way around the Portland, Oregon area we encountered hard frozen slush on the highway and the driving, even for a seasoned Canadian winter driver, got a little on the "touchy" side. I was glad I had my winter tires on the car which crunched the frozen stuff with loud cracking noises. Along the road were many semitrailer trucks in the ditches, including quite a few moving vans, which didn't give us a warm and fuzzy feeling .

At four o'clock in the afternoon we reached Salem, Oregon, and the valve noise in the engine was getting louder. I decided to drive to the local Buick dealer, and let him have a look at the engine. The service manager listened to what I told him, and then listened to the engine. He said not to worry about it, because it could easily be fixed. He suggested we go to the nearest restaurant just a block away and have a good steak and at 5:30 pm we could pick the car up. I was worried, because I had read about the many rip-offs by automotive shops. When we came back to the dealer the car was finished and the charge was less than the price of the steaks we had eaten. When I asked how they had fixed the problem that fast, the manager grinned and pointed to an oil passage between the engine block and the oil filter. He said that they had drilled that passage bigger and I would never have any problems again. We drove off impressed with this man's business integrity.

We were in a hurry now because we had made reservations at the Holiday Inn in Grants Pass, Oregon, close to the California border, and that was 200 miles away. As I drove south it rained in the lower elevations and snowed when we got up to higher hills. It was dark and the driven snow illuminated by the headlights impaired the forward visibility and the snow on the road surface obscured the center line of the highway. I was fortunate to get behind a big tanker truck on its way south so we made good headway and at 11:15 pm arrived at the hotel. We had a hot shower and sank into beds knowing that tomorrow we would be in sunny California and our weather problems would be over.

Moving into Murphy Country

The next morning the world looked white again, more snow had fallen. I called the Highway Patrol office about road conditions and was told that they wouldn't let anybody on the road without chains, and that vehicles were being convoyed through Siskiyou Pass. Good grief, here we come from the cold north of Canada, where I had driven for seven years without owning tire chains, and just before entering sunny California I had to have chains on my tires? I felt like the Greek god Sisyphus who had to roll rocks uphill all the time. I drove around Grants Pass to buy a set of chains.

I was miffed because I was certain that with my snow and mud tires I could easily get through. But the idea of what constitutes a "real winter" changes as one goes south. Finally, armed with chains, I drove towards California. We soon reached the end of the long line of vehicles backed up waiting for the snow plows to convoy them through. It took about two hours until it was our turn, and we would have easily made it over the pass without chains, but these southern drivers were peeing their pants when they saw something white on the road. When we finally drove down the southern slopes of the Cascades and into Redding, the temperature was 70°F.

We continued south to San Jose and stayed in a motel for a few hours of sleep. We took off at 5 am. It was the 15th of December and I was determined not to celebrate my 38th birthday on the road. As we neared Buellton, Santa Barbara County, Martha suggested driving to Solvang, staying over night there, and inviting the Master's over for my birthday dinner in Solvang. That was an excellent idea, and we checked into the Hamlet Motel. "To be, or not to be in California" was no longer a question, we had arrived!

We took a leisurely walk through Solvang, and were impressed by the high quality of goods imported from Scandinavia, but the main attractions were the delicious Danish pastries and coffee shops.

For breakfast we had Danish pancakes, and spent more time driving around the Santa Ynez valley. In the late afternoon the Masters came up from Santa Barbara to join us for dinner at the Windmill Restaurant. We had reserved a large table and had a good dinner and several bottles of California wine to celebrate my 38th birthday.

The next morning we drove to Santa Barbara through San Marcos Pass. I stopped at one of the view points on San Marcos Pass Road, which on that clear December day let us look over Santa Barbara, the ocean and the offshore islands. It was a breathtaking introduction to our new home. It had been a long way to Santa Barbara. I was convinced I had finally arrived at my "non plus ultra" location.

The trip to Santa Barbara, 1961

Finally, Santa Barbara, California, December 16, 1961

Oh' say, can you see? Observations by an immigrant
Hans B. Thielemann

From Bär to Bear, ISBN 1-890634-15-8

Cold War, Hot Love, ISBN 1-890634-13-1
Luck alone is not enough, ISBN 1-890634-05-0
Glück allein genügt nicht, ISBN 1-890634-06-9

Not published yet
Retirement, Yielding a Chainsaw?
From Mephisto's Metropolis to Hicktown, USA

Check website <www.germanhistory.net>
To contact the author: hanspogi@shasta.com

Also by Hügelwilhelm Publishing:
Whitmore Shasta County, A History
Author: Janice C. Thielemann

Hügelwilhelm Publishing Publishing Co.
813 Country Oak Drive, Redding, CA 96003-2747 USA